Critical Political Theory and Radical Practice

Series Editor
Stephen Eric Bronner
Department of Political Science
Rutgers University
New Brunswick, NJ, USA

The series introduces new authors, unorthodox themes, critical interpretations of the classics and salient works by older and more established thinkers. A new generation of academics is becoming engaged with immanent critique, interdisciplinary work, actual political problems, and more broadly the link between theory and practice. Each in this series will, after his or her fashion, explore the ways in which political theory can enrich our understanding of the arts and social sciences. Criminal justice, psychology, sociology, theater and a host of other disciplines come into play for a critical political theory. The series also opens new avenues by engaging alternative traditions, animal rights, Islamic politics, mass movements, sovereignty, and the institutional problems of power. Critical Political Theory and Radical Practice thus fills an important niche. Innovatively blending tradition and experimentation, this intellectual enterprise with a political intent hopes to help reinvigorate what is fast becoming a petrified field of study and to perhaps provide a bit of inspiration for future scholars and activists.

More information about this series at
http://www.palgrave.com/gp/series/14938

Frank Cunningham

The Political Thought of C.B. Macpherson

Contemporary Applications

Frank Cunningham
Departments of Philosophy & Political Science
University of Toronto
Toronto, ON, Canada

Critical Political Theory and Radical Practice
ISBN 978-3-319-94919-2   ISBN 978-3-319-94920-8 (eBook)
https://doi.org/10.1007/978-3-319-94920-8

Library of Congress Control Number: 2018950664

© The Editor(s) (if applicable) and The Author(s), under exclusive license to Springer Nature Switzerland AG, part of Springer Nature 2019. Corrected Publication 2019
This work is subject to copyright. All rights are solely and exclusively licensed by the Publisher, whether the whole or part of the material is concerned, specifically the rights of translation, reprinting, reuse of illustrations, recitation, broadcasting, reproduction on microfilms or in any other physical way, and transmission or information storage and retrieval, electronic adaptation, computer software, or by similar or dissimilar methodology now known or hereafter developed.
The use of general descriptive names, registered names, trademarks, service marks, etc. in this publication does not imply, even in the absence of a specific statement, that such names are exempt from the relevant protective laws and regulations and therefore free for general use.
The publisher, the authors and the editors are safe to assume that the advice and information in this book are believed to be true and accurate at the date of publication. Neither the publisher nor the authors or the editors give a warranty, express or implied, with respect to the material contained herein or for any errors or omissions that may have been made. The publisher remains neutral with regard to jurisdictional claims in published maps and institutional affiliations.

Cover credit: Frank Cunningham
Cover design by Fatima Jamadar

This Palgrave Macmillan imprint is published by the registered company Springer Nature Switzerland AG
The registered company address is: Gewerbestrasse 11, 6330 Cham, Switzerland

The original version of this book was revised. Correction to this book can be found at https://doi.org/10.1007/978-3-319-94920-8_11

Preface

The goal of all of C.B. Macpherson's writings was to put his sophisticated and unique political theory to the service of progressive political practice. 'The political scientist,' he writes in an early essay, 'will be a better scholar if he is a protagonist' (1942, 458).[1] This book is similarly motivated. In the chapters of Parts I and II, it explains Macpherson's essential views, which are appealed to in Part III for help in addressing a selection of challenging issues in the twenty-first century. While problematic dimensions of his theories will be noted, as will some of the few significant matters on which he changed his mind, I contend that his work constitutes a coherent whole that has well stood the test of time and can make original contributions in confronting current challenges. The book is not meant to be an exhaustive scholarly study, and secondary literature is only attended to when doing so helps to explicate, defend, and apply Macpherson's core theses.

This book has been rather a long time in the making. I first conceived of writing it shortly after the death of Macpherson (in 1987), whose work greatly influenced me and who counselled and supported me in my efforts in political theory at the University of Toronto. The more time that passed, the more relevant to current challenges to progressive politics his ideas became—even more 'contemporary' than when he first developed them in the 1960s and 1970s, that is, at a time when the welfare state led many to

---

[1] C.B. Macpherson. 1942. The Position of Political Science. *Culture* 3: 452–459, 458. Re 'he': until the late 1970s Macpherson unfortunately employed gendered pronouns. This is discussed at the beginning of chapter nine.

question whether an attack on the capitalistic culture and politics of what Macpherson famously labelled 'possessive individualism' was needed. Then came the neoliberal politics and economics of the Reagan and Thatcher years, which continue today, even strongly enough to have survived their having ruined the world's economies in the crash of 2008, and possessive individualism now stares one in the face at every turn.

Current resurgence of interest in Macpherson's theories is a reaction to this situation. It reflects not just opposition to neoliberal values and practices but discontent with current alternatives: weak forms of social democracy and insufficient attention to economic-structural matters in mainstream liberal theory.

Though the chapters of this book may be read independently, the book is written as an integrated whole. In particular, the applications in Part III presuppose expositions and arguments presented in the first two parts of the book.

Thanks are due to those who helped me with one or more of the book's chapters: Derek Allen, Edward Andrew, Ronald Beiner, Nicolas Blomley, John Calvert, Duncan Cameron, Marjorie Cohen, Harry Glasbeek, Alison Jaggar, Lynda Lange, Ian McKay, Charles Mills, Philip Resnick, Richard Sandbrook, Ingrid Stefanovic, Richard Stren, and Mel Watkins.

Thanks are due, too, for the patience of my wife, Maryka Omatsu, who appreciated the healthy scepticism of Brough Macpherson's wife, Kay, about the power of theory alone.

Macpherson's major writings have been reissued: *Democracy in Alberta* [DA] by the University of Toronto Press, 2013. By Oxford University Press: *The Real World of Democracy* [RWD] 1972 (also Anansi Press 1992); *Possessive Individualism* [PI] 2011; *Democratic Theory* [DT] 2012; *The Life and Times of Liberal Democracy* [L&T] 2012; *Burke 2013*; *The Rise and Fall of Economic Justice* [EJ] 2013. A nearly complete list of all Macpherson's writings is in Ray, B.N. (1996) *C.B. Macpherson and Liberalism*. New Delhi: Kanishka Publishers.

Toronto   Frank Cunningham
2018

Contents

Part I	Macpherson's Project	1
1	Overview of Macpherson's Works	3
2	Macpherson and Liberal Democracy	23
3	Macpherson's Socialism	39
Part II	Questions of Theory	57
4	Political Theory and Political Philosophy	59
5	Core Themes	73
Part III	Contemporary Challenges	91
6	Neoliberalism	95
7	Global Problems	117

8	Intellectual Property	139
9	Racism and Sexism	153
10	Urban Challenges	171

Correction to: The Political Thought of C.B. Macpherson   C1

Index   195

PART I

Macpherson's Project

CHAPTER 1

Overview of Macpherson's Works

Consumerism, commodification of nearly everything, unbounded acquisitiveness, fixation on private property—C.B. Macpherson saw all these things as distinctive features of life and work in the modern world. Contrary to those who think that they have their roots in human nature, Macpherson devoted his entire scholarly career to showing that they are products of a specific sort of society, namely, one dominated by a capitalist market, to which he proposed an alternative mode of life and work based on a form of robust democracy.

In the often appropriated term coined by him, Macpherson describes the world view he opposes as one of 'possessive individualism.' By the twentieth century this had become an explicit and dominant political orientation. It also implicitly informed the major political theorists in the early capitalism of the seventeenth century, especially Thomas Hobbes and John Locke. On this world view:

> The human essence is freedom from any relations other than those a man enters with a view to his own interest. The individual's freedom is rightfully limited only by the requirements of others' freedom. The individual is proprietor of his own person, for which he owes nothing to society. He is free to alienate his capacity to labour, but not his whole person. Society is a series of relations between proprietors. Political society is a contractual device for the protection of proprietors and the orderly regulations of their relations. (PI, 269, and see *ibid.*, 3, 263–264)

Macpherson came to designate this perspective an 'ontology.' By this he means a conception of human nature presupposed, if not always explicitly expressed, by political theorists and in popular political cultures that carries with it judgments about what is morally desirable, or at least acceptable, and realistic. A possessive-individualist ontology is both engendered by and sustains a capitalist 'market society' where 'exchange of commodities through the price-making mechanism of the market permeates the relations between individuals, for in this market all possessions, including men's energies, are commodities.' (*ibid.*, 55)

Publication in the early 1960s of his analyses of Hobbes, Locke, and others of their times in terms of this world view almost immediately established Macpherson's reputation as an innovative scholar of political-theoretical history. His subsequent articulation of a rival ontology to possessive individualism ('developmental democracy') attracted an international following among left-wing theorists and a broader public through the 1980s, and, with the rise of neoliberalism, his theories are currently experiencing a revival.

Macpherson subjected an early version of neoliberalism to sustained critique (recounted in this book's chapter six), in which, as in all his other writings, his stance was not as a detached scholar. Rather, he wished to contribute to efforts on the political left to combat conservative orientations. He pursues this task not by offering an answer to the 'what is to be done' question, that is, not by making detailed institutional recommendations or prescriptions about activist politics, but by interventions in political culture to articulate a progressive vision and to counter claims that such a vision flies in the face of human nature. After a biographical sketch, an overview of Macpherson's works will be given. Then his stances on liberal democracy and on socialism will be reviewed, and in Part II of the book theoretical complexities of these stances will be examined. Part III will apply Macpherson's theories to a selection of current challenging topics.

C.B. Macpherson

Crawford Brough Macpherson was born in Toronto in 1911 to a comfortable though not wealthy family. His father was a teacher of education, his mother of music. The family's religion was Presbyterian, though Brough (as he was called) never exhibited any strong religious commitments. His secondary school education was at the prestigious University of Toronto Schools. He pursued his undergraduate

(*continued*)

(continued)

work in the University of Toronto's Department of Political Economy and his graduate work at the London School of Economics (LSE) under Harold Laski. While at the LSE (from 1932 to 1935) he also interacted with R.H. Tawney and other scholars whose Fabian and other progressive views would have a lasting influence on him. He then returned to the University of Toronto, where, with the exception of some visiting positions, he taught in the Department of Political Economy from 1935 to his retirement in 1982.

The Department of Political Economy (established in 1924) included the largest number and among the best known of political economists in Canada and perhaps in North America. The head of the department from 1937 to 1952 was Harold Innis, whose studies of the political and economic importance of the staples trades was a defining accomplishment of Canadian political economy and who was also a pioneer in communications studies. Other leading political-economic colleagues of Macpherson included E.J. Urwick, Vincent Baden, W.J. Easterbrook, Harry Easton, Abraham Rotstein, and Mel Watkins. Macpherson saw himself as in the tradition of political-economic theory dating from Adam Smith and including Karl Marx and J.S. Mill, all of whom 'thought of economic analysis as valuable for what it could contribute to the development of social and political principles' (EJ, 134). In the year Macpherson retired, his department was disbanded and replaced by the separate departments of Political Science and Economics.

Though Macpherson interacted with political activists, especially in his capacity as a founder of a Faculty Committee on Vietnam at the University of Toronto, which participated in demonstrations, lobbying campaigns, and an international teach-in against the war, his activities outside the study and the classroom were, with the exception of a stint as Secretary to the Canadian Civil Liberties Association, academically oriented: lead author of a report in 1968 resulting in dismantlement of an elitist division of students in the Faculty of Arts and Science in the University of Toronto and introduction of formal student input to the Faculty's governance and curricular decision making; a founding member of a faculty group in support of students in these matters (the Faculty Reform Caucus);

(continued)

(continued)
head of the University's Faculty Association (an analogue of a faculty union); President of the Canadian Association of University Teachers; and President of the Canadian Political Science Association.

Brough Macpherson with Kay and Alkis Kontos, 1979. (Photo courtesy of University of Toronto Archives. Taken by David Lloyd.)

(*continued*)

(continued)

These mainly university-centred activities contrast with the prodigious and influential grass-root endeavours of his wife, Kay. Originally from England, she met her husband early in his career when he was a guest lecturer at the University of New Brunswick. Their marriage issued in a son (who predeceased his mother, shortly after Brough's death in 1987) and two daughters. In addition to (unsuccessfully) running for Parliament for Canada's social-democratic, New Democratic Party and for a short-lived Feminist Party, Kay Macpherson was a founder and for periods of time president of an influential and still extant organization of women for peace, the Voice of Women, and of an equally influential organization campaigning for women's rights, the National Action Committee on the Status of Women, as well as several other ventures recounted in her autobiographical book *When in Doubt, Do Both* (1994). Kay died in Toronto in 1999. Her interests were not in political theory but in activism. Brough often expressed pride in his wife's political life, and his understanding of the importance of ground-level, participatory politics was largely gained in virtue of it.

Fuller descriptions of Macpherson's life and the early development of his thinking may be found in Townshend (2000, ch. 1), Ray (1996, ch. 2), Leiss (2009, ch. 2), and McKay (forthcoming).

Synopses of Macpherson's Books

Macpherson's first book-length publication, *Democracy in Alberta: Social Credit and the Political Party System* (1953), sought to explain the dominant strength of a right-wing populist political party, Social Credit, which had formed the government of the Province of Alberta for 18 years before Macpherson published his book and was to continue in power for another 18 years. His explanation was by reference to that party's appeal to its large agricultural population. This class of *petit bourgeois*, independent entrepreneurs who, though champions of the private property system, were hostile to Eastern Canadian capitalism and receptive to Social Credit's attacks on it. (218–224) Although Macpherson did not pursue such Marxist-like class analysis in subsequent works, two themes in this early one (summarized in its chapter eight) were to be taken up in his last writings: the danger of a 'corporatist or plebiscitarian state' displacing democracy in hard times (EJ, 16) and anti-democratic features of politics dominated political parties. (L&T, 64–69, 86–91)

In his 1962 *The Political Theory of Possessive Individualism: Hobbes to Locke*, Macpherson saw in the capitalism gelling at the time of Thomas Hobbes and John Locke and eventually subsuming all aspects of society a growing acquiescence to market forces and a concomitant, possessive-individualist conception in popular culture of one's society and of one's self. He lamented the absence in twentieth-century Western societies of an equally persuasive alternative world view in keeping with non-capitalistic social, political, and technological potentials but still 'consistent with the maintenance of liberal institutions and values.' (PI, 276)

Macpherson challenges the conventional reading of Hobbes as deriving political norms from a supposed prehistoric human state, arguing instead that the society for which Hobbes was seeking legitimate state comportment was the nascent capitalist one contemporary to him: 'Natural man,' on Macpherson's interpretation of Hobbes, 'is civilized man with only the restraint of law removed' (PI, 29). His treatment of John Locke focuses on the latter's enthusiasm for property, conceived of as the right of owners to exclude others from the use of what they own, and of Locke's violation of his own, natural law-based injunction against unfettered acquisitiveness. Macpherson similarly exposes possessive-individualist suppositions in the theories of James Harrington (the seventeenth-century English essayist who defended a gentry-led republic) and even in the otherwise progressive Leveller movement of the 1640s, in both cases contrary to conventional understanding. Later he takes the same approach to the views of the prominent eighteenth-century Whig, Edmund Burke (1980).

In *Possessive Individualism*, Macpherson's own political-theoretical ideas were advanced in the course of interpreting the theories of Hobbes, Locke, and others. While he certainly believed that he had successfully exposed dominant dimensions of these thinkers orientations, Macpherson's expositions are part of a project with contemporary political intent, and it is therefore misleading to classify him as primarily an historian of ideas. The nature of his efforts as an intellectual historian is addressed in an appendix to this chapter.

In *The Real World of Democracy*—a series of public lectures published in 1965 and receiving a very wide international readership—Macpherson contrasts the liberal-democratic 'first world,' the socialist 'second world,' and the developing or 'third world' countries with respect to their different, but he thought potentially complementary, values of, respectively, liberal rights, economic equality, and communalism. Though he had not yet explicitly advanced a conception of developmental democracy, Macpherson is here proposing the combination of these three things as essential for full democracy, where liberal-democratic principles and institutions of the first world would be conjoined with socialist material equality and third-world community values.

The question of whether Macpherson's positive attitude towards existing socialism and his endorsement (albeit circumscribed) of vanguard leadership in some third-world national liberation struggles detract from his liberal-democratic credentials will be taken up in the next chapter. Here it is appropriate to identify the context within which he delivered the lectures. In 1965 there was pressure both in the leadership of the Soviet Union and in the West to relax the pressures of the Cold War, which had come dangerously close to becoming hot with the earlier Cuban Missile Crisis and which resulted a few years later in arms reduction pacts. Khrushchev had denounced Stalin at the 20th Congress of the Soviet Union, and the (short-lived) Kosygin economic reforms had begun there. African national liberation movements had formed and resulted in the gains associated with Kwame Nkrumah in Ghana in 1958 and Patrice Lumumba in the Congo in 1960. In this environment *The Real World of Democracy*, as Ian McKay puts it: 'was a plea for détente and the recognition of the dignity and complexity of decolonizing states' (2014, 317). Macpherson's description of his guiding question in these lectures is: 'Can we keep what is really valuable in our democracy while adjusting ourselves sufficiently to the new world to acknowledge their claims to co-exist with us?' (RWD, 3)

In his next major work, *Democratic Theory: Essays in Retrieval* (1973), Macpherson returns to the challenge he put to himself at the end of *Possessive Individualism* to identify an alternative to possessive individualism, and he proposes 'developmental democracy' as his candidate. On this conception a person is regarded 'as a doer, a creator, an enjoyer of his human attributes' (DT, 4), and a good society maximizes the development and exertion of these attributes equally by everyone. The attributes he has in mind include such things as 'the capacity for rational understanding, for moral judgment and action, for aesthetic creation or contemplation, for the emotional activities of friendship and love, and, sometimes, for religious experience.' (*ibid.*, expanded at DT, 53–54) Unlike in market-dominated societies that are focused on competition for profits or jobs, the development of what Macpherson calls a person's 'truly human potentials' is not achieved at the expense of others developing theirs, but on the contrary depends upon cooperation.

Macpherson sees possessive-individualist and developmental-democratic ontologies as uncomfortably coexisting in the history of liberal democracy. The first of these is at the centre of the political-scientific approaches of twentieth-century power-political, 'Pluralist' theorists, and it informs as well the radically pro-capitalist views of Milton Friedman and the softer, welfarist theories of such as John Rawls. Also in this book Macpherson distinguishes an approach to liberty consonant with developmental democracy from one in keeping with possessive individualism, and he contrasts two opposing conceptions of property: as entailing a right to exclude others from the use of one's possessions and as socially responsible trusteeship.

A major thrust of *Democratic Theory* is to argue that elements of the idea of developmental democracy have historical antecedents. A morality favouring the exercising of people's truly human potentials rather than seeking fame or wealth was well expressed by Aristotle, and its later incorporation in a democratic ideal advocating distribution of resources and opportunities for everyone equally to develop their potentials was to be found in varying degrees in the works of John Stuart Mill, John Dewey, and the English Idealist philosopher, T.H. Green. Macpherson's overarching aims were to show, on the one hand, that possessive-individualist values and attitudes are social-economic constructs not essential to human nature and, on the other hand, that a developmental-democratic alternative has cultural bases subject to 'retrieval' in the history of political thought.

The first demonstration is important for combating a fatalistic viewpoint that there is no alternative to accommodating politics and social/economic interactions generally to self-centred competition or to accepting the idea that everything is a marketable commodity. Retrieval refers to the exercise of drawing on elements of past traditions to explicate a developmental-democratic ontology. It may be seen as an effort at the level of political theory similar to left-wing projects to overcome an opposition between a politics that is realistic but not socially transformative (reform) and one that is transformative but not realistic (revolution). Macpherson's orientation regarding this matter is more like that of Gramsci than of Lenin in attempting to supersede a reform/revolution dichotomy. In Macpherson's case this means surveying liberal-democratic traditions to expose and reject components supportive of possessive individualism and to accentuate and build upon those conducive to developmental democracy.

This is not to say that Macpherson should be classified as a follower of Gramsci, to whom he devoted no attention in his works, but only that there are some broad similarities with Gramscism. There are also similarities between Macpherson's views and those of his contemporary Herbert Marcuse (with whom he developed a personal friendship), particularly in Macpherson's concerns about consumerist society and the self-images that support it. The prior radical thinking he explicitly employs most extensively is that of Marx. But, as will be urged in an appendix to chapter three, there is little to be gained by trying to classify Macpherson as a Marxist either, notwithstanding debates over whether or to what extent he was one.

Similarly, Macpherson is sometimes interpreted as a political philosopher, but while in *Democratic Theory* he made approving references to several philosophers there is no indication that Macpherson wished to place himself in any of the philosophical schools associated with them. His work remains instead within the domain of political theory where his principal efforts are to trace the origins of and implications for economic and political practices of alternative conceptions of, among other things, democracy, property, liberty, individualism, liberalism, rights, and justice, and to evaluate mainstream political theories according to how far they suppose or support either possessive-individualist or developmental-democratic thought and action. Macpherson's relation to philosophy is addressed in chapter four.

In *The Life and Times of Liberal Democracy* (1977) Macpherson describes four models of democracy, two of which—'protective' and 'equilibrium'—are informed by a possessive-individualist ontology. A third, 'developmental,' model is compatible with full democracy, but only if it is conjoined with rejection of an economy based on a capitalist market and includes an emphasis on the extensive citizen participation in governance endorsed in a fourth, 'participatory,' model. In this book it is clear that Macpherson saw possessive individualism and developmentalism as mutually exclusive alternatives, not world views and attendant politics that could complement one another or that could somehow be melded into a unified whole.

Macpherson's interest in participatory democracy is especially evident in this book. That interest dates at least from his graduate studies at the London School of Economics. Prominent in this milieu were proposals for guild socialism and other forms of what today democratic theorists call associational democracy, where collective decision making is devolved as much as possible to local-level associations. Macpherson's thesis for Harold Laski explored the specifics of the British trade union movement viewed as a voluntary association constrained by the state to preserve existing (capitalist) industrial structures.

The version of participationism Macpherson advocates should not be confused with the anti-state stance associated with anarchism. He does not see states with representative governments being dismantled. Rather, he envisages transforming them insofar as they support market societies and are beholden to powerful economic interests. In this book he devotes attention to the role of political parties, which in a market society, he maintains, mainly function to allow for negotiation among dominant capitalist interests while foreclosing access to major decisions regarding the form and activities of governments for most people, thereby also encouraging political apathy. Still, in a world without major class divisions and with substantial bottom-up participation, Macpherson sees a need for political parties to 'allow issues to be effectively proposed and debated' such as 'the overall allocation of resources, environmental and urban planning, population and immigration policies, foreign policy, military policy,' and he speculates on how parties might function in this world. (L&T, 112–113)

Macpherson's last book, *The Rise and Fall of Economic Justice and Other Essays* (1984), comprises essays on a range of subjects, all of which relate in one way or another to his major polemic. He once again criticizes the possessive-individualist conception of property. Political theorists are sorted into eight categories depending on how their views are compatible with either possessive individualism or developmentalism. In an essay on the prospect for achieving industrial democracy, he concludes that developmental democracy largely depends upon working people 'changing their priorities from consumer satisfaction to work gratification' (EJ, 41). Several essays centrally include exhortations to Macpherson's fellow political theorists: to challenge the assumption that democracy must be traded off against economic efficiency; to retrieve a largely abandoned tradition to develop 'grand theories of the state' that relate it to 'essentially human purposes and capacities' (56); and to pursue visionary theories that look for conditions in which 'the demand for material satisfactions might give way increasingly to demand for a better quality of life and work.' (129)

In the lead essay of this book, Macpherson argues that demands for economic justice will likely diminish as first-world societies move towards one of two possible futures. One future is developmental-democratic transcendence of market capitalism where 'a concept of human fulfilment will surpass the concept of economic justice' (20); another is the triumph of anti-democracy where 'a corporatist or plebiscitarian state would neither have to accede to demands for distributive justice nor need to defend itself in those terms.' (16) Macpherson had witnessed this scenario in his own country and written about it in his first book, where he saw early support for delegate democracy in Alberta morph into 'a plebiscitarian system from which the essential quality of delegate democracy—the close and continuous pressure of local opinion and demands on concrete issues—was conspicuously absent.' (DA, 217)

Macpherson is not prepared in *The Rise and Fall* to predict which possible future will prevail. This book reflects a less optimistic prognosis than earlier works, in which he opined that people would come to see a non-possessive-individualistic society as both possible and desirable. Macpherson counted for this on a combination of the overcoming of scarcity made possible by technology (if properly employed) and the example of a humanistic, egalitarian alternative to capitalism exhibited in socialist countries and increasingly attractive as these countries underwent liberal reforms. The Gorbachev efforts were in accord with Macpherson's anticipation of socialist liberalization, though they obviously were too little and too late to provide a real-world model for a transformation of liberal-democratic societies. Analogous to the disjunctive prediction by Rosa Luxemburg, attributed by her (probably incorrectly) to Engels, of 'either transition to socialism or regression to barbarism' (2010 [1915], 204), in this last book Macpherson sees the possibility of either a humanistic socialist future or a right-wing corporatist one. (EJ, 16)

Though some of Macpherson's views underwent changes through these writings, he steadfastly maintained commitment to basic principles both of liberal democracy and of socialism. How he accomplished this combination, thought by many as an implausible or even impossible task, is the topic of the next two chapters.

Appendix: *Possessive Individualism*'s Critics

Macpherson's interpretation of the theories of Hobbes, Locke and others sparked energetic criticisms from scholars including Quentin Skinner, Isaiah Berlin, John Dunn, David Miller, John Pocock, and James Tully. References and summaries of most of the criticisms can be found in Tully (1993, ch. 1), who is one of the main critics of Macpherson's reading of Locke, and in defences of Macpherson by Jules Townshend (2000, chs. 2 and 3) and Ian McKay (forthcoming). The generic criticism of Macpherson as an intellectual historian is that his interpretation of the seventeenth-century political thinkers in economic terms is at least one-sided in missing non-economic intents and influences and at worst simply wrong.

Townshend, McKay, and other defenders of Macpherson argue that the critics' readings of Macpherson are simplistic caricatures, which, among other things, ignore Macpherson's qualifications and disclaimers regarding extra-economic intents of the seventeenth-century thinkers. 'It cannot be said,' Macpherson writes in the first pages of *Possessive Individualism*, 'that the seventeenth-century concepts of freedom, rights, obligation, and justice are all entirely derived from [the] concept of possession, but it can be shown that they were powerfully shaped by it.' (PI, 3) Or he writes 'the assumptions of possessive individualism are not unalloyed in Locke. He refused to reduce all social relations to market relations and all morality to market morality' (PI, 269). Contrary to criticisms of Macpherson for depicting Hobbes as defending unbridled laissez-faire capitalism (e.g., by Berlin 1964, 455) or the related criticism that he failed to see that the dominant economic system of the seventeenth century was not industrial capitalism but mercantilism (e.g., Tully 1993, 85), for him the 'possessive-market model ... does not require a state policy of laissez-faire; a mercantilist policy is perfectly consistent with the model' (PI, 58; Townshend and McKay give more examples). Moreover, Macpherson notes in *The Life and Times of Liberal Democracy* that prior to the nineteenth century, the contours of class-divided societies are less sharply drawn than subsequently. (L&T, 9–11)

Correcting for straw-man characterizations, however, does not get at the heart of these critics' attacks. They would not be distressed by a demonstration that Macpherson's attribution of capitalist market assumptions to Hobbes, Locke, and others is nuanced, since they maintain that these thinkers are wrongly interpreted by such attribution, nuanced or otherwise. There is here a fundamental standoff. For instance, Macpherson makes much of Hobbes's assertion that:

> The Value or WORTH of a man, is as of all other things, his price; that is to say, so much as would be given for the use of his power: and therefore is not absolute, but a thing dependent on the need and judgment of another. (Hobbes 1968 [1651], 151–152, pt. 1 ch. x, emphases in original)

One of the critics, Keith Thomas, argues that Macpherson's economic interpretation of this passage, though it 'probably would have had the support of Marx,' is misleading: 'It is quite possible that ... Hobbes's statement is not concerned with economic transactions in early capitalist society at all, but rather with the nature of human reputation,' suggesting further that it may have had to do with feudal notions of praise or fame. (1965, 230)

A central thesis of Locke on which Macpherson focuses is about the related concepts of self-ownership and property, as in Locke's central assertion that:

> Though the Earth and all inferior Creatures be common to all men, yet every Man has a Property in his own Person. This no Body has any Right to but himself. The Labour of his Body, and the works of his Hands, we may say are properly his. Whatsoever then he removes out of the State that Nature hath provided, and left it in, he has mixed his Labour with, and joyned to it something that is his own, and thereby makes it his Property. (1960 [1689], 305–306, §27)

Tully's interpretation of this thesis relates it to the views of Hugo Grotius who, according to Tully, used the concept of self-ownership to mean self-preservation to which everyone has a right and which governments should respect. The concept is, as Tully puts it, a 'moral, political and military, not economic one.' (1993, 82) Regarding property, on this reading, Locke was just referring to 'the civil and religious rights of Dissenters and their possessions, which were confiscated during the great persecutions of the Restoration.' (84)

Thomas's non-economic interpretation of the passage about the worth of a man being his price is strained in light of the language of Hobbes's own explication: 'And as in other things, so in men, not the seller, but the buyer determines the Price.' (Hobbes *ibid.*, 152) Contrary to the charge of some critics (e.g., Miller 1982, 123; Ryan 1988, 101) that Macpherson ignores the emphasis Hobbes places on honour, he attends at some length to this notion in his discussion of the 'worth' passage. (PI, 37–40) Quoting Hobbes's assertion that 'Honourable is whatsoever possession, action, or quality, is an argument and signe of power,' Macpherson sees Hobbes as treating the degree of honour (or of dishonour) afforded a person by others as a manifestation of their estimation of that person's 'power to command the services of others.' (PI, 38ff; Hobbes 1968, 155) No doubt there is room for interpretative debate here, but Hobbes's language gives at least prima facie credence to Macpherson's interpretation. Perhaps this is why another critic, D.D. Raphael, characterizes Hobbes as being 'deliberately satirical' in the 'worth of a man' passage. (cited in Townshend, 42)

Similarly, much of Locke's language in his discussions of self-ownership and property lends itself most conveniently to economic understanding, as for example:

> Thus the Grass my Horse has bit; the turf my Servant has cut; and the Ore I have digg'd in any place where I have a right to them in common with others, become my Property, without the assignation or consent of any body. The labour that was mine, removing them out of that common state they were in, hath fixed my Property in them. (1960, 307, §28)

Perhaps, with the ingenuity characteristic of Tully's historical surveys, such passages can be interpreted as part of a non-economic, political theory about government responsibility to respect self-determination in general, and this would be at odds with Macpherson's approach to Locke; though, again, the economic intent of the quoted passage suggests otherwise. In lieu of pursuing all the interpretative disagreements between Macpherson and his critics, this appendix flags three pertinent features of Macpherson's approaches to the classic texts and to political-economic history generally.

Interpretation of texts: Regarding textual interpretation, Tully contrasts 'understanding' and 'explanation,' where the former 'turns on recovering the meaning [an] author intended to convey by reading the text in light of the available conventions and assumptions, and so of coming to understand it in those terms.' (1993, 99; Skinner 1988, 78) Tully and other critics of Macpherson view him as trying not to understand but to explain Hobbes, Locke, and the rest by reference to a Marxist-like historiographical theory of capitalism in terms the classic authors would not recognize as reflecting their intentions. Neither of these describes Macpherson's approach. In section two of his introduction to *Possessive Individualism*, 'Problems of Interpretation,' Macpherson outlines a method that is neither the entirely internal one Tully recommends nor an external, historiographical approach.

Macpherson aims instead to identify authors' 'assumptions,' some of which they do not state, either because they take them for granted or because they do not fully understand their implications. He gives as an example of the first sort of assumption that the Levellers never doubted that 'servants are rightly excluded from the franchise.' (PI, 6) Much of the book is devoted to exposing the second sort of assumptions. An example is a position Macpherson sees as implied in Hobbes that only in a market society could people be in the perpetual competition for power that concerns him (PI, 59) Macpherson does not see such assumptions as entirely foreign to the viewpoints of Hobbes and Locke, and in agreement with Tully on this point he distinguishes identification of not clearly understood assumptions from the imputation to an author of unconscious views 'which we take for granted but which a writer of an earlier century would not.' (PI, 6–7)

For Macpherson, one is still justified in attributing these unarticulated assumptions to an author when:

> Such assumptions do make sense of [an author's overall] argument (or more sense than can otherwise be made of it), and are ones that we can now see might readily have arisen from that thinker's experience of his own society, and when, moreover, they are repeatedly implied in various of his incidental arguments. (PI, 6)

Macpherson applies these criteria in detail to Hobbes, Harrington, and Locke, and he buttresses his interpretations by showing how recognition of an assumption helps to resolve problems, or what he calls 'inconsistencies,' in an author's theories. One of these is an apparent contradiction in Harrington's treatment of preconditions in the commonwealth he recommends where he sometimes sees the bulk of property residing in a majority, sometimes in a minority. Or there is vacillation on the part of Locke between characterizing 'property' as 'Lives, Liberties, and Estates' (1960, 137, §§123, 131, 137) and a more limited characterization as only goods or land. (193, §138–140) Another inconsistency, called a paradox by Macpherson, is the question for Hobbes of how people perpetually in conflict can agree to support an overriding sovereign.

Macpherson maintains that if Locke's assumption of an unavoidable class division between property holders and the propertyless is taken into account the inconsistency in use of the term 'property' is explained: 'The ambiguity as to who are members of civil society by virtue of the supposed original contract allows Locke to consider all men as members for the purposes of being ruled and only the men of estate as members for the purposes of ruling.' (PI, 248–249) Harrington's contradiction is resolved on the assumption that the initially excessive power of a minority gentry must be constrained in order to enlist support for achieving a bourgeois commonwealth, where subsequently a shared belief that market forces favour everyone obscures the ability of this minority to acquire a disproportionate amount of property. (PI, 188–190)

As to the apparent paradox in Hobbes, Macpherson argues that this can be resolved by reference to the exigency in a competitive-market society of enforcing rules that facilitate ongoing competition in part by preventing mutual destruction of the competitors. (PI, 100–101, 103–106) While in each case assumptions are not explicitly formulated and may not be fully comprehended by Hobbes, Harrington, or Locke, their attribution is not entirely foreign to their ways of thinking and helps to explain their aims.

Political focus. A second general feature of Macpherson's approach pertains to its focus. Macpherson was not pretending to offer comprehensive and synoptic accounts of all dimensions of the historical thinkers addressed in *Possessive Individualism*. Though he thought that his political-economic readings of them provide more accurate accounts than those that ignore or play down economic and class-sensitive aspects, Macpherson was motivated by contemporary political concerns in proffering these accounts. When it is seen how deeply and persistently possessive-individualist assumptions are embedded in the earlier theories, he maintains, 'we can consider how far [their continuing persistence] is responsible for the difficulties of liberal-democratic theory in our own time.' (PI, 4)

In his chapter on James Harrington, Macpherson quotes a claim by John Pocock that Harrington 'has no conception whatever that there exists a complex web of economic relationships between men which can be studied in itself and which determines the distribution of power among them.' (quoted in PI, 175, from Pocock 1957, 128–129) Macpherson credits Pocock for correcting an overly economic interpretation of Harrington's motives, but against Pocock's allegation he describes several economic features of seventeenth-century England to which Harrington devoted explicit attention. (PI, 175–181) If Pocock's phrase, 'which can be studied in itself,' is taken to deny that Harrington attended only to economic features of his society, Macpherson agrees. In one of his treatments Pocock acknowledges that Harrington paid attention to some economic matters, but holds that the ascendant gentry for Harrington did not purchase their main property, land, 'in order to sell it' or that they saw it as 'a commodity and source of profit.' (1975, 67) Pocock's argument is that the gentry accumulated property for the purpose of gaining the resources to allow them to lead virtuous lives as republican citizens. (e.g., 1985, 68, 107)

Macpherson does not address this motivational question, but in principle he could acknowledge some plausibility in it. 'If Harrington's gentry were bourgeois,' he writes, 'they were still gentry, with a sufficiently different way of life and code of behaviour that a separate place had to be found for them,' and Harrington 'did not resolve all relations between men into relations of the market.' (PI, 193) These allowances are compatible with depicting the gentry as one component of an ascending, non-feudal economic class performing 'capitalist functions, by which private accumulation would increase national wealth.' (*ibid.*) The contemporary applications Macpherson finds in his study of Harrington are that a capitalist market society can avoid anarchistic competition through intra-class cohesion (PI, 267) and that revolutionary discontent can be resisted by allowing for equality but restricting it just to legal equality of opportunity. (PI, 185–186)

Historical processes. A third pertinent feature of Macpherson's orientation towards economic history is an implied conception of historical periods. Macpherson was interested in *la longue durée* of intellectual history (McKay 2014, 322), which he saw as comprised of processes. This perspective is at odds with that of David Miller, who, citing features of seventeenth-century politics and economics that differentiate it from modern capitalism, writes that 'English society in the period we are now considering ... should be regarded as *sui generis*, neither feudal nor market, and its ideology likewise.' (1982, 126)

Macpherson's contrasting orientation is that the period in question was part of a protracted process stretching from fully feudal society to developed industrial capitalism. As noted, he viewed seventeenth-century capitalism as not primarily industrial, and he allowed that 'Hobbes was addressing men who did not yet think and behave entirely as market men.' (PI, 105) In explaining how Hobbes could sanction much more in the way of limitations to individual property than Locke, Macpherson avers that 'Hobbes was writing in an economy in which the process of primary accumulation of capital was still of first importance [and] to facilitate that accumulation, a sovereign power which could cut through all the traditional restraints was needed.' (EJ, 145)

In his criticism of Macpherson on this topic Berlin asks:

[I]s it truly the case that England in Hobbes's youth was a market society already so free from medieval survivals and the older hierarchical world, that its power-seeking men ... formed in the Marxist sense a competitive capitalist society, rather than a less neatly classifiable social whole, pregnant with the new bourgeois order, but still heavy with the landed and hierarchical past? (1964, 452)

This is an apt question, asked from a 'process' perspective. Macpherson differs from Berlin in thinking that the birth of some form of market society had already taken place by the time of Hobbes and Locke. On this perspective, identifying any pre-capitalist elements in seventeenth-century England does not provide decisive proof in such disputes.

As in the case of all analyses of a thing in process of change, there is room for debate about what is required to merit attributing significant changes in it, but the task of understanding something is different if one is looking for new features and trends, recognizing that they will coexist with prior features, than if one sees any continuity with the past as proof that the thing has not undergone change. Macpherson believed that in this period England 'approximated closely to a possessive market society,' and he provided a list of characteristics to substantiate this view (PI, 61–62), but this is consistent with realizing that it was not a full-blown capitalist society of the twentieth-century sort.

Since the focus of the present book is on the contemporary relevance of Macpherson's political views, not much hinges on the soundness or otherwise of his critics' allegations. For his political purposes, Macpherson could have limited himself just to exposing possessive-individualist assumptions of contemporary twentieth-century theorists, or, as Miller suggests (1982, 127), he could have started with the thought of James Mill and Jeremy Bentham. Still, something would be lost by abstracting from the interpretations of *Possessive Individualism*. Macpherson's explication of twentieth-century theorists by relating them to those of the seventeenth century exhibits the longevity and tenacity of a possessive-individualist culture.

References

Berlin, Isaiah. 1964. Hobbes, Locke and Professor Macpherson. *The Political Quarterly* 35 (4): 444–468.
Hobbes, Thomas. 1968 [1651]. *Leviathan*. Harmondsworth, UK: Penguin Books.
Leiss, William. 2009 [1988]. *C.B. Macpherson: Dilemmas of Liberalism and Socialism*. 2nd ed. Montreal and Kingston: McGill-Queen's University Press.
Locke, John. 1960 [1689]. *Two Treatises of Government*. Cambridge: Cambridge University Press.
Luxemburg, Rosa. 2010 [1915]. *Socialism or Barbarism: The Selected Writings of Rosa Luxemburg*. London: Pluto Press.

Macpherson, Crawford Brough. 1953. [DA] *Democracy in Alberta.* Toronto: University of Toronto Press. Reissued with an Introduction by Nelson Wiseman. Toronto: University of Toronto Press, 2013.

———. 1962. [PI] *The Political Theory of Possessive Individualism: Hobbes to Locke.* Oxford: Oxford University Press. Reissued with an Introduction by Frank Cunningham. Toronto: Oxford University Press, 2011.

———. 1965. [RWD] *The Real World of Democracy.* Toronto: Canadian Broadcasting Corporation. Reprints: Oxford: Oxford University Press, 1966; also Toronto: House of Anansi Press, 1992.

———. 1973. [DT] *Democratic Theory: Essays in Retrieval.* Oxford: Oxford University Press. Reissued with an Introduction by Frank Cunningham. Toronto: Oxford University Press, 2012.

———. 1977. [L&T] *The Life and Times of Liberal Democracy.* Oxford: Oxford University Press. Reissued with an Introduction by Frank Cunningham. Toronto: Oxford University Press, 2012.

———. 1980. *Burke.* Toronto: Oxford University Press. Reissued with an Introduction by Frank Cunningham. Toronto: Oxford University Press, 2013.

———. 1984. [EJ] *The Rise and Fall of Economic Justice.* Oxford: Oxford University Press. Reissued with an Introduction by Frank Cunningham. Toronto: Oxford University Press, 2013.

Macpherson, Kay. 1994. *When in Doubt Do Both: The Times of My Life.* Toronto: University of Toronto Press.

McKay, Ian. Forthcoming. *A New Method of Liberty: C.B. Macpherson and the Global Crisis of Liberal Order.*

———. 2014. A Half-Century of Possessive Individualism: C.B. Macpherson and the Twenty-First Century Prospects. *Journal of the Canadian Historical Association* 25 (1): 306–340.

Miller, David. 1982. The Macpherson Version. *Political Studies* 30 (1): 120–127.

Pocock, John G.A. 1957. *The Ancient Constitution and the Feudal Law.* Cambridge: Cambridge University Press.

———. 1975. Early Modern Capitalism: The Augustan Perception. In *Feudalism, Capitalism, and Beyond*, ed. Eugene F. Kamenka and R.S. Neale, 62–83. Canberra: Australian National University Press.

———. 1985. *Virtue, Commerce, and History.* Cambridge: Cambridge University Press.

Ray, B.N. 1996. *C.B. Macpherson and Liberalism.* New Delhi: Kanishka Publishers.

Ryan, Alan. 1988. Hobbes and Individualism. In *Perspectives on Hobbes*, ed. Graham A.J. Rogers and Alan Ryan, 81–105. Oxford: Oxford University Press.

Skinner, Quentin. 1988. Meaning and Understanding in the History of Ideas. In *Meaning and Context: Quentin Skinner and His Critics*, ed. James Tully, 29–78. Oxford: Polity Press.

Thomas, Keith. 1965. The Social Origins of Hobbes' Political Thought. In *Hobbes Studies*, ed. Keith C. Brown, 185–236. Cambridge, MA: Cambridge University Press.
Townshend, Jules. 2000. *C.B. Macpherson and the Problem of Liberal Democracy.* Edinburgh: University of Edinburgh Press.
Tully, James. 1993. *An Approach to Political Philosophy: Locke in Contexts.* Cambridge: Cambridge University Press.

CHAPTER 2

Macpherson and Liberal Democracy

For many, both liberal democrats and socialists, the notion of liberal-democratic socialism is oxymoronic. For example, arguing in favour of a Rousseau-inspired socialism and against Macpherson, Andrew Levine concludes that: 'Neither adding a theory of justice to liberal-democratic theory nor expunging "possessive individualist" elements from [it] will suffice to produce a genuine and satisfactory "supersession" of liberal democracy.' (1981, 206) Macpherson himself was cognizant of the intimate association of liberal democracy and capitalism: 'It cannot be too often recalled that liberal democracy is strictly a capitalist phenomenon.' (DT, 173, and see RWD, 4) And he notes that 'what is usually … considered to be the liberal tradition' has 'from the beginning included an acceptance of the market freedoms of a capitalist society.' (L&T, 20)

Nonetheless, Macpherson conceived his vision as a version of liberal democracy, specifically a socialist version. That liberal democracy has historical roots in capitalism does not mean for him that it must always be capitalistic: 'The reason "liberal" did mean acceptance of the capitalist market society, during the formative century of liberal democracy, does not apply any longer.' (*ibid*., 21) Nor does it preclude egalitarian and democratic reforms being made within liberal states, since, as noted in the overview of his writings in the previous chapter, he saw values compatible with socialism and in fact requiring it for full realization in the history of democracy even predating a liberalism that unquestionably accepted capitalism.

In *The Rise and Fall of Economic Justice* Macpherson distinguishes among liberal theorists who accept the status quo, theorists who, like John Stuart Mill, see liberal-democratic practices as falling short of its developmental-democratic potentials, and those who reject liberal democracy, which they would replace 'totally by Marxian theory and practice,' and he places himself in the second category. (EJ, 56) Macpherson concludes *The Life and Times of Liberal Democracy* by maintaining that the form of participatory democracy he defends in this book 'would be in the best tradition of liberal democracy.' (L&T, 115) His stated aim in *The Political Theory of Possessive Individualism* is not to abandon but to 'repair' liberal democracy by bringing back 'a sense of the moral worth of the individual, and combine it again with a sense of the moral value of community.' (PI, 2)

It is abstractly conceivable that Macpherson was not sincere in labelling himself a liberal democrat but was opportunistically posing as one to sell a non-liberal-democratic, likely Marxist, agenda to political theorists and in popular forums. Against such a conspiratorial interpretation is that Macpherson's main works were written in post-McCarthyist times and moreover in Canada, which is less virulently anti-socialist than the United States. In fact, he took at least as much flak from the relatively large number of leftist scholars in the academy of his times for his friendly stance towards liberal democracy as he did from the anti-socialists. In this milieu there was little incentive to disguise left-wing ideas. A more challenging claim is that Macpherson was mistaken in thinking that liberal democracy and socialism can be conjoined. Some headway towards meeting this challenge is made by taking a refined approach to political orientations.

Rather than regarding political terms like 'freedom,' 'equality,' 'democracy,' or 'justice' as having univocal and unambiguous meanings, such concepts are all, as the philosopher William Gallie puts it, 'essentially contested.' (1955) Or in a similar vein they are what Ernesto Laclau and Chantal Mouffe, borrowing from semiotic linguistic theory, designate 'floating signifiers,' amenable to alternative interpretations. (1985, 112–114) For them, contests in political culture to win people to a favoured point of view are not matters of abstractly persuading them of the soundness of some political theory, but are embedded in oppositional politics. This suggests one way of conceiving Macpherson's project. He anticipates the sort of analysis of Mouffe and Laclau in arguing that the ideological dominance or hegemony of Western capitalism has been achieved by fusing 'the values of liberal democracy, of possessive individualism, and of anti-communism.' (DT, 168) His counter-hegemonic project is to provide for social activists, the media, educators, and the like a well-articulated and historically motivated orientation towards liberal democracy that integrates it with developmentalism.

Important for Macpherson's project thus conceived is to maintain some points of contact between hegemonic conceptions and counter-hegemonic ones. That a term is subject to contestation does not mean that there are no limits on how to interpret it. Alternative signifiers 'float,' so to speak, within common river banks. For example, if it is not conceptually impossible for an imaginative enough theorist, it would surely be entirely futile to try suturing liberal democracy with the anti-democracy and anti-egalitarianism of theocracy, Nazism, or Stalinism. So the question remains of how liberal democracy is to be generically characterized in order to specify the sense in which Macpherson can be classified as a liberal democrat.

Liberal Democracy

In agreement with a traditional conception of liberal democracy, Macpherson identifies as its three principal values individual liberty, equality, and democracy. The first of these marked a dramatic shift in political thought from the seventeenth century to 'a new belief in the value and the rights of the individual.' (PI, 1) Even in its most rudimentary form where 'liberty' is sometimes distinguished from 'freedom' to pertain just to legal protection of certain rights, this concept includes a notion of equality among people with respect to this protection that broke with aristocratic conceptions of a hierarchy of entitlements, and it was further enhanced to become political equality when individual liberty was conjoined with electoral democracy.

The notion of a union of liberty, equality, and democracy as Macpherson treats it is both narrow and broad. It is narrow in focusing on the morally normative side of liberal democracy. Claims that liberal democracy requires a competitive capitalist market or that elected parliamentary assemblies and leaders are all that is required for a democratic polity are not about the value of liberal democracy but about how its values are best, or can only, put into practice. They are not, that is, claims about the moral values infusing liberal democracy but claims about how these values are to be realized. At the same time the values of liberty, equality, and democracy are broad in the sense that each of them admits of alternative interpretations. This is what allows for contestation, not only between liberal democrats and anti-liberal democrats but among liberal democrats themselves, even though contests not infrequently take the form of champions of an interpretation alleging that those who do not share their viewpoint are therefore not genuine liberal democrats. (These issues are addressed in Cunningham 1987, ch. 7 and 2002, ch. 3.)

In the case of each core value, interpretations can be arranged along a spectrum from thin or minimal conceptions to thick or robust ones. Liberty may be regarded as no more than the legal ability to try to achieve certain of one's present preferences or as the possession of resources and opportunities required to attain one's most important life goals. Equality may be thought of just as legally enforced equality of certain opportunities or in a substantive way such that enjoying a society's benefits and bearing its burdens are equitably distributed. Thin democracy is the bare ability to vote for or against candidates presented in elections, while more robust democracy includes the ability actively to participate in all aspects of electoral processes as well as in many other collective endeavours. With his most favoured liberal-democratic thinkers, J.S. Mill and John Dewey, Macpherson endorses robust interpretations.

INDIVIDUALISM

A core aspect of the liberal dimension of liberal democracy pertinent to Macpherson's location in it is his commitment to normative individualism. In an essay reproduced in *The Rise and Fall of Economic Justice*, 'Pluralism, Individualism and Participation,' he lists eight species of pluralism, all of which champion individualism—'pluralism *is* individualism writ large' (EJ, 92)—though they differ in their assumptions about human nature, ranging from those that take 'the individual to be essentially a maximizing consumer of utilities' to ones for which the individual is 'essentially an exerter and developer of his/her human capacities.' (*Ibid.*) Six of the versions are seen by Macpherson as broadly in keeping with his own view, which he here designates 'developmental individualism.' (96)

Macpherson's commitment to normative individualism is combined by him with rejection of an 'atomistic' conception. Atomism has both normative and descriptive dimensions. In an essay on this topic Charles Taylor approvingly refers to Macpherson's 'affirmation of individual rights which presuppose[s] society' (Taylor 1979, 40), just as in a later work he endorses Macpherson's alternative to Locke's version of individualism. (1989, 195–196) Taylor identifies one kind of normative atomism as investing the protection of individual rights with political primacy abstracting from the human capacities (save the minimal ability simply to make choices) that are worthy of respect and encouragement (1979, 40–51), and he might also have referred to Macpherson's endorsement of 'positive liberty' as 'the ability to live in accordance with one's own conscious purposes, to act and decide for oneself rather than to be acted upon and decided for by others.' (DT, 109)

In accord with Taylor's recommendation, Macpherson's positive conception of liberty ties it to an essential human capacity, and while the capacity may not be as fulsome as Taylor would like, it is more than the bare ability to make choices. In chapter five Macpherson's notion of positive liberty will be addressed in more detail. Suffice it for present purposes to observe that he intends his conception of it (as 'counter-extractive liberty') to 'serve the libertarian purpose of warning people off the kind of debased liberty which negates liberty.' (DT, 119) That is, he sees this nonatomistic conception not in competition with individual liberty, but in aid of it.

If Macpherson cannot be described as an atomist in Taylor's sense, he is not a communitarian either as is manifest in an exchange between him and Alasdair MacIntyre. In this exchange, the nature of Macpherson's individualism, both normative and descriptive, is exhibited. MacIntyre calls Macpherson's approach 'cooperative and creative individualism' (1976, 178), and, though agreeing with much of its political thrust, he criticizes Macpherson for failing to break with individualism. Macpherson reacts that to be charged with 'being too individualist is a pleasant change' (1976, 195), and he then he reiterates earlier assertions that society 'is a positive agent in the development of human capacities, that those capacities are socially derived, that their development must also be social, and that society is the medium through which human capacities are developed.' (*ibid.*, 199, and see DT, 57)

It is in this spirit that Macpherson approvingly cites Marx's view that 'the human essence' is the 'ensemble of [one's] social relations' (EJ, 95; Marx 1976, 4), and he could as well have referred to a view of Marx and Engels quite in keeping with one of his central tenets: 'Only in the community has each individual the means of activating his gifts in all directions; hence personal freedom becomes possible only within the community.' (Marx and Engels 1976, 78) Macpherson's orientation rests on a distinction between (morally) normative and (social-scientifically) descriptive individualisms to urge, like some other liberal-democratic theorists, for example, Will Kymlicka (1990, 207–216, and see Mills 2017, 18–19), that the question of how individuals' aspirations are formed is different from the question of whether the aspirations are worthy of support.

Also, placing a high value on an individuals' achieving goals consonant with the full exercise of their truly human capacities is compatible with recognition that these may sometimes favour, and justly so, the advancement of collective rights, for example:

> [M]embership in a national or cultural community which has defined itself historically is part of what it means to be human, and is sometimes the most important part. And the right to national self-determination may be humanly more important to its claimants than any of the individual rights (as well as being seen as necessary to securing the latter). And the right of a subjected native people to its traditional way of life and to the resources necessary to maintain it may be the greater part of what it means to them to be human (as well as being, in the extreme case where genocide is threatened or in is process, prerequisite to any other rights). (EJ, 23)

Effectively and sincerely to defend the right of individual native people to preserve (or regain) the group-based traditions that give their lives meaning requires supporting the social (economic, political, etc.) conditions essential for the existence and flourishing of their groups. Thus, respecting individual rights sometimes requires endorsing collective rights.

That some rights accrue to people in virtue just of their being members of some group is consistent with acknowledging that the rights are enjoyed or their denial is suffered by the (present and future) individuals who make up the group, as opposed to by some mysterious super-individual entity. However, still compatibly with Macpherson's orientation, an also mystifying concept of what Harry Glasbeek labels 'sovereign individuals' should also be rejected. (1985, 284) An apt example is given by Larry Savage and Charles Smith, who report a declaration by George Brown (one of Canada's founding fathers) that while 'the law to the fullest extent provides for the protection and preservation of individual or personal liberty, it is equally against combinations [e.g.] for the purpose of raising wages.' (quoted in Savage and Smith 2017, 24) This is from an attack on a strike in Canada of typographical workers employed by Brown. Mitigated for a time in the twentieth century, this anti-collectivist perspective resurfaced with a vengeance with the later ascendancy of neoliberal governments in legislation restricting unions, which is typically justified in the name of a supposed right of an individual worker not to be union member or to join a strike action. (*ibid.*, chs. 1 and 4) This not the kind of stance Macpherson endorses or that his group-sensitive individualism commits him to.

Virginia Held, whose specifically feminist criticisms of Macpherson will be discussed in chapter nine, recognizes Macpherson's individualism and sees it as a defect in his thinking. For her Macpherson cannot 'appreciate the value of shared, relational activity' unless it 'would contribute to the maximization of individual development.' (1993, 149–150) But Macpherson argues that transcending a society imbued with possessive-individualist values and structures is required to enable people to develop and enjoy 'truly human powers,' some of which are intrinsically social—friendship, love, and others that could be included in his open-ended list—all of which require social cooperation and are incompatible with selfishly individualistic comportment.

The compatibility of such individual development with the enjoyment, promotion, and protection of certain social interactions ('shared, relational activity') is seen by Macpherson as a feature of the human condition, not, as Held puts it, as an 'evaluation of gains and losses to individuals in isolation from one another.' (*ibid.*, 151) Macpherson's version of normative individualism is close to J.S. Mill's notion of 'individuality.' While this involves freedom from social pressures or traditional customs to permit individuals to develop their unique potentials, it is not at all at odds with social sensibilities and commitments:

> In proportion to the development of his individuality, each person becomes more valuable to himself, and is therefore capable of being more valuable to others. There is a greater fulness of life about his own existence, and when there is more life in the units there is more in the mass which is composed of them. (Mill 1977a [1859], 266)

Macpherson maintains that to be fully human, the exercise of someone's capacities 'must be under one's own conscious control rather than at the dictate of another' and that 'a man's activity is to be regarded as human only insofar as it is directed by his own design' (DT, 56). The relation of this endorsement of Macpherson's normative individualism to his descriptive views on the social conditions for and origins of people's endeavours may be illustrated by contrasting his approach with Steven Lukes's discussion of 'abstract individualism':

Social and political rules and institutions are, on this view, regarded collectively as an artifice, a modifiable instrument, a means of fulfilling independently given individual objectives; the means and the ends are distinct. The crucial point about this conception is that the relevant features of individuals determining the ends which social arrangements are held (actually or ideally) to fulfil, whether these features are called instincts, faculties, needs, desires, rights, etc., are assumed as given, independently of a social context. (Lukes 1973, 75)

Macpherson's understanding is compatible with the first sentence of this passage, but not with the second, which Lukes seems to assume is entailed by the normative claim. 'A society of *some* kind,' Macpherson maintains, 'is a necessary condition of the development of individual capacities. A *given* society, with all its enabling and coercive institutions may be judged more of a help than a hindrance, or more of a hindrance than a help, at any given time ... The objective is to find a form of society which will be more of a help and less of a hindrance.' (DT, 57) Thus Macpherson does not, as Lukes later charges, see individuals 'in abstraction from the social relations and forms of community' that impede or facilitate their development. (Lukes 1979, 151)

Acknowledging social determinants of individuals' aspirations and opportunities is compatible with making normative political prescriptions centred on individuals. The morally normative dimension of Macpherson's overall project may be viewed as taking sides, not with communitarians against liberal individualists, but with one stream of liberal theory against another. Regarding the possessive-individualist strain he sees in Bentham, which he criticizes, and the developmental one of Mill, which he endorses, Macpherson maintains that both are advanced 'in the name of individual personality,' but that 'the essential character of that personality is seen differently.' (DT, 4, and see EJ, 93–96) The similarity between Bentham and Mill is that for each of them, as for Macpherson, social arrangements ought to serve individuals.

More on Macpherson's Liberal-Democratic Credentials

John Stuart Mill and John Locke are often designated prototypical liberal democrats in virtue of their advocacy of combining democracy with the protection of rights. In Locke's case, democracy means majority rule (though a 'majority,' as Macpherson with several other critics observes, within a narrow range of the population). Also, like many subsequent liberal democrats, Locke centrally includes property rights among those to be protected. Mill makes it clear that majority rule is mainly exercised by parliaments that should be elected by a portion of the population much larger than Locke's (mainly due to Mill's prescribed inclusion of women), and his list of rights is in keeping with those generally thought of as liberal such as freedom of speech and conscience. Macpherson also favours some form of representative democracy, but he wants this to be conjoined with provision for participatory democracy.

On one interpretation, this conjunction would challenge classifying Macpherson as a liberal democratic, but it would also exclude Mill, whom Macpherson designated 'the first serious liberal-democratic theorist' (DT, 174) since, as Carole Pateman and other participatory democrats approvingly note, Mill, too, was in favour of democratic participation beyond just voting. (Pateman 1970, 28–35) What Macpherson and Mill share is the view that representative and participatory democracy are potentially complementary, as when Mill prefaces his conclusion that government in a political entity as large as a state must be representative and argues that this form of government requires a public-spirited citizenry nurtured by local participation that 'should everywhere be as great as the general degree of improvement of the community should allow.' (1977b [1861], 412; Macpherson EJ, 53)

As to property, there are continuing debates in several liberal-democratic countries, including Macpherson's Canada, over whether private property should be constitutionally protected (it is not in Canada, but is in the United States). Claims that in virtue of his views favouring participation Mill is not a consistent liberal democrat or that countries that exclude private property from constitutional entrenchment cannot be liberal democracies need to appeal to some independent, universally agreed-upon standard for what counts as liberal democratic. The absence of such a standard highlights the contested nature of this concept.

Another possible ground for challenging Macpherson's liberal-democratic credentials pertains to his privileging some potentials as truly human and his related defence of positive liberty. In his treatment of liberty, Mill famously announces that the 'the only freedom that deserves the name is that of pursuing our own good in our own way' (1977a [1859], 226), thus giving expression to the 'pluralist' dimension of liberal democracy. On a pure version of this Millian principle, the democratic state should favour no particular values or views about what constitutes a good person or a good society but should confine itself to mitigating destructive conflict and to pursuing those goals about which at least a majority are in accord.

For Macpherson, by contrast, the state should facilitate people developing certain of their potentials—the 'truly human' ones referred to earlier. 'Democracy' is defined by Macpherson as 'the equal development of everyone's truly human potentials.' He criticizes Isaiah Berlin's restriction of liberty to 'negative freedom' or the ability of people to do whatever they wish unimpeded by the deliberate interference of others (Berlin 1969, 122) and defends instead a version of positive liberty, where people enjoy the abilities to develop their truly human potentials and to participate in collective, democratic activities. (DT, essay v) However, like Berlin, Macpherson excludes counting as liberty a situation where people are coerced by a minority of the self-declared 'fully rational.' (*ibid.*, 108–109)

Still it is not hard to identify circumstances when a policy favouring positive liberty in Macpherson's sense conflicts with somebody's negative liberty. But so will the exercises of negative liberties sometimes be in conflict with each other, and, as Macpherson notes, some freedoms of individuals are unavoidably constrained when they are out of accord with majority decisions. (1942, 417) Short of somehow realizing the dream (or nightmare) of a society having attained utter homogeneity of interests among their citizens, conflicts will remain a feature of human interactions.

Faced with persisting conflict the tasks of the political theorists are: modestly, to insist on the rule of law and recommend informal ways to avoid violence; more ambitiously, to identify and encourage conditions the alteration of which mitigates the severity of destructive conflicts, in Macpherson's view scarcity and the capitalist market; or, most ambitiously, actively to promote adoption of values that do not lend themselves to such conflict—for Macpherson, those of developmental democracy. Largely because mainstream liberal-democratic theorists have been unwilling to challenge capitalist markets, they have confined themselves to the first of these strategies. Dropping passive or active support for capitalism and attacking the possessive-individualist values that accompany it require what Macpherson calls a 'post-liberal-democratic theory,' which, far from being opposed to liberal democracy, is essential for 'justifying the liberal-democratic state and society as they now are or might be improved.' (DT, 172)

Central to such a theory, as Macpherson envisages it, is that the state should pursue policies that privilege nurturing and exercising people's truly human powers. He thus positions himself in basic tension with the orientation of those towards the libertarian pole of liberal-democratic theorists. On their view, with a very few exceptions a state should not impede people exercising any of their powers or endorse policies favouring some powers. Macpherson anticipates this orientation when he argues that any democratic theory 'must start with the assumption that there are specifically or uniquely human capacities.' (DT, 53) The neoliberal state is a good example, informed as it is by free market-friendly views in keeping with values favouring capacities for unconstrained material acquisition and competition, that is, the values of possessive individualism.

Liberal political theorists come at an aspect of this question in addressing 'the paradox of liberalism': if the state in a liberal democracy favours some values or visions over others, it is in violation of Mill's pluralist dictum, but if it maintains strict neutrality, it can find itself sanctioning values conducive to the destruction of a liberal-democratic society. Political theorists who address this question may be classified according to how far and in what respects they think either value neutrality or value commitment on the part of a state should be embraced. Macpherson is found in the company of John Rawls (1996), William Galston (1991), Jean Hampton (1989), and many others who favour active state endorsement of certain values. Though there are differences among these theorists over just what values a state should promote, they all represent themselves as liberal democrats. Absence of an independent ground to deny liberal-democratic status to such theorists provides another example of the contested nature of this phenomenon.

Vanguardism

In *Democratic Theory* Macpherson warns against the anti-democratic degeneration of vanguardism citing Stalin's Russia, and regarding African national liberation movements he observes that the only ones where a vanguard did not degenerate is where the vanguard 'made it its business to develop a grass-roots democratic participation.' (DT, 107) Peter Lindsay's point is well taken that 'the cases for [democratic] participation and vanguardism are irreconcilably contradictory' (1996, 92), and in an interview on the anniversary of Marx's death Macpherson is in accord with this opinion: 'rule by a vanguard is simply inconsistent with participatory democracy.' (1983, 10) However, Macpherson's stance is not unequivocally anti-vanguardist. In *The Rise and Fall*, he maintains that the suppression of civil liberties 'in an immediate post-revolutionary period may be defensible, but it is not defensible in any longer run.' (R&F, 53) In *Democratic Theory*, just after the passage quoted above, he makes the puzzling statement that even when not degenerating into anti-democracy, national liberation leadership's reliance on a 'perverted doctrine' of vanguardism 'is not a necessary feature of even a revolutionary regime which is *for a time necessarily illiberal*.' (DT, 107, emphasis added)

The starkness of what seems a straightforward contradiction here can be muted by distinguishing between vanguardism with respect to civil liberties and with respect to democracy. Macpherson's allowances for vanguardism usually pertain to the liberal dimension of liberal democracy, not to its democratic dimension, and (despite Lindsay's assertion that for Macpherson, liberalism is 'democracy by another name,' 1996, 101), these dimensions are different for him. Otherwise Macpherson's historical claim that liberalism antedated democracy and was only later wedded to it, which is seen as an insight with important theoretical implications by many, such as Ernesto Laclau (1993), would make no sense. So there is a difference between shelving democracy and suspending some civil liberties. But the civil liberties that could legitimately be set aside are limited for anyone who agrees with Mill that democracy and civil liberty are generally mutually reinforcing. (1977a [1859], 305–310)

Macpherson, himself, expresses agreement with this thesis: 'Without the civil liberties there can be no responsiveness of governments to the will of the people, for then that will have no way of making itself felt' (EJ, 53). Moreover, some of Macpherson's comments in support of *pro-temp* vanguard rule pertain specifically to democracy. In *The Real World of Democracy* he argues that in a revolutionary period 'when a substantial part of the society senses uneasily that it is dehumanized but does not know quite how … there is no use relying on the free votes of everybody to bring about a fully human society' (RWD, 19–20), and he goes on to assert that in such a situation a vanguard state 'may be called democratic.' (*ibid.*, 22) Since he sees such rule as temporary, Macpherson cannot mean by the latter assertion that vanguardism is a unique 'kind' of democracy, as was often claimed by defenders of Soviet rule, but he must mean that it is democratic in the sense of being, in certain circumstances, a necessary precondition for achieving future democracy.

B.N. Ray concludes that for Macpherson 'both democracy and freedom may be effectively proscribed or postponed indefinitely.' (1996, 109) This allegation is contrary to Macpherson's stated views on this topic which are guarded and of greatly limited scope. They are also sensitive to the actual circumstances within which national liberation efforts take place. The newly liberated countries Macpherson has in mind:

> want to move to a humanistic society, both without any 'dictatorship of the proletariat' and without setting up a capitalist market society internally. It is an open question whether they can …. Much will depend on the attitudes of the capitalist nations—aid and trade which will allow them to get on their feet, or political and economic pressure to reduce them to 'neo-colonialism.' (UTA 1971, 67a)

A charitable interpretation of Macpherson on this topic is that he was genuinely conflicted—unlike those who do not harbour liberal-democratic sentiments, or who are indifferent (or hostile) to the efforts of socialist countries or national liberation movements in difficult circumstances, or who are ignorant of these circumstances. Whether the views of Macpherson, who was acutely aware of the constraining circumstances, are evidence against his being a consistent champion of liberal democracy depends in part on how stringently criteria for being such are to be applied and in part on whether the limitations on liberal rights he has in mind would in fact advance liberal-democratic goals and are unavoidable for this purpose. Full development of examples by Macpherson, unfortunately lacking, might have strengthened his case on this score.

Though it does not justify Macpherson's comments in support, albeit qualifiedly, of vanguardism, it is apt to note that every modern democracy has sometimes deviated in its actions from liberal and/or democratic principles in ways that go far beyond anything Macpherson was prepared to sanction. Formally these include proroguing legislative assemblies and enabling police infringement on civil liberties. Informally, democracy is also knowingly undermined by wholescale reneging on campaign promises, rigging elections, and selling votes to moneyed interests. When international comportment is taken into account more, and more extreme, examples are common, as in active support to the point of subversion for anti-democratic regimes that brutally violate human rights. If such domestic and international measures exclude a country from being liberal democratic, this means that there are not now nor have there likely ever been any liberal-democratic states.

Unlike Mill, who saw despotism as appropriate for whole civilizations in 'those backward states of society in which the race itself may be considered as in its nonage' (1977a [1859], 224) Macpherson's comments about curtailing democracy are restricted to national liberation struggles which confronted severely limiting options. Notwithstanding his understanding of these limitations, Macpherson remained a champion of liberal democracy and was no supporter of the dictatorship of the proletariat. What kind of a socialist he should be taken to be is the topic of the next chapter, where his opposition to vanguardism with respect to the developed world will be treated.

REFERENCES

Berlin, Isaiah. 1969. Two Concepts of Liberty. In *Four Essays on Liberty*, ed. Isaiah Berlin, 118–172. Oxford: Oxford University Press.
Cunningham, Frank. 1987. *Democratic Theory and Socialism*. Cambridge: Cambridge University Press.
———. 2002. *Democratic Theory: A Critical Introduction*. London: Routledge.
Gallie, W.B. 1955/1956. Essentially Contested Concepts. *Proceedings of the Aristotelian Society* 56: 167–198.
Galston, Willliam. 1991. *Liberal Purposes: Virtue and Diversity in the Liberal State*. New York: Cambridge University Press.
Glasbeek, Harry. 1985. Law: Real and Ideological Constraints on the Working Class. In *Law in a Cynical Society? Opinions and Law in the 1980's*, ed. Dale Gibson and Janet K. Baldwin, 282–301. Calgary: Carswell.
Hampton, Jean. 1989. Should Political Philosophy Be Done Without Metaphysics. *Ethics* 99 (4): 791–814.
Held, Virginia. 1993. Freedom and Feminism. In *Democracy and Possessive Individualism: The Intellectual Legacy of C.B. Macpherson*, ed. Joseph Carens, 137–154. Albany: State University of New York Press.
Kymlicka, Will. 1990. *Contemporary Political Philosophy: An Introduction*. Oxford: Oxford University Press.
Laclau, Ernesto. 1993. The Signifiers of Democracy. In *Democracy and Possessive Individualism: The Intellectual Legacy of C.B. Macpherson*, ed. Joseph Carens, 221–234. Albany: State University of New York Press.
Laclau, Ernesto, and Chantal Mouffe. 1985. *Hegemony and Socialist Strategies*. London: Verso.
Levine, Andrew. 1981. *Liberal Democracy: A Critique of Its Theory*. New York: Columbia University Press.
Lindsay, Peter. 1996. *Creative Individualism: The Democratic Vision of C.B. Macpherson*. Albany: State University of New York Press.

Lukes, Steven. 1973. *Individualism*. New York: Harper & Row.
———. 1979. The Real and Ideal Worlds of Democracy. In *Powers, Possessions and Freedom: Essays in Honour of C.B. Macpherson*, ed. Alkis Kontos, 139–152. Toronto: University of Toronto Press.
MacIntyre, Alasdair. 1976. On "Democratic Theory: Essays in Retrieval" by C.B. Macpherson. *Canadian Journal of Philosophy* 6 (2): 177–181.
Macpherson, Crawford Brough. 1942. The Meaning of Economic Democracy. *University of Toronto Quarterly* 11 (4): 403–420.
———. 1962. [PI] *The Political Theory of Possessive Individualism: Hobbes to Locke*. Oxford: Oxford University Press. Reissued with an Introduction by Frank Cunningham. Toronto: Oxford University Press, 2010.
———. 1965. [RWD] *The Real World of Democracy*. Toronto: Canadian Broadcasting Corporation. Reprints: Oxford: Oxford University Press, 1966; and Toronto: House of Anansi Press, 1992.
———. 1971. [UTA] Marxian Theory. University of Toronto Archives, B1987-0069, Box 2a, file 4.
———. 1973. [DT] *Democratic Theory: Essays in Retrieval*. Oxford: Oxford University Press. Reissued with an Introduction by Frank Cunningham. Toronto: Oxford University Press, 2012.
———. 1976. Individualist Socialism? A Reply to Levine and MacIntyre. *Canadian Journal of Philosophy* 6 (2): 195–200.
———. 1977. [L&T] *The Life and Times of Liberal Democracy*. Oxford: Oxford University Press. Reissued with an Introduction by Frank Cunningham. Toronto: Oxford University Press, 2012.
———. 1983. Interview on the Centenary of Marx's Death. *Socialist Studies Annual*. Winnipeg: University of Manitoba Publication, 7–12. Reproduced in Frank Cunningham, *The Real World of Democracy Revisited* (1994). Atlantic Highlands, NJ: Humanities Press, 14–21.
———. 1984. [EJ] *The Rise and Fall of Economic Justice*. Oxford: Oxford University Press. Reissued with an Introduction by Frank Cunningham. Toronto: Oxford University Press, 2013.
Marx, Karl. 1976 [1845]. Theses on Feuerbach. In *Karl Marx, Frederick Engels Collected Works*, vol. 3, 3–5. London: Lawrence & Wishart.
Marx, Karl, and Frederick Engels. 1976 [1845–1847]. *The German Ideology*. In *Karl Marx, Frederick Engels Collected Works*, vol. 5. London: Lawrence & Wishart.
Mill, John Stuart. 1977a [1859]. *On Liberty*. In *The Collected Works of John Stuart Mill*, ed. J.M. Robson, vol. 18, 212–310. Toronto: University of Toronto Press.
———. 1977b [1861]. *On Representative Government*. In *The Collected Works of John Stuart Mill*, vol. 18, 371–577. Toronto: University of Toronto Press.

Mills, Charles. 2017. *Black Rights/White Wrongs: The Critique of Racial Liberalism*. Oxford: University of Oxford Press.
Pateman, Carole. 1970. *Participation and Democratic Theory*. Cambridge: Cambridge University Press.
Rawls, John. 1996. *Political Liberalism*. New York: Columbia University Press.
Ray, B.N. 1996. *C.B. Macpherson and Liberalism*. New Delhi: Kanishka Publishers.
Savage, Larry, and Charles W. Smith, eds. 2017. *Unions in Court: Organized Labour and the Charter of Rights and Freedoms*. Vancouver: University of British Columbia Press.
Taylor, Charles. 1979. Atomism. In *Powers, Possessions and Freedom: Essays in Honour of C.B. Macpherson*, ed. Alkis Kontos, 39–61. Toronto: University of Toronto Press. (Reprinted in Taylor's *Philosophical Papers*, vol. 2. Cambridge: Cambridge University Press, 1985. Essay 7.)
———. 1989. *Sources of the Self*. Cambridge, MA: Harvard University Press.

CHAPTER 3

Macpherson's Socialism

There are fewer challenges to the portrayal of Macpherson as a socialist than as a liberal democrat. Ellen Wood allows that Macpherson wished to classify himself as a socialist, but within a version of socialism eviscerated of progressive political impact by abandoning class struggle and having 'fallen under the spell of liberalism.' (1978, 239, and see the critique of Wood on this point by Leo Panitch 1981, 147–152) Andrew Levine echoes some other commentators in labelling Macpherson a social democrat, where social democracy for Levine 'has become an effort to reform and moralize capitalism.' (1976, 192) Progress can be made in evaluating such allegations by distinguishing among three aspects of theories and debates about socialism: those that concern themselves with socialist *visions*, that is, with conceptions of socialism's basic character and value; projections of governmental and economic *institutions* required to implement a socialist vision; and proposals about the *activities* required to secure the institutions.

Macpherson's almost exclusive emphasis is on a socialist vision. With reference to a criticism that he did not undertake an empirical assessment of the class forces conducive to socialist transformation, and reflecting his general orientation on such matters, he describes the contribution he thinks he can make:

At a level of some abstraction and by the principle of comparative advantage in any social division of labour I have thought myself better occupied with seeking to improve theoretical understanding. (1976, 425)

He regards his own major task as to articulate a developmental-democratic alternative to a social vision based on possessive-individualist principles and to expose and criticize the latter: 'We need a revolution in democratic consciousness' to which he hopes his theoretical work will contribute. (DT, 184) The vision Macpherson defends is developmental democracy itself in which, as discussed in the overview in chapter one, everyone enjoys the resources and opportunities to develop his or her truly human potentials to the fullest and where, whatever else these potentials may be, their development by some is not unavoidably at the expense of others but thrive on cooperation. Two aspects of this vision make it socialist.

EGALITARIANISM

First, Macpherson's vision places him within the tradition of socialist egalitarianism beginning at least with Claude-Henri Saint-Simon and Robert Owen (who independently coined the term 'socialism' in the early nineteenth century) through Louis Blanc and Louis-August Blanqui, Pierre-Joseph Proudon, Charles Fourier, Etienne Cabet, both wings of the first socialist international organization, the one represented by Ferdinand Lassalle, the other, which included Marx and Engels, by William Liebnknecht, and extending into socialist advocates in the twentieth century. (A useful survey is G.D.H. Cole's *A History of Socialist Thought*, 2003 [1931–1939]) Some of these socialists were more thoroughgoing egalitarians than others. Some ranked social cooperation or collective economic production on a par with or higher than equality, and they differed on just what should be equalized as well as on institutional and activist questions, but they all decried the inequalities of their times.

Further, they all saw as inadequate the mere absence of legal impediments to try to secure equality of opportunity or condition, and they promoted a conception of societies where equality is a core norm instead of being regarded as a barrier to more highly ranked goals such as (alleged) economic efficiency or freedom from regulatory government measures. This feature of socialist thought provides a criterion to sort social-democratic or other orientations that avoid using the term 'socialist' into those that are nonetheless socialistic and those that are not. For the non-socialist social democrat, for example, egalitarian policies are permissible only to the extent that they do not substantially inhibit private ownership and deployment of major means of production and distribution; whereas a socialistic social democracy is prepared to challenge core capitalist structures and policies.

ANTI-CAPITALISM

This brings us to the second socialist aspect of Macpherson's vision, its anti-capitalism. He defines 'capitalism,' whether *laissez-faire* or welfarist, as:

> [The] system in which production is carried on without authoritative allocation of work or rewards, but by contractual relations between free individuals (each possessing some resource be it only his own labour-power) who calculate their most profitable courses of action and employ their resources as that calculation dictates. (DT, 181)

When it is added to this that a few privately own the overwhelming bulk of a society's capital and other resources, the result is that the remaining members of the society have no option but to exchange the one thing they do own, their ability to work, for wages. This yields what Macpherson described as 'a continuous net transfer of part of the power of some men [workers] to others [capitalists], thus diminishing rather than maximizing the equal individual freedom to use and develop one's natural capacities.' (DT, 10–11)

The capacities of the large majority who possess only their ability to work are directly diminished in this process by denying them use of their productive powers for purposes they would otherwise chose themselves. Individuals' powers are indirectly diminished to the extent that extra-productive activities (hobbies, learning, artistic creation or enjoyment, local political engagement, pursuit of a full social life, etc.) are severely impeded due to inadequate remuneration and to the mind-numbing and time-consuming nature of much employed labour. (DT, 63–70) More than one commentator has noted that Macpherson's notion of the net transfer of powers is akin to Marx's theory of exploitation, that is, capitalist extraction of surplus value from wage labour, or even, according to Victor Svacek, an improvement on this theory. (1976, 405–406) The question of Macpherson's relation to Marxism is discussed in the appendix to this chapter.

INSTITUTIONS

True to his intention to focus on visionary theory, Macpherson has very little to say about governmental and economic institutions or about pro-socialist activism. In *The Life and Times of Liberal Democracy* he suggests that pyramiding governing structures would be the most compatible with the participatory democracy he endorses in that book, specifying that these should not be of the Soviet type but should include political parties (presumably genuinely competitive ones) and 'operate through a parliamentary or congressional structure.' Such speculation, he concludes, is 'as far as it is now feasible to go by way of a blueprint.' (L&T, 114)

Though he does not spell out projections for a socialist constitution and certainly did not think that the existence of formal rights alone suffices to realize a developmental-democratic vision, Macpherson remarks that whatever the detailed provisions of a socialist constitution, it should include 'constitutional guarantees of civil liberties and a legal system able to enforce them.' (DT, 153) With reference to the existing socialist societies of his time, he held that 'absence or severe restrictions of civil liberties' in them 'diminish men's powers *more* than does the market transfer of powers.' (DT, 14, emphasis added) It should be registered that Macpherson was an active civil libertarian. As Secretary of the Canadian Civil Liberties Association, he prominently engaged in an effort during the late 1940s to secure a constitutionally entrenched charter of rights (35 years in advance of this finally being achieved), and he drafted a petition to this end. (UTA 1947)

Macpherson engages in even less speculation about socialist economic institutions. Again, his focus is on a vision which could guide thought about economic structures. For example, in a criticism of welfare capitalism he writes:

> A fully democratic society requires democratic political control over the uses to which the amassed capital and the remaining natural resources are put. It probably does not matter whether this takes the form of social ownership of all capital, or a social control of it so thorough as to be virtually the same as ownership. But more welfare-state redistribution of the national income is not enough: no matter how much it might reduce class inequalities of income it would not touch class inequalities of power. (L&T, 111)

However, the part of his vision that decries a market society does commit him to be sceptical of the place of economic markets, however institutionally constrained.

An attempt to show that Macpherson was not hostile to such markets is made by Peter Lindsay, who offers an interpretation according to which Macpherson only wants the benefits of privately owned goods and services to be immune to market forces. Lindsay's interpretation is based on strained readings of isolated passages in essays by Macpherson (Lindsay 1996, 144–145; Macpherson 1978, 4, 206), and his related assertions that Macpherson was not a foe of exclusive property rights *per se* and even saw infinite desire as compatible with a democratic society (Lindsay 139, 129) are explicitly contradicted by Macpherson.

Another effort to make Macpherson's views more market friendly than Macpherson himself could allow is by William Leiss. Referring to a description by Macpherson of state regulation of markets in welfare capitalism as creating a 'quasi-market society.' (DT, 133–134) Leiss sees as a realistic implementation of Macpherson's orientation—already achieved in many OECD countries—extension of state intervention and provision of some public goods in a society that still maintains characteristics of capitalism. A quasi-market society for Leiss includes substantial state ownership and regulation of the economy with welfare floors, but in it 'labour is a commodity' and '[i]ncome and wealth distributions show large and persistent inequities.' As well, Leiss thinks Macpherson's hostility to consumerism should be tempered. (2009 [1988], 115–142) As Jules Townshend notes, this perspective is simply out of accord with both the letter and the spirit of Macpherson's critique of market societies and with his future visions. Townshend sees Leiss's view as suffering 'from an unwillingness to see the significance of the net transfer of powers concept,' the overcoming of which is central to Macpherson's conception of developmental democracy. (2000, 110, 116–119)

Despite his expression of agnosticism about social ownership referred to above, Macpherson's views on economic markets could drive him towards endorsement of something approaching thoroughgoing economic planification, and perhaps he would have accepted this outcome provided planning is integrated with full democratic guidance and oversight. This would make the economic-institution most in keeping with his views what is called by David Schweickart, referring not to Macpherson but to more recent socialist theorists, including Michael Albert and Robin Hahnel (1991), 'marketless participatory socialism,' the feasibility and desirability of which Schweickart criticizes. (1996, 329–334) However, Macpherson's views on markets are not totally dismissive of them. In his polemic against Milton Friedman he allows that 'the absence of a complete capitalist market economy does not entail the absence of markets' in some things. In the specific context of this polemic, he gives the examples of the paper, presses, and meeting halls, required for independent political campaigning. (DT, 153)

Macpherson's orientation in this matter is not and need not be, a thoroughgoing statist alternative to neoliberalism. This would be the stance that John Meyer calls 'absolutist.' Citing Karl Polanyi's view that actual markets are 'embedded' in specific social and political contexts, he notes that property rights and their exercise are always formally and informally constrained in various ways. (Meyer 2009, 112–121) A similar point is urged by Avner de-Shalit, who also appeals to *de facto* limitations of private property to conclude, with special reference to property in the natural environment, that 'the question is not so much one of possession—who legally owns the property—but a question of the limitations on the use of property resources, whether public or private.' (2000, 204–205) Though Macpherson's recommendations surely require extensive government regulation, his focus is not on the *mechanisms* (formal or informal) of an economy consonant with the vision he advances, but on the vision itself and on impediments to it posed by a market society.

In *The Life and Times of Liberal Democracy*, Macpherson cites as an example of movements that challenge acceptance of the cult of economic growth and other features of possessive-individualist culture ones for 'democratic participation in decision-making at the workplace' (L&T, 103): '[T]hose involved in workers' control are participating *as producers*, not as consumers or appropriators. They are in it not to get a higher wage or a greater share of the products, but to make their productive work more meaningful to them.' (*ibid.*, 104–105) This raises the question of whether Macpherson's theories are compatible with an economic system based on workers' cooperatives or workers self-management. Such a system, as Schweickart is at pains to argue, is different from a form of market socialism where wage labour will be retained. (1996, 319–329) In a conversation shortly before his death, Macpherson told this author that he considered the concept of market socialism 'a contradiction in terms.' This is unsurprising coming from one who had devoted the preceding 30 years to a critique of the pernicious effects of market economies, but perhaps Macpherson could have accepted some version (probably a weakened one) of Schweickart's market socialism, which is combined by him with workers self-management and which makes room for economic planning. (*ibid.*, 334)

Be this as it may, there is one important area where it is doubtful that markets can or should be entirely suppressed. According to Friedrich von Hayek: 'The whole acts as one market, not because any of its members surveys the whole field, but because their limited individual fields of vision sufficiently overlap so that through many intermediaries the relevant information is communicated to all' (1948, 86). This is part of Hayek's general thesis that a society's economy is efficient only if left entirely to individual market transactions, but his specific claim is not without merit. In a society where most economic exchanges are face-to-face, market prices can be directly negotiated. Large-scale economies, where parties to exchange are usually anonymous to one another, however, admit just of two generic mechanisms for establishing the prices of goods and services: central command and individual market exchanges.

Soviet planification was a version of the first mechanism. No doubt it could have been improved, but among its failings was that planners had to make unreliable estimates of consumer demand, or else political authorities tried to force a populace to conform their consumer behaviour to the goods made available to them. The alternative, market mechanism where consumers signal preferences in their individual economic activities is superior to full planning to the extent that it is less wasteful, where waste occurs when goods are produced that people do not want or when goods that are widely wanted are priced above what most can afford or not produced at all.

Recognizing advantages of markets with respect to consumer information does not support the claim that markets are indispensable for ascertaining the value (i.e., the use value) of all goods and services. Things about which it is clear that they are highly valued by nearly everyone (housing, clean air and water, education, good health, etc.) do not need to be subjected to market transactions for their values relative to other things to be well enough known to assign their provision a high priority without fear of wasteful investment. Also, subordination of some things to a market can yield *unreliable* information. For example, while labour force deployment is probably relatively efficient when sensitive to market demands, the same is not true of salary levels. Claims are dubious that the enormous incomes of corporate executives, movie stars, or professional athletes compared to those of day-care workers, secretaries, or corner store managers are, or are generally thought to be, less wasteful than a more egalitarian distribution of wealth.

Still, regarding many categories of consumer goods, markets look to be indispensable, at least regarding the provision of information about consumer demand for them.

Setting aside the wholescale recommendations of Leiss, it seems that Macpherson's resistance to markets should at least be qualified to confront this situation. In fact, Macpherson, himself recognized this when in a letter to Leiss he wrote that:

> A centrally-planned and administered socialist economy may use markets as a distributive mechanism without permitting market incentives to determine investment or pricing decisions or the whole direction of the economy. It may be risky for them to do so, but the fact that they use the market doesn't mean that they are letting the market use them. It is a simple error to equate 'market' with 'capitalist' and I can only regret that I seem to have contributed to that error by calling the main entry in my *Democratic Theory* 'Problems of a Non-Market Theory of Democracy,' rather than 'of a Non-Capitalist Theory.' (UTA 1980)

Whether accommodation to economic markets would place Macpherson closer than he would like to the welfarists whom he sees as propping up possessive-individualist societies depends upon the scope of goods and services left to market forces and on how the acquisition and sale of goods can be regulated in the interests of preserving the availability of resources for people to develop their potentials without denuding these market transactions of their informational functions.

Here is a domain that can be considered a problem-solving challenge for Macpherson. The problem is how to prevent a society including markets—a 'market economy' in Polanyi's term—from becoming a society completely dominated by an economic market, that is, a 'market society.' (1944, see 57) On Macpherson's perspective real and artificial scarcity is a main contributor to a market-society culture. Fear of deprivation supports a fixation on private ownership; insecurity about employment or business success foments stances of looking out primarily for oneself and to attitudes of competitiveness towards others (argued in Cunningham 2005). In the first two essays in *Democratic Theory* Macpherson relates this topic to technology: 'since the emergence of modern technology, we should be able to see that scarcity, whatever it was for many millennia, is not an invariable natural phenomenon but a human construction.' (DT, 63) Thus the elimination of scarcity made possible by modern technology weakens the hold of possessive individualism in a society. However, technological advances do not automatically translate into general wellbeing. Three problems remain.

An Ideological Problem

The problem to which Macpherson devotes most attention is that while technology can remove an impediment to addressing real scarcity, that is, scarcity in the means to afford everyone the basic necessities of life and to develop their truly human potentials, resources can never be enough to satisfy consumerist, infinite desires. As 'technology multiplies productivity, profitable production will require the creation of new desires,' and 'the tendency will be for the directors of the productive system to do everything in their power to confirm Western man's image of himself as an infinite desirer.' (DT, 38) This means that 'the difficulty to be overcome within the advanced liberal democracies is not primarily material but ideological.' (DT, 63) Political theorists, Macpherson concludes, can play a role in confronting this problem by doing 'something to demolish the time-bound and now unnecessary and deleterious image of man as an infinite consumer … whose rational purpose in life is to devote himself to an endless attempt to overcome scarcity.' (DT, 38) Macpherson saw himself, along with his friend Herbert Marcuse and several others, as embarked on this task.

When he advanced the views quoted above, Macpherson thought that the required ideological campaign would be abetted as the egalitarian socialist countries advanced in economic productivity as well as liberalizing and democratizing. This, he opined, would prompt a shift from economic competition to 'moral competition' over providing the conditions for truly satisfying lives for their populations. (DT, 22) As noted in chapter one, Macpherson later abandoned anticipation of such progress in the socialist countries, thus removing one potential support in efforts to combat possessive-individualist attitudes in popular culture.

However, Macpherson did not pin his hopes entirely on this unrealized source of support since he also counted on 'cumulative popular pressures, already in evidence, which arise, not from relative deprivation in the usual sense, but from … the want of esteem, autonomy, and community' he regarded as endemic to market societies. (L&T, 51) He saw this discontent manifested in a variety of social movements—environmental, urban, the women's movements, and others—already prominent in his times. (1983a, 5) In support of Macpherson on this point is that such pressures have continued into the twenty-first century, and with the ascendance of neoliberalism have been conjoined with both morally and economically motivated opposition to gross inequality, as in the anti-1% demonstrations.

The second problem to be confronted is, in a broad sense, political. Perpetuation of a capitalist market society is in the interests of those who profit from it, and through a variety of means they have been successful in preventing effective opposition by standard electoral-political means. Macpherson's approach to this problem is best discussed with reference to his orientation towards active opposition to capitalism.

Political Action

Macpherson's relatively few comments about activist politics largely concern what is not to be done. As most explicitly expressed in his interview on the anniversary of Marx's death, he was wary of two main dimensions of proletarian revolution. Regarding proletarians as the primary agents of a socialist transformation, at least in North America the working class 'has not used its power in the way socialists have wanted and shows very little sign of using its power [for socialist transformation]. It has used its power to get immediate material benefits or to hold on to its share but has not gone much beyond what Lenin called trade union consciousness.' He thus concludes that 'we cannot count on the traditional working class as an adequate resource' for this purpose. (1983a, 11–12)

Working-class activism. Macpherson saw more promise in social movements such as the ecological, peace, and women's movements. Because 'a lot of these other movements are propelled rather more by middle-class people than by the working class' (*ibid.*), he focused on prospects for radical action coming from them. An example is in some notes he wrote on 'Marx for the Middle Class':

> We may soon reach the point where either democracy or capitalism must go under. At that point the liberal middle class will have to take sides: take chances on a more or less liberal socialism or a thinly disguised capitalist police state. The risk is substantial. The chances of a liberal socialism diminish the longer the choice is not seen. (UTA 1983b)

Macpherson is not alone among socialist theorists in despairing of working-class impetus for radical change, but the views cited above are in tension with his inclusion among the social movements that give him hope listed in his 1983 interview itself those 'for participation in the work place, workers' control or industrial democracy' (1983a, 4), and with his observations published earlier about discontent with the conditions of work beyond wages.

There he predicted that the 'trade unions will be increasingly impelled not just to concern themselves with labour's share of the national income but to recognize the structural incompetence of managed capitalism':

> It cannot be said that trade union leaders generally have yet seen this, but they are being increasingly hard pressed by shop steward activity and unofficial strike action. It is to be expected that working-class participation in political and industrial action will increase, and will be increasingly class-conscious. (L&T, 106, and see his discussion of the preconditions for movements for industrial democracy in *Economic Justice*, EJ, 38–39)

What Macpherson had called 'the cult of economic growth at whatever cost to the environment and the quality of life' (DT, 76) has in fact spawned activism around a broad range of issues undertaken by social movements including some trade unions. Examples are 'social' as opposed to 'business' trade union practices which attend to environmental, social justice, poverty, and other issues and look to forge alliances with other social movements around such matters (see Ross and Savage 2012).

A democratic transition. Several of the notes Macpherson prepared for his classroom lectures are devoted to the other main dimension of proletarian revolution, the seizure and consolidation of state power by force. Macpherson approaches this question from a moral point of view. He describes the use of force by a class state, 'either bourgeois or proletarian,' as 'bad in itself' since 'it is directed against individuals of a certain class designed to prevent them having rights ... to enjoy and develop their lives in their own way,' and it is destructive of human community and civil liberties. (UTA 1968a, 61c)

The question Macpherson asks himself is whether in the interests of securing a good end (democratic socialism) such bad means can be justified. Despite Macpherson's criticisms of Benthamite Utilitarianism as it pertains to economic theory, the exercise undertaken in these notes is a standard utilitarian calculus: 'There is a frightful margin of error, since one cannot be sure that the prospective good *will* be attained, but the weighing of the present balance of good and evil against the prospective balance of good and evil in means and end together cannot very well be avoided.' (*ibid.*, 61f)

Macpherson does not conclude that the risk is worth taking. Instead he devotes attention to preconditions for any form of a potentially successful movement for socialism. These include: a change in popular consciousness away from acceptance of the values of possessive individualism, such as consumerism; technological advances that make possible freedom from debilitating labour and material abundance; and 'a partial breakdown of the political order (national or international) of the market society.' (DT, 76) He agrees with the claim of Svacek that he does not have a theory of socialist transition (Svacek, 418) but specifies that 'I am not persuaded that forcible revolution is the only way to a new society or that Marx always thought it was.' (1976, 425)

In notes written in 1975 Macpherson opined that: 'Some capitalist nations with parliamentary systems (France, Italy) may now reach socialism by parliamentary means, not via a social-democratic reformist party, but by increase in the already great strength of their Communist parties.' (UTA 1975, 68a) This was during the time of Eurocommunism, to which Macpherson devoted no attention except for this comment, but which, along with approving references to the political and economic reforms of the Dubček government of Czechoslovakia, forcibly put down by the Soviet Union in 1968 (L&T, 133), might come the closest to an attempt at a theory of socialist transformation consistent with his views.

This effort, especially as undertaken in Italy, advanced a humanistic anti-capitalist democratic vision not unlike Macpherson's, and it strove, by working both within governments and in labour and other movements, to garner support in the working and middle classes strong enough to avert capitalist counter-revolution to a socialism achieved by electoral means. (Macpherson adds to his comments about these parties that their support would be enhanced due to 'the increasing attractiveness of Soviet Union prospects.' (*ibid.*) What happened instead was that, notwithstanding its having distanced itself from Soviet-style Communism, Eurocommunism faltered in no small measure due to the discrediting of socialism generally with the collapse of the Soviet Union.)

Realism and Utopianism

A third problem is one Macpherson shares with any social theorist who focuses on visions while leaving aside questions of institutions and means to achieve them. Unless there is some defensible way of institutionalizing a vision or a political programme, a vision is utopian in a pejorative sense of being nothing but wishful thinking. If it supposes any activist prescription at all this is only to describe the vision with such rhetorical force that people will be won over and somehow make it happen. A charge that Macpherson must, then, take seriously is that absent plans for implementation and transformative action, his socialist developmental-democratic vision is no more than such an exercise. Macpherson was not unaware of this charge and addressed two aspects of it.

One reaction is in a table-turning challenge to what might be called the 'argument from revolutionary realism' to maintain that institutional and activist prescriptions themselves stand in need of visions. In the essay 'Democracy, Utopian and Scientific,' reproduced in *The Rise and Fall*, Macpherson criticizes the self-described political-scientific Realists—Schumpeter and the power-political Pluralists—not for failing to attend to the existing political world where democratic politics is limited to competition among political parties and among interest groups (e.g., L&T, 83) but exactly for thus narrowing their focuses to the *status quo*. Macpherson's alternative is non-utopian in the sense of projecting visions that he sees as continuous with past dimensions of political culture (the developmental-democratic ones), but utopian in refusing to try squaring his visions with existing institutions or established channels for political action.

Elaborating on this criticism, Macpherson also argues that a theory attending exclusively to existing institutions taken out of historical context and with no regard to new directions for a political society is 'inadequate as science because it is not visionary.' The Realists 'have all failed ... to take account of the necessary and possible forces of change inherent in capitalist democracy.' (EJ, 129) Visions are required to identify objectionable features of an existing situation and to direct inquiry towards finding resources to counter them. This is what Macpherson's humanistic vision enabled him to do, first in criticizing possessive-individualist society and then in finding bases in the history of liberal democracy for an alternative perspective to possessive individualism.

Most socialist theorists agree with Macpherson's criticisms of the political-scientific Realists, but his criticisms also apply to an analogous revolutionary realism that requires socialist visions to conform to estimates about what are taken to be possible institutions or activist programmes. In the spirit of Macpherson's orientation it could be said that any such requirement will, just like those of the power-political Pluralists, presuppose views about what a desirable society will be; so implicit visions are already at work. Macpherson's task is explicitly to articulate a vision that can guide institutional and activist considerations even if the vision is at odds with existing conditions.

In this articulation Macpherson's views on vanguardism in general (i.e., aside from the tentative remarks about national liberation movements discussed in the last chapter) become clear. Regarding socialist efforts in developed, liberal-democratic societies he takes a stand in rejecting vanguardism. He addresses this topic by challenging the distinction between means and ends. If goals and activities to achieve them affect one another, then full and careful articulation of a goal, that is, a vision, is especially important:

> [If] what I consider the basic liberal and the basic Marxist value of individual self-development is not made the mainstay of the whole attempt at transition to a good society, then there won't be any transition; it won't even get started. And you can't make individual self-development a central value if you resign your judgment to a vanguard at the beginning. (1983a, 11)

It might be said that for Macpherson democracy is not like tap water that can be turned off and then turned back on at one's convenience. Antidemocratic measures set in motion self-entrenching political and social dynamics that militate against discarding them when they are thought no longer needed to achieve a democratic end. Surely he was right about this, as we have seen where the stance he resists led.

Appendix: Macpherson and Marxism

Victor Svacek's view that Macpherson lacked a theory of socialist transformation is in an article entitled 'The Elusive Marxism of C.B. Macpherson' in which he lists six central tenets of Marxism and claims that Macpherson's theories are in accord with all but one, namely, the necessity of proletarian revolution, thus making him 'five-sixths of a Marxist.' (1976, 419) In a reply Macpherson concurs with this assessment (1976, 424), thus adding fuel to debates from the late 1970s in journal exchanges and in left-wing academic conference sessions about whether he was a Marxist, and, if so, how much of one or of what kind.

For some, Macpherson may be classified as a variety of Marxist since he held to a class-based theory of society and saw the interests of workers and capitalists as necessarily at odds due to the latter's requiring exploitation (the net transfer of powers) for their profits. For others, that Macpherson does not endorse proletarian revolution suffices to deny him membership in the club. Also, while agreeing with much of Marx's analysis of the genesis of capitalism, the model of a possessive market society Macpherson criticizes 'does not require any particular theory of the origin or development of such society.' (PI, 48)

Macpherson was certainly influenced by Marxism. First, he found much that resonated with his thinking in Marx's *The Economic & Philosophic Manuscripts of 1844* (1975, see 270–282) and in the later study for *Capital, The Grundrisse* (1986/1987) along with an influential article on the latter work by Martin Nicolaus (1968). Chief among the themes which attracted Macpherson in these works were as follows:

- Marx's views as expressed in the *Manuscripts* about the thwarting of what Macpherson called 'truly human potentials,' which views are retained in Marx's economic theory as outlined in the *Grundrisse*;
- Similarities in this work with Marcuse's views in *One Dimensional Man* about the ability in capitalist society to 'prevent or contain critical understanding' of the capitalist system on the part of workers (UTA 1968b, 68–62);
- The contradictory effects of automation on prospects for working-class revolutionary consciousness and action (*ibid.*, 68: 3–8);
- The thesis in the *Grundrisse* that 'impoverishment' means 'not material impoverishment, but impoverishment of power' (UTA 1968c, 46d) such that the contemporary proletariat could become 'a new revolutionary force because of a consciousness of its powerlessness to have a "good life" and to promote a good life for mankind more generally' (*ibid.*, 46g);
- Marx's observation, also in this study that, as Nicolaus summarizes it, 'the process of production, historically considered, creates not only the object of consumption but also consumer need and the style of consumption.' (Nicolaus 1968, 56; Macpherson DT, 182–183)

A second broad area of influence is evident in Macpherson's advice to political theorists in Chap. 5 of *Economic Justice*, 'Do We Need a Theory of the State?,' where he distinguishes his approach to political theory from that of Marxism (EJ, 56ff.) while also making use of Marxist theories. There he approvingly refers to some contemporaries whom he places in the tradition of Marxism or neo-Marxism (*ibid.*, 74), namely, Jürgen

Habermas (1973), Nicos Poulantzas (1973), Ralph Miliband (1969), and James O'Connor (1973) and to some related discussions in *The New Left Review* (no. 92, 1975, and no. 98, 1976).

These authors address such questions as: the nature and extent of state independence from a capitalist economy (a special concern of O'Connor); whether states should be conceived of on the model of agents (Miliband) or structurally (Poulantzas); and on strains on the legitimacy of the capitalist state (Habermas). Earlier, Macpherson had specified one way that Marxist theories of the state are important for overcoming the anti-developmentalism of market societies. He sees an electoral role in this task, but only if it is recognized, with the Marxists, that electoral politics are relatively impotent in effecting major changes as long as a state remains 'devoted to maintaining capitalism.' (1980, 29)

In *The Rise and Fall* chapter Macpherson urges fellow democratic-socialist theorists to learn from the endeavours of Habermas and the others instead of being at pains to differentiate themselves from Marxism, and he describes an 'euphoric, even utopian vision' in which liberal-democratic and Marxian theories merge. (75) Macpherson does not try to specify just what such a merger entails. As between Marxist socialism and liberal-democratic socialism, Panitch describes Macpherson as essentially a champion of the former who 'has been preparing liberal theory for [a] "raid" by Marxism' (1981, 164), but one could just as easily portray Macpherson as laying the ground for a liberal-democratic raid on Marxism.

Macpherson's stance on this question has most often simply prompted charges of social-democratic revisionism from socialists and of crypto-Marxism from liberal-democratic theorists. Macpherson, himself, was not very much interested in such classificatory questions, preferring to get on with his critiques of capitalist markets and their attendant cultures and with his promotion of a democratic-socialist alternative. He would likely have agreed with the opinion of Lindsay:

> I have not taken up this issue of whether the developmental ideal is liberal or Marxist, or whether Macpherson's thought is more one or the other, as I personally see little point in such exercises. This type of categorization would seem to lend itself to reductionist error more than it would to genuine insight. (1996, 42)

References

Albert, Michael, and Robin Hahnel. 1991. *The Political Economy of Participatory Economics*. Princeton: Princeton University Press.
Cole, G.D.H. 2003 [1931–1939]. *A History of Socialist Thought* (7 volumes). London: Macmillan.
Cunningham, Frank. 2005. Market Economies and Market Societies. *Journal of Social Philosophy* 36 (2, Summer): 129–142.
de- Shalit, Avner. 2000. *The Environment Between Theory and Practice*. Oxford: Oxford University Press.
Habermas, Jürgen. 1973. *Legitimation Crisis*. Boston: Beacon Press.
Hayek, Friedrich von. 1948. *Individualism and Economic Order*. Chicago: University of Chicago Press.
Leiss, William. 2009 [1988]. *C.B. Macpherson: Dilemmas of Liberalism and Socialism*. 2nd ed. Montréal and Kingston: McGill-Queen's University Press.
Levine, Andrew. 1976. The Political Theory of Social Democracy. *Canadian Journal of Philosophy* 6 (2): 183–193.
Lindsay, Peter. 1996. *Creative Individualism: The Democratic Vision of C.B. Macpherson*. Albany: State University of New York Press.
Macpherson, Crawford Brough. 1947. [UTA] National Committee for a Bill of Rights. University of Toronto Archives, B2003-0016 Box 1, May 27.
———. 1962. [PI] *The Political Theory of Possessive Individualism: Hobbes to Locke*. Oxford: Oxford University Press. Reissued with an Introduction by Frank Cunningham. Toronto: Oxford University Press, 2010.
———. 1968a. [UTA] Marxian Theory. University of Toronto Archives, B1987-0069, Box 2a, file 4.
———. 1968b. [UTA] Impoverishment & Expectation of Revolution. University of Toronto Archives, B1987-0069 Box 2a, file 5, Oct. 13.
———. 1968c. [UTA] Last Day of Lectures. University of Toronto Archives, B1987-0069 Box 2a, file 5, Oct. 21.
———. 1973. [DT] *Democratic Theory: Essays in Retrieval*. Oxford: Oxford University Press. Reissued with an Introduction by Frank Cunningham. Toronto: Oxford University Press, 2012.
———. 1975. [UTA] Marxian Theory. University of Toronto Archives, B1987-0069, Box 2a, file 4, Oct. 13.
———. 1976. Humanist Democracy and Elusive Marxism: A Response to Minogue and Svacek. *Canadian Journal of Political Science* 9 (3): 423–430.
———. 1977. [L&T] *The Life and Times of Liberal Democracy*. Oxford: Oxford University Press. Reissued with an Introduction by Frank Cunningham. Toronto: Oxford University Press, 2012.
———. 1980. [UTA] Publications after Festschrift. University of Toronto Archives B1987-0069, Box 4, Jan. 13.

———. 1983a. Interview on the Centenary of Marx's Death. *Socialist Studies Annual*. Winnipeg: University of Manitoba Publication, 7–12. Reproduced in Frank Cunningham, *The Real World of Democracy Revisited* (1994). Atlantic Highlands, NJ: Humanities Press, 14–21.

———. 1983b. [UTA] Marx for the Middle Class. University of Toronto Archives, B1987-0069, Box 5, July 24.

———. 1984. [EJ] *The Rise and Fall of Economic Justice*. Oxford: Oxford University Press. Reissued with an Introduction by Frank Cunningham. Toronto: Oxford University Press, 2013.

Marx, Karl. 1975 [1844]. *The Economic & Philosophic Manuscripts of 1844*. In *Karl Marx Frederick Engels Collected Works*, vol. 3, 229–346. London: Lawrence & Wishart.

———. 1986/1987 [1857–1858]. *Outline of the Critique of Political Economy (The Grundrisse)*. In *Karl Marx Frederick Engels Collected Works*, vols. 28 (49–537) and 29 (5–417). London: Lawrence & Wishart.

Meyer, John M. 2009. The Concept of Private Property and the Limits of the Environmental Imagination. *Political Theory* 37 (1): 99–127.

Milliband, Ralph. 1969. *The State in Capitalist Society*. New York: Basic Books.

Nicholas, Martin. 1968. The Unknown Marx. *New Left Review* (48, March–April): 41–61.

O'Connor, James. 1973. *The Fiscal Crisis of the State*. New York: St. Martin's Press.

Panitch, Leo. 1981. Liberal Democracy and Socialist Democracy: The Antinomies of C.B. Macpherson. *Socialist Register 1981* 18: 144–168.

Polanyi, Karl. 1944. *The Great Transformation*. Boston: Beacon Press.

Poulantzas, Nicos. 1973 [1968]. *Political Power and Social Classes*. London: Sheed & Ward.

Ross, Stephanie. 2012. Business Unionism and Social Unionism in Theory and Practice. In *Rethinking the Politics of Labour in Canada*, ed. Stephanie Ross and Larry Savage, 33–46. Halifax: Fernwood Publishing.

Schweickart, David. 1996. *Against Capitalism*. Boulder: Westview Press.

Svacek, Victor. 1976. The Elusive Marxism of C. B. Macpherson. *Canadian Journal of Political Science* 9 (3): 395–422.

Townshend, Jules. 2000. *C.B. Macpherson and the Problem of Liberal Democracy*. Edinburgh: Edinburgh University Press.

Wood, Ellen Meiksins. 1978. C.B. Macpherson: Liberalism, and the Task of Socialist Political Theory. *The Socialist Register: 1978* 15: 215–240.

PART II

Questions of Theory

INTRODUCTION TO PART II

Writings of Macpherson, especially from *Democratic Theory*, include expositions of an imposing list of much-debated theoretical issues: human nature, positive and negative liberty, conceptions of democracy, equality, needs, the individual and the community, and other core matters to which political theorists address themselves. Secondary literature about Macpherson, additionally to those about his interpretations of seventeenth-century British thinkers, concerns itself with his stances on these topics. Chapter five of this part of the book reviews Macpherson's general theoretical approaches in preparation for applying his theories to the contemporary challenges addressed in Part III.

Macpherson is first and foremost a political theorist. The accessible style that makes him, in the words of Isaiah Berlin, 'one of the very few rational and lucid and altogether admirable writers' (1971) is on a par with that of political essayists such as Gore Vidal, Christopher Hitchens, Joan Didion, and Angela Davis, to name a few. However, his work goes beyond that of the traditional essay by bringing to bear on the topics he addresses extended, sophisticated, and sometimes speculative theory in support of his conclusions.

At the same time, Macpherson does not advance his views as fundamental, philosophical justifications of the political theses he wishes to defend. He is best viewed as a political theorist rather than as either an essayist or a political philosopher. The efforts of some scholars of Macpherson to interpret his theories philosophically are seen in this book not just as inaccurate depictions, but as unnecessary and even disadvantageous for the practical purposes that he had in mind. Chapter four explains and defends situating Macpherson as a non-philosophical political theorist.

Reference

Berlin, Isaiah. 1971. University of Toronto Archives B1987-0069, Box 5 ('Isaiah Berlin'). Letter to Macpherson, May 25.

CHAPTER 4

Political Theory and Political Philosophy

Partly due to the intense attention paid to Macpherson's treatment of seventeenth-century theorists by the intellectual historians discussed in the appendix to chapter one, his other writings have received less scholarly attention than they deserve. Among the exceptions are books by Leiss (2009 [1998]), Ray (1996), Lindsay (1996), Townshend (2000), and Hansen (2015), and the collections edited by Kontos (1979b) and Carens. (1993) *Possessive Individualism* was not written just as an exercise in intellectual history but to flag what Macpherson took as a major problem in his own times, namely, to defend an alternative to a still all-too-alive possessive-individualist conception of humans and society. This is the overriding task in his writings from 1965 to 1985. The chapter argues that the methodology Macpherson employs is one of political theory rather than of political philosophy. The distinction is not a pedantic one, but will be seen in Part III of the book to play a role in applying Macpherson's work to current challenges.

Philosophy

Throughout his writings Macpherson refers to philosophers—Hobbes, Locke, Aristotle, Marx, Mill, Dewey, and others. This has led some to ask whether his own views are, can be, or should be philosophically based. One commentator, Phillip Hansen, maintains that Macpherson was himself a philosopher of the Critical-Theoretical, Frankfurt school associated with Théodor Adorno, Max Horkheimer, and Jürgen Habermas, though he 'suppressed' acknowledgement and explicit employment of this school's tenets. Robert Meynell sees substantial Hegelian elements in Macpherson's theories. Alkis Kontos holds that Macpherson's endorsement of the values of developmental democracy stands in need of philosophical justification. Ian Angus argues that rejection of possessive individualism calls for epistemological support. Steven Lukes holds that Macpherson presupposed and should have made explicit a perfectionist ethical theory.

One difficulty in assessing these claims is that there are disputes among philosophers themselves about what philosophy is. As used here the term refers to critical thinking about fundamental matters. What counts as fundamental is itself a matter of philosophical contention, but Macpherson's concerns about what a good political society is or what makes for a fully human life are good examples. At one limit, critical thinking involves justification of views on topics like these by reference to metaphysical or ethical principles. At another limit, it challenges even trying to identify first principles or foundations. Macpherson certainly addresses fundamental questions, but despite his occasional use of philosophical language, his texts reveal a political-theoretical approach to them that abstracts from matters of philosophical justification.

MACPHERSON AS A CRYPTO PHILOSOPHER

If Macpherson was hiding philosophical commitment to Frankfurt-style philosophy, as Hansen urges, he was doing a good job of it. He refers to Herbert Marcuse's attention to 'the phenomenon of men hugging their chains' (DT, 76), but there is no attempt to incorporate Marcuse's unique deployment of Hegelian dialectics. There are no references at all to Horkheimer or Adorno or to the merits or otherwise of the dialectics of the Enlightenment that centrally occupied them. Macpherson approvingly cites Habermas's *Legitimation Crisis* as an example of attention to the state that he found lacking in most contemporary political theory (EJ, 61), but no attention is paid to Habermas's theories in that book about the 'immanent relation to truth' of values and norms or the 'transcendental character of ordinary discourse.' (Habermas 1973, 95, 110) (An exchange between Hansen and myself, from which some of the arguments in his chapter are drawn, is at Cunningham 2016.)

Similar to Hansen's view is Meynell's claim that 'Macpherson unwittingly engaged in the restoration of the original and much maligned Hegel' (2011, 61). In his published works Macpherson makes a few references to Hegel, praising him for pursuit of a 'grand theory of the state' (EJ, 55), while criticizing his views on private property. (*ibid.*, 89–90) He does not, however, discuss Hegel's dialectical metaphysics and phenomenology or his philosophy of history. Hegel's *Philosophy of Right* is more extensively dealt with by Macpherson in his unpublished notes. There he questions whether Hegel makes concessions to possessive individualism or, worse, constructs 'a metaphysical system which allows him to embrace possessive individualism.' He also takes note of Hegel's view that persons exist for each other 'only as owners' and of his endorsement of self-ownership. (UTA 1981; Hegel 1967 [1821], paragraphs 40 & 57)

Nor does Macpherson employ the dialectical approach Hansen attributes to him of proffering an 'immanent critique' of possessive individualism where the seeds of a developmental-democratic ontology are already present in it. (2015, 286) It is hard to sustain this interpretation of *Possessive Individualism*. There Macpherson portrays possessive-individualist values and conceptions of the human essence not as concepts that 'point beyond themselves' (15), but as parts of the coherent and pernicious world view for which Macpherson was seeking an alternative. The developmental ontology he identifies for this purpose antedates possessive individualism and stands in opposition to it. Macpherson is not seeking the supersession of two ontologies in a higher synthesis but the complete triumph of developmental democracy. (see DT, 24)

To be sure there are affinities between many of Macpherson's views and those of philosophers. As noted earlier Macpherson shared the problematic Marx set down in his *Economic & Philosophic Manuscripts of 1844*, where humans are depicted as social creatures seeking to engage in meaningful work but whose ability to realize their humanistic potentials is blocked by oppressive economic forces. (1975 [1844]) Macpherson shares John Dewey's characterization of democracy as 'a kind of society' rather than 'a system of government.' (DT, 51; Dewey 1984, 325 and see 388–389) The linchpin of Aristotle's approach to ethics—happiness—includes the development of individuals' potentials in virtuous lives which is impeded by unconstrained greed for possessions. (1984 [350 BCE], 1733–1736 [1097a–1098b]) In holding that one's capacities 'must be under one's own conscious control' Macpherson refers to Aristotle (DT, 56; Aristotle 1984 [350 BCE], 1746 [1105b]), but as in his appeals to theories of Marx,

Dewey, Mill, and T.H. Green, Macpherson only cites Aristotle with respect to the content of this view without reference to his metaphysical or other philosophical theories. One can agree with the *conclusions* about fundamental matters expressed by philosophers without also embracing the philosophical *grounds* they give to support them.

Ethics and Morality

An illustration of Macpherson's approach to normative political theory is seen in the ways he treats issues that involve morality. Macpherson is critical of political scientists who 'claim to have abstained from any value judgment about the processes they are analysing.' (EJ, 57) He sees them as presupposing value judgments in spite of their pretence of value neutrality, and his own accounts are replete with morally normative views. One reason some assume that Macpherson invoked philosophy pertains to his frequent use of the term 'ethics.' A pertinent distinction is between morality and ethics. Morality has to do with prescribed norms of behaviour: thou shall not kill, inflicting pain on innocents is wrong, people should not be indifferent to the wellbeing of others, and so on. Terms like 'ethical' in ordinary discourse are typically used interchangeably with 'moral' in this sense, or one talks of such things as 'a work ethic.'

A treatment by Shelly Kagan of ethics in its technical philosophical sense is helpful. He distinguishes among normative ethics, meta-ethics, and applied ethics. The first of these comprises two components. It 'involves substantive proposals concerning how to act, how to live, or what kind of a person to be,' and it 'attempts to state and defend the most basic principles governing these matters.' (1998, 2) This is the key dimension of ethics. Positions advanced in normative ethics are the ones applied to specific realms (medical ethics, business ethics, etc.), and meta-ethics addresses abstract views assumed in normative ethics, such as about the nature or existence of moral facts. Macpherson certainly does proffer substantive proposals on fundamental questions, for instance, regarding a good society or desirable human potentials. But making claims about substantial matters does not by itself constitute philosophy. For this Macpherson would need to have engaged the second component of normative ethics as described by Kagan, namely, adducing basic principles to justify the claims.

Macpherson holds that any viewpoint on 'specifically human capacities different from, or over and above, animal ones,' will carry with it a 'value postulate' since in such matters 'the very structure of our thought and language puts an evaluative content into our descriptive statements about "man."' (DT, 53) He draws support for this claim from theses of H.L.A. Hart and Isaiah Berlin. Hart describes as a 'simple truism' reflected in structures of thought and language that all people wish to survive and are vulnerable to harm inflicted by others. Like other truisms, this carries with it value judgments about things that may impede or promote avoidance of harm. (1961, 188–189)

Berlin is arguing that, unlike the putatively value-free empirical social sciences, descriptions of human attributes by political theorists involve 'models and paradigms' that include moral evaluations. The conceptions of humanity Berlin has in mind differ depending on the nature of the models or paradigms employed, for example, religious or secular. (Berlin 1962, 26–30) Despite obliquely referring to his claims as philosophical, Hart simply asserts them without reference to philosophical theories of the nature of thought or language. Full justification of one paradigm over the others for Berlin would no doubt require philosophical argumentation, but he does not offer such, any more than does Macpherson try philosophically to prove that a developmental view of the human essence is superior to a possessive one from the point of view of ethical theory.

The only places where Macpherson clearly expresses a philosophical-ethical opinion are at the level of meta-ethics. In *Democratic Theory* he echoes a thesis prevalent in Anglo-American philosophical circles when he was writing that 'the truth or falsity of [a core norm of possessive individualism] is not in question' since 'it is an ontological postulate, and as such, a value postulate.' (DT, 37) In *Possessive Individualism* he devotes several pages to a discussion of the view, popular among philosophers in the tradition of David Hume, that 'no moral principle can logically be deduced from any statements of fact.' (PI, 81–90, 81) Were Macpherson concerned to advance and defend specifically philosophical principles in support of political value judgments, the assertion in *Democratic Theory* would be damaging as it calls into question the rationality of claims about what is morally desirable.

However, Macpherson does not apply this Humean thesis to philosophical justifications. In the section of *Democratic Theory* where the value postulate comment is made he is arguing that, partly due to the potentials of modern technology (if denuded of its negative potentials), discarding a possessive-individualist conception of human nature in popular consciousness is now feasible. (DT, 38) This, in turn, makes endorsing the project of achieving the equal development of human potentials a realistic possibility.

The point about value postulates not being true or false is introduced precisely to justify *not* being obliged to give ethical arguments in favour of developmentalism. (*ibid.*, 37)

In *Possessive Individualism* there is a more extended discussion about moral norms not being derivable from non-moral facts. In this treatment Macpherson repeatedly makes use of philosophical terms, such as 'deduction' and 'valid,' as in his assertion that Hobbes's 'deduction of obligation from fact [is] logically unobjectionable.' (*ibid.*, 90) Read in context, it is apparent that Macpherson is using such terms in a colloquial way. He does not, in fact, disagree with the Humean dictum, writing that it 'must be granted that on the model of formal calculi, moral utterances cannot be entailed by factual statements' (*ibid.*, 82) and that it is possible to deduce obligation from fact 'in any sense *short of* strict logical entailment.' (*ibid.*, 81, emphasis added) No follower of Hume would demand more than these disclaimers. However, Macpherson does not pursue such questions. Rather, in his discussion of Hobbes the sense of what Macpherson calls a deduction becomes apparent.

In a society the culture of which replaces the notion of a natural hierarchy with that of equality, a question arises about what moral mandates people might recognize as equally binding on them all, and the answer will depend on the respect in which they are thought to be equal. Aside from the ability each person has to kill another (equality in a state of nature), Hobbes, on Macpherson's interpretation of him, depicts people as equally subject to economic market forces where there is 'equal subordination of every individual to the laws of the market.' (PI, 85) So if economic competition is not to turn into mutually destructive anarchy, obedience to a political authority that can maintain order in market interactions is required. Acceptance of this authority is in everyone's interests and 'may as well be called moral as prudential; it is the highest morality of which market men are capable.' (*ibid.*, 87) To say, then, that obedience to authoritative political regulation of economic markets is 'deduced' from subordination to market forces is just to say that in the absence of an alternative, people are disposed to obey a political authority that serves these forces, both as a prudential matter and as one of common-sense (business) morality.

In *Possessive Individualism* extended attention is devoted to Hobbes's deployment of a hypothesized social contract to justify his political recommendations. (PI, 81–106) But Macpherson does not evaluate the philosophical merits of social contract theory *per se*. Instead, he concerns himself with the sense described above that Hobbes and those receptive to his political conclusions gave to the idea that people are equal in a state of nature. In Macpherson's subsequent treatment of Locke's theories he again refrains from addressing the philosophical aspects of Locke's contractarianism and instead argues that Locke appeals to tacit contracts to 'remove all the [egalitarian] natural law limits from ... property right.' (PI, 199, see 229–247) Yet another famous contract theorist discussed by Macpherson is John Rawls, where he declares that his concern is 'not with Rawls's central case that a contractarian theory of justice is preferable to a utilitarian one.' (DT, 89) Instead, Macpherson argues that Rawls's theory of justice suffers from an unwarranted assumption that class divisions with attendant inequalities are inevitable. (Macpherson, *ibid.*, and 87–94)

As to his own evaluations, when Macpherson expresses opinions about the (bad) values of possessive individualism or the (good) ones of developmental democracy, he is writing at the level of morality, not of philosophical ethics. He remarks that for a liberal-democratic model of democracy to be 'workable' it must be in accord with how people actually think, and it 'must contain, explicitly or implicitly, an ethically justificatory theory.' (L&T, 6) This remark may betray a confusion on Macpherson's own part about the morality/ethics distinction. However, literally read his point is not that the developmental model is ethically *justified*, but that liberal democrats must *claim* ethical justification for whatever model they endorse, and this includes two models—'protective' and 'equilibrium'—that Macpherson emphatically rejects.

Or again, when characterizing a good society as one that facilitates maximum development of its citizens' truly human potentials, Macpherson adds that:

> It is important to notice that this concept of powers is an ethical one, not a descriptive one. A man's powers, in this view, are his potential for realizing the essential human attributes said to have been implanted in him by Nature or God, not (as with Hobbes) his present means, however acquired, to ensure future gratification of his appetites. (DT, 9)

Macpherson is not alleging that a morality favouring the development of human potentials is based on Nature or God (in which case he would have needed extended elaboration of the point) but contrasting Hobbes's approach with natural law or religious approaches that he elsewhere notes antedate Hobbes. The essential point is that for the Hobbesist, as for the 'value-free' descriptive political scientists, 'a man's powers [are just] the powers he has, not the powers he needs to have in order to be fully human.' (*ibid.*) The term 'ethical' is being used to emphasize the importance of moral evaluations in political theory rather than to adduce any one ethical theory in support of them.

Macpherson's concern is to argue: that political theories generally, and those of democracy in particular, presuppose some value-laden viewpoints about what makes humans unique; that visions of a good society are justified by appeal to such a viewpoint; that the viewpoint he endorses is centred on developmental powers; and that the normative dimension of the viewpoint is not subject to being proven true or false. Of these components, only the last is a philosophical claim. Were Macpherson trying to develop a philosophical theory, he would have at least made reference to the extensive meta-ethical debates about whether or how moral claims can be, if not proven, then otherwise supported. But his political theory only aims to throw into relief favoured and disfavoured visions of political society and to explicate the core role ideas about human powers play in these alternative visions.

Ontology

Another source of confusion is Macpherson's use of the term 'ontology.' Unlike 'ethics,' this is an unambiguously philosophical term, coined in the seventeenth century by Leibniz to refer to the metaphysical study of being. The term is also used in social and political philosophy to describe ways of conceptualizing political forces and structures. An example is Bertell Ollman's interpretation of Marx as employing a conception of internal relations among all the political, economic, and other features of society viewed as a totality. (1976, appendix 2, and see Harvey 2009, 288–296) It was possibly Alkis Kontos who prevailed upon his senior colleague to use the term 'ontology' in an effort to persuade Macpherson to adduce philosophical grounding for his normative theories.

However, Kontos also allows that Macpherson 'does not agonize over crucial ontological and metaphysical problems' because the political-theoretical context of his endeavour 'forces his analysis toward the concrete political reality and disallows him from undertaking any abstract philosophical analysis.' (1979a, 30–31) That Macpherson did not address Kontos's counsel, let alone follow it, supports the view that he was using this term in an idiosyncratic manner to describe value-infused conceptions of human nature. He would not be alone in such usage. For example, *The Journal of Social Ontology* explicitly accepts contributions either of a philosophical or of a social-scientific nature.

Does Macpherson Need Philosophy?

In his critique of Isaiah Berlin on positive and negative liberty Macpherson writes that his 'plea is certainly not to abandon logic or philosophy, which have never been more needed than now' (DT, 107), thus seemingly acknowledging that he thought he needed philosophical grounding for his views. However, Macpherson's ensuing critique of Berlin and his exposition of a democratically acceptable theory of positive liberty do not include philosophical argumentation or refer for support to philosophers. Moreover, the conception of philosophy he thinks needed does not involve seeking philosophical grounding:

> we can no longer rely on the sort of logic which, though it starts, as Berlin does, from solid historical observation of the lengths to which certain philosophical positions have in fact been taken in political practice, is content to analyse those positions on their own terms, that is, to analyse them at their own abstract level. They need to be judged in terms of the actual impediments to liberty in concrete historical situations. (DT, 108)

Thus, despite the phrasing of his comment about needing philosophy, Macpherson warns against abstract philosophical theorizing. His reasoning about moral matters is in keeping with what Aristotle calls *phronesis*, or 'practical wisdom,' which he distinguishes from philosophical wisdom. The person who reasons in this way already has some idea of what is morally good and hence is not engaging in foundational ethical argumentation but instead is deliberating about what morality requires in specific circumstances. (Aristotle 1984 [350 BCE], 1800–1802 [1139b–1141b], and see MacIntyre 1981, 144–145)

It might be granted that Macpherson's writings do not include explicit or disguised philosophical views and that he is concerned, *phronesis*-like, to employ moral judgments rather than to discover or justify them, but be maintained that his conclusions still stand in need of philosophical support. Several of the claims of Hansen and Meynell suggest one version of such an approach. Macpherson believes that possessive-individualist values exist in tension with alternative developmental-democratic ones, and he looks to the former being replaced by the latter. Hansen avers that here 'the issue of Macpherson's suppressed philosophical dimension emerges' (2015, 119) and that what 'he was really doing' was advancing a philosophical theory about how human conceptions of themselves can and do change which is 'most fully at home ... with Hegel's "objective spirit," or Wittgenstein's "form of life," as well as the work of Horkheimer' (121). Meynell maintains that 'Hegel helps us to better understand Macpherson and clarifies what Macpherson might have missed' in his endorsement of a community-friendly individualism through Hegel's theory of recognition. (2011, 99)

To understand how these claims relate to Macpherson's theories, they may be thought of as something like Immanuel Kant's transcendental deductions. Kant famously and obviously correctly noted that 'everything actual is possible' (2003 [1788], 250 A231), and his overriding project was to uncover the grounds of possibility for that which is actual in the realms of morality, science, and the appreciation of beauty. Hansen and Meynell think that the possibility of value transformations or of individual/communal compatibility is demonstrated in the philosophical theories of Hegel (or Wittgenstein, or Horkheimer). A variation of such a strategy is Ian Angus's argument that possessive individualism is philosophically supported by an empiricist epistemology, while the ground of developmentalism is in a contrasting neo-Kantian one. (1982, 148)

But in evaluating Macpherson's conclusions and putting them to political use, why not stick to the realm of the actual? He wished to explicate what he took as the two major conceptions of humanity in the history of liberal democracy, each with its own morality, in order to identify conditions where the developmental one could displace possessive individualism. Either the values and prescribed behaviours of these conceptions, independently of putative philosophical support, are incompatible or not. Either Macpherson has or has not identified conditions conducive to changes in political culture. Either the potentials he favours can be compatibly developed by everyone or not. On some philosophical theory it might be that some of these alternatives *must* be accurate, but appeal to historical examples, everyday experience, or generally accepted social-scientific conclusions can suffice as evidence for the ones Macpherson endorses. To be sure, such appeals are always contestable, however, as those in the philosophical profession well know, so are philosophical theories.

As to why it is desirable to uncover philosophical dimensions in Macpherson's theories, or to read them as if they were philosophical, Hansen maintains that this gives the theories 'richness and meaning.' (*ibid.*, 269) No doubt, for some a theory must be philosophically understood to be rich and meaningful. But, though myself trained in philosophy, I find Macpherson's theories exciting and refreshing partly *because* they are close to the political ground.

Advantages to Philosophical Agnosticism

According to the interpretation of Macpherson's enterprise in this chapter, he draws on what he takes as established social-scientific facts and everyday experience: to articulate a vision, to examine the stances, pro and con, of a variety of other political theorists, to identify problems for achieving the visions for those who find them attractive, and to indicate sorts of solutions. Regarding one of his key theoretical notions, Macpherson argues against Kenneth Minogue that 'the reason I have dealt with developmental power in terms of access [to resources] and transfer [of powers] and quantities [of aggregate liberties] was to make that concept concrete and useable.' (1976, 428) Macpherson's methodology is largely pragmatic. He wants to identify and explicate problems, and, like John Dewey, propose solutions to them in real-world circumstances.

By not tying political theories to philosophical grounds Macpherson avoids getting embroiled in intra-philosophical controversies. It also allows those with differing philosophical views to agree with him politically in spite of these differences. One need not subscribe to consequentialism, deontology, natural law, or some other ethical theory to be in accord with Macpherson's appraisals of the potentials he designates truly human. Similarly, agnosticism on questions of philosophical grounding facilitates support for Macpherson's political views by members of diverse philosophical schools: Frankfurt philosophers, Neo-Aristotelians, Post-Structuralists, Hegelians, Marxists, and more generally philosophers in both the 'Analytic' and the 'Continental' traditions. Indeed, theorists from all of these have approvingly cited and made use of Macpherson's work.

Moreover, in the interests of getting straight to the politically relevant points of a theory, the question of what kind of philosophy should be appealed to in defence of Macpherson is avoided. As will be discussed in the next chapter, Carol Gould offers the alternatives of pro-, anti-, or quasi-foundationalism and thinks it important to locate Macpherson in one of them. (1988, 19) Meynell argues that Macpherson was a Hegelian. Lukes sees him as supposing some form of perfectionist ethics (*ibid.*, 1979). The merits or otherwise of foundationalism and of perfectionism are currently much debated, and there are significant differences among the Frankfurt philosophers and between them and Hegel.

Hansen links Macpherson with Wittgenstein, Gadamer, Marx, and Mill (9), as well as with the Critical Theorists, but there are also important differences among these philosophers and schools. Surely one cannot be expected to sift through their philosophies as a precondition for understanding, evaluating, and making use of Macpherson's theories. Yet another disadvantage is that in trying to frame Macpherson's political conclusions in philosophical terms, one invites the charges Marx and Engels levelled against the 'Young Hegelian' philosophers of obfuscation and the submersion of concrete political and economic analysis in abstract concepts, where 'a philosophical *phrase* about a real question is the real question itself.' (Marx and Engels 1976, 99) Or where the Young Hegelians' philosophy and the study of the world 'have the same relation to one another as onanism and sexual love.' (*ibid.*, 236)

In general, philosophical agnosticism of the sort here attributed to Macpherson invites one directly to grapple with pressing social and political problems without awaiting settlement on philosophical issues, and by remaining on the level of factually based political theory, Macpherson's views have a better chance of making actual political impact than they would if appreciating his contributions required buying into a philosophical theory. Further explication of Macpherson's specifically political-theoretical approach will be provided in the next chapter. Examples of deployment of his extra-philosophical ideas will be given in Part III of this book.

To acknowledge that Macpherson did not concern himself with questions of philosophical grounding is not to portray him as an *anti*-philosopher. He admired several philosophers and respected their efforts to defend social and political views in accord with his own. Should a philosophical theory provide incontrovertibly sound philosophical grounding for these views, he would surely welcome it. This chapter has maintained that Macpherson's inattention to questions of philosophical justification is not a defect of his thought. On the contrary, his strength was and remains that of an engaged political theorist.

REFERENCES

Angus, Ian. 1982. On Macpherson's Developmental Liberalism. *Canadian Journal of Political Science* 15 (1, March): 145–150.
Aristotle. 1984 [c350BC]. *Nichomachean Ethics*. In *The Complete Works of Aristotle*, vol. 2. Princeton: Princeton University Press.
Berlin, Isaiah. 1962. Does Political Theory Still Exist? In *Philosophy, Politics and Society*, ed. Peter Laslett and W.G. Runciman, 2nd ed. Oxford: Oxford University Press.
Carens, Joseph, ed. 1993. *Democracy and Possessive Individualism: The Intellectual Legacy of C.B. Macpherson*. Albany: State University of New York Press.
Cunningham, Frank. 2016. Was C.B. Macpherson a Crypto Philosopher?, Review essay of Phillip Hansen's *Reconsidering C.B. Macpherson*, with a reply by Hansen and a rejoinder to the reply, *Canadian Journal of Political Science* 49 (3): 559–574.
Dewey, John. 1984 [1927]. *The Public and Its Problems*. In *John Dewey: The Later Works*, vol. 2, 235–372. Carbondale, IL: Southern Illinois Press.
Gould, Carol. 1988. *Rethinking Democracy: Freedom and Social Cooperation in Politics, Economy, and Society*. Cambridge: Cambridge University Press.
Habermas, Jürgen. 1973. *Legitimation Crisis*. Boston: Beacon Press.
Hansen, Phillip. 2015. *Reconsidering C.B. Macpherson: From Possessive Individualism to Democratic Theory and Beyond*. Toronto: University of Toronto Press.
Hart, H.L.A. 1961. *The Concept of Law*. Oxford: Oxford University Press.
Hegel, G.W.F. 1967 [1821]. *Hegel's Philosophy of Right*. Oxford: The Clarendon Press.
Kagan, Shelley. 1998. *Normative Ethics*. Boulder, CO: Westview Press.
Kant, Immanuel. 2003 [1788]. *The Critique of Pure Reason*. London: Palgrave Macmillan.
Kontos, Alkis. 1979a. Through a Glass Darkly. *Canadian Journal of Political and Social Theory* 3 (1, Winter): 25–45.
———, ed. 1979b. *Powers, Possessions and Freedom: Essays in Honour of C.B. Macpherson*. Toronto: University of Toronto Press.
Leiss, William. 2009 [1988]. *C.B. Macpherson: Dilemmas of Liberalism and Socialism*. 2nd ed. Montréal and Kingston: McGill-Queen's University Press.
Lindsay, Peter. 1996. *Creative Individualism: The Democratic Vision of C.B. Macpherson*. Albany: State University of New York Press.
Lukes, Steven. 1979. The Real and Ideal Worlds of Democracy. In *Powers, Possessions and Freedom: Essays in Honour of C.B. Macpherson*, ed. Alkis Kontos, 139–152. Toronto: University of Toronto Press.
MacIntyre, Alasdair. 1981. *After Virtue*. South Bend: Notre Dame Press.

Macpherson, Crawford Brough. 1962. [PI] *The Political Theory of Possessive Individualism: Hobbes to Locke*. Oxford: Oxford University Press. Reissued with an Introduction by Frank Cunningham. Toronto: Oxford University Press, 2010.

———. 1973. [DT] *Democratic Theory: Essays in Retrieval*. Oxford: Oxford University Press. Reissued with an Introduction by Frank Cunningham. Toronto: Oxford University Press, 2012.

———. 1976. Humanist Democracy and Elusive Marxism: A Response to Minogue and Svacek. *Canadian Journal of Political Science* 9 (2, September): 423–430.

———. 1977b. [L&T] *The Life and Times of Liberal Democracy*. Oxford: Oxford University Press. Reissued with an Introduction by Frank Cunningham. Toronto: Oxford University Press, 2012.

———. 1981. [UTA] On Hegel. University of Toronto Archives, Box 2 B87 (0069).

———. 1984. [EJ] *The Rise and Fall of Economic Justice*. Oxford: Oxford University Press. Reissued with an Introduction by Frank Cunningham. Toronto: Oxford University Press, 2013.

Marx, Karl. 1975 [1844]. The Economic & Philosophic Manuscripts of 1844. In *Karl Marx Frederick Engels Collected Works*, vol. 3, 229–346. London: Lawrence & Wishart.

Marx, Karl, and Frederick Engels. 1976 [1845–1847]. *The German Ideology*. In *Karl Marx Frederick Engels Collected Works*, vol. 5. London: Lawrence & Wishart.

Meynell, Robert. 2011. *Canadian Idealism and the Philosophy of Freedom: C.B. Macpherson, George Grant, and Charles Taylor*. Montréal and Kingston: McGill-Queen's University Press.

Ollman, Bertell. 1976. *Marx's Conception of Man in Capitalist Society*. 2nd ed. Cambridge: Cambridge University Press.

Ray, B.N. 1996. *C.B. Macpherson and Liberalism*. New Delhi: Kanishka Publishers.

Townshend, Jules. 2000. *C.B. Macpherson and the Problem of Liberal Democracy*. Edinburgh: University of Edinburgh Press.

CHAPTER 5

Core Themes

In this chapter Macpherson's approaches to a selection of core theoretical themes are reviewed, each of which is important for the task in subsequent chapters of applying his views to contemporary challenges. Macpherson's treatments of these themes also illustrate the previous chapter's account of the general nature of his approach to political theory.

True and False Needs

In an exchange on the relation between needs and wants Macpherson and Alkis Kontos find themselves agreeing that a fundamental distinction between these things should not be made; rather needs are a kind of wants (Macpherson 1977a; Kontos 1979). Kontos also agrees with Macpherson's sorting those wants that are called needs into ones consonant with a developmental ontology and ones compatible with possessive individualism, but he further insists that 'from a strictly philosophical point of view' rejection of the latter ontology and embrace of developmentalism require 'independent grounds for the validation of ontological postulates' (Kontos, 32). He is thus urging Macpherson not just to identify needs by reference to these two main, competing ontologies, but to interpret them in philosophical terms. As noted in chapter four Macpherson does not address Kontos's entreaty, and there it was concluded that this is because he was not interested in engaging in debate over philosophical theories.

In a subsequent treatment of the topic, Macpherson retains use of the term 'need' because it is familiar to English-speaking theorists, and he distinguishes between needs that are 'imposed by relations of production which require domination'—'false needs'—and needs that 'could be met by a rational, non-class-dominated, organization of production ... given present available technology.' These are the 'true needs' that are compatible with developmentalism. (1979, 48–49) Of course, Macpherson favours meeting the needs he calls 'true,' and he thought that most contemporary readers would also favour this once they are presented with an alternative to possessivism and are persuaded that developmental democracy is a realistic possibility.

Macpherson would likely also recognize that some are so strongly wedded to possessive individualism that no alternative would be attractive to them (the 'greed is good' crowd) and that some are fatalistically unshakable in their conviction that things can never change. Macpherson was not trying to argue such people out of possessive-individualist commitment or resignation. His approach to this core theme, as to the others, is therefore relatively modest: to articulate what he sees at the main rival orientations in current political culture and to identify problems and opportunities for realizing the developmental-demcratic alternative.

Truly Human Powers

In *Democratic Theory* Macpherson distinguishes between power as someone's 'potential to use and develop one's uniquely human attributes or capacities' and as 'his present means ... to ensure future gratification of his appetites,' calling the first of these an 'ethical' concept, the second a 'descriptive' one (DT, 8–9). Later he qualifies this terminology (DT, 52), but its force remains. The bare ability to do or get whatever someone wants is a matter of descriptive fact. The ability to develop a person's truly human capacities is called ethical by Macpherson since it pertains to human purposes that are morally worthy of pursuit whether or not anyone actually pursues them.

As noted in the last chapter any morally relevant concept of human powers for Macpherson must 'start from the assumption that there are specifically human capacities different from, or over and above, animal ones.' (DT, 53) He defends this point by reference to the views of H.L.A. Hart and Isaiah Berlin described in that chapter that thought and language about human purposes implicate such an assumption. Contrary to Peter Lindsay's claim that he bases his views about the human essence on a philosophical theory that is 'independent of human experience' (Lindsay 1996, 96), Macpherson characterizes the assumption as 'an empirical postulate, verifiable in a broad way by observation.' (DT, 53) Macpherson allows that his sample lists of truly human capacities (for aesthetic creation, rational understanding, friendship, and others, DT, 4, 53–54) exhibit a certain 'looseness,' and he observes that, despite some thinking that 'the capacities should be shown to be in an ordered relation, with one as the first principle and the others as derivative,' he does not attempt to rank them. (DT, 54)

Steven Lukes sees this looseness as a shortcoming. Noting that there can be disagreements about just what the uniquely human powers are, Lukes argues that Macpherson's view of truly human capacities 'is basically a form of individual moral perfectionism' and that this ethical theory is required to specify what capacities should be valued. (1979, 148–149) In Thomas Hurka's exposition of perfectionist ethics—the view that a morally good life requires the development of certain features of human nature—Macpherson is cited as an exponent. (1993, 195n19) Macpherson's views do lend themselves to inclusion within one species of perfectionism sometimes called 'the capabilities approach' as deployed by Amartya Sen and Martha Nussbaum (e.g., Sen 1993). On this approach people should be provided with the means successfully to exercise certain capabilities, for example, for Nussbaum, the abilities to live a healthy life, maintain emotional attachments, participate in political decision making, and (in one of her lists) seven other things. (1999, 41–42) Macpherson's approach to human potentials is akin to this capabilities version of perfectionism. Each draws on aspects of Aristotle's views about human happiness, and what Macpherson calls 'capacities' are the same things as capabilities, but this does not make Macpherson's views a form of philosophical perfectionism.

Deliberately lacking in his treatment is an effort to provide a complete and prioritized list of capacities worthy of development. Lukes is right that this would require going beyond describing the capacities Macpherson favours and appealing to foundational ethics to motivate a complete list of capabilities and philosophically to justify the moral superiority of this list over capabilities compatible with possessive individualism. As to the latter task, Macpherson thought that, as he put it in a related context, the 'concept of man as an exerter and enjoyer of his human capacities' is 'more morally pleasing' than a possessive-individualist one (DT, 34), and he thought that most, if not all, people would agree.

He saw his task as to explicate the notion of human capacities and to identify impediments to their full development. Chief among the impediments are: the ability some possess in a market society to force the transfer of others' powers to themselves ('extractive power'); inadequate resources for many to access the conditions for developing their capacities (real scarcity); false beliefs ('intellectual errors') about the inevitability of such scarcity, that is, 'ideologies inherited from ages of scarcity' (DT, 52–57); and the active promotion of consumerist desires in a capitalist society. (DT, 38)

Macpherson's view that a full and ordered list need not be sought is based on his vision of a democratic society. Since the definition of such a society is that everyone enjoys the ability to develop his or her capacities to the fullest, its attainment is obstructed to the extent that some people's exertion of their powers can only be undertaken at the expense of others not being able to exert theirs. Hence, unlike currently existing societies deemed democratic, which are based mainly on voting and assume continuing irreconcilable conflict, a fully democratic one requires that 'the essentially human capacities may all be used and developed without hindering the use and development of all the rest.' (DT, 54) Thus, membership of a capacity in a list of truly human ones is warranted when it is not of an unavoidably conflictual nature. Examples of both the realism and the difficulty of determining what capacities meet his criteria (not developed by Macpherson, but invited by the framework for addressing these questions he provides) come readily to mind.

The capacity to develop and sustain friendships requires, among other things, free time, which in market societies is scarce for many. The capacities for rational understanding and aesthetic appreciation or creation require educational and cultural resources, also scarce, and similarly for most candidates for being truly human capacities. Macpherson can agree that provision of sufficient resources needed for development of everyone's truly human capacities is a prodigious undertaking, but this consideration by itself does not prove that projects to develop and employ technology in humanistic directions and to implement social and economic policies also to this end are impossible. The claim that they are impossible has a self-serving character to it.

There have already been examples in human history of major successes in this domain: the abolition of slavery, breaking ties of the franchise to property and gender, invention of the printing press and access to information and education for general literary, regulations of working hours, restrictions on the length of work weeks, provision of pensions and social assistance, and so on. Macpherson is not prescribing radically new measures, but strengthening and expanding those that have already been at least partially achieved.

Just as Macpherson's approach to truly human potentials does not provide an exhaustive list of these potentials, it does not pretend to offer full guidance about just what capacities one should seek to develop. Somebody may choose to devote all their free time to doing crossword puzzles, playing bridge, bird watching, or some other activity considered by others trivial and detracting from more worthy pursuits, even if they meet Macpherson's criterion that their undertaking by some does not unavoidably prohibit others from developing their capacities. Ethical considerations, not addressed by Macpherson, are appropriate here. For example, animal rights advocates may well marshal arguments against the development and exercise of a talent for hunting. Someone for whom sloth is a cardinal vice may mount arguments from within virtue theory against trivial pursuits.

Some activities may violate Macpherson's principles indirectly; for example, developing a talent for playing golf requires there to be environmentally destructive golf courses, which, when added to other environmental degradations, threaten the natural sustainability required for the exercise by anyone of many undeniably worthy potentials. Were a fully developmental-democratic world in Macpherson's sense ever achieved, where everyone had access to the opportunities and resources to pursue any chosen life activities, important morally relevant problems would therefore remain, but this would not be a bad world from within which to address them.

A concern internal to Macpherson's approach is that in a society with a smoothly running market economy to which people are acculturated everyone will be either a willing and happy seller or a willing and happy buyer of labour power, so a market society could meet his criteria at least regarding labour. No doubt there are some who fully accept market-society life, just as there are some so irredeemably selfish that they cannot tolerate any distribution of wealth that diminishes their own incomes. Macpherson is not committed to denying these things, and indeed recognition of them prompts his exposition of the pervasiveness of a culture of possessive individualism and identification of counteracting, developmental-democratic ideas. It is not enough for this argument that there *might* be a society of happy wage slaves and (even happier) capitalists. Rather, the argument must be that should such a society ever come into existence, Macpherson's theories would be inappropriate to it. The application of Macpherson's views to neoliberalism will bear on this topic.

Positive Liberty

In chapter two it was registered that Macpherson saw his notion of positive liberty as not only compatible with but required for liberal commitment to individual freedom. A question this raises is whether this viewpoint is coherent. As earlier noted, Isaiah Berlin famously limited the concept of liberty to the ability to do what one wants without the deliberate interference of others—'negative liberty'—and he resisted positive conceptions where the *goals* of freedom are specified. The particular goal Berlin had in mind was 'self-mastery' or the ability 'to be self-directed, to be moved by [one's] own conscious purposes, to act and decide rather than be acted on upon and decided for by others.' (DT, 10, Berlin 1969, 131)

Against Berlin, Macpherson endorses a 'self-directed' conception of positive liberty (labelled PL1 by him), which, along with the ability fully to participate in governance (PL3), is an essential component of his notion of developmental power. However, he challenges as unwarranted Berlin's further view that a conception of positive liberty unavoidably invites acceptance of coercion 'by the fully rational or by those who have attained self-mastery, of all the rest' or what Macpherson designates as PL2. (DT, 109, Berlin, 131–132, 154) PL1, Macpherson argues, does not entail PL2, and it need not in practice be transformed in an illiberal way.

The 'predicament,' which Macpherson credits Berlin as having highlighted, of 'wholescale denial of liberty' being undertaken and justified in paternalistic ways is due:

> not to the logic of positive liberty nor to the assumptions of the Idealist and rationalistic theorists who have pushed positive liberty, in thought, to positions which have supported repulsive extremes ... [but] to a specific failure of liberal theory, and of those who hold power in the societies which justify themselves by liberal theory, to take account of the concrete circumstances which the growing demand for fuller human realization has encountered and will encounter. (DT, 107)

The required circumstances are removal of impediments to the development of people's capacities to the fullest endemic to a capitalist market: scarcity, artificially sustained by inadequate use of technology; promotion of competitive practices and culture; and perpetuation of the ability of some 'to extract benefit from the use of others' or 'extractive power.' (*ibid.*, 42) In light of the severity of the last of these impediments, Macpherson recommends substituting the terms 'counter-extractive liberty' or 'developmental liberty' for 'positive liberty.' (*ibid.*, 118)

Someone might still try to defend anti-democratic means to attack impediments to developmental liberty or to justify coercive perpetuation of extractive power on trickle-down grounds. But placed on the terrain of concrete political and economic realities, such defence could not be deduced from abstract principles. In this essay Macpherson allows that in some circumstances a degree of coercion might be justified, but generally, and 'clearly in our time,' it is not justified. (DT, 106–107) On the contrary, removal of impediments to positive liberty can also increase negative liberty, in a sense broader than Berlin's, to confront structural as well as deliberate constraints (*ibid.*, 118–119).

False Consciousness

In place of the abstract speculations by Herbert Marcuse, Georg Lukács, and others, Macpherson's discussion of false consciousness, as of human powers or positive liberty, is pragmatic: articulate goals; identify impediments to reaching them; and look for ways to overcome the impediments. Some obstacles to developmental democracy are 'external' to people's values—prominently, inadequate resources to pursue full lives, confinement of work to wage labour, and oppressive class relations. 'Internal' impediments are ones that shape peoples' values in ways that perpetuate possessive-individualist practices and institutions. This is 'the phenomenon of men hugging their chains' and becoming willing 'slaves of their own possessions.' (DT, 76)

In *Democratic Theory* Macpherson addresses structural, economic supports for values and self-conceptions that inhibit one's challenging possessive individualism. There he sees a connection between external and internal impediments: 'A man whose productive labour is out of his control, whose work is in that sense mindless, may be expected to be somewhat mindless in the rest of his activities.' (DT, 67) This recognition is compatible with Macpherson holding out little hope for *directly* attacking internal impediments, that is, arguing people out of completely internalized possessive-individualist values. Instead, he opines that the staying power of possessive-individualist values depends in large measure upon whether a society is experiencing political, economic, and environmental crises. In these circumstances, 'a partial breakthrough of consciousness is not out of the question.' Political theorists can supplement this process through 'rational analysis of the external impediments' (DT, 76) highlighting the deficiencies of market societies and describing realistic alternatives.

The topic is pursued by Macpherson in subsequent writings. As noted in chapter three, in *The Rise and Fall of Economic Justice* he sees demands for industrial democracy as potentially involving 'workers' awareness of the dynamics of capitalism, and (consequently) ... changing their priorities from consumer satisfaction to work gratification.' (EJ, 41) Taking stock of the conditions required for this awareness he again emphasizes external factors: 'The demand for industrial democracy will increase in the measure that the capitalist economy ... is seen to have become incompetent to provide the economic goods which it has led the working class to expect.' (*ibid.*, 38) Later in this essay Macpherson challenges a prevalent view that human rights—in a broad sense that includes women's, workers', civil, and environmental rights—must be traded off against economic efficiency. Though most participants in social movements for these rights are not in the grips of a possessive-individualist culture, they do not all possess 'clarity of understanding' of the impediments to human rights posed by a market society. Macpherson concludes with a self-effacing comment that political theorists can contribute to this understanding as 'scribblers whose ideas do sometimes percolate through to the media.' (*ibid.*, 49)

Macpherson's most extensive treatment of ways that internal impediments can be overcome is in his discussion of citizen participation in part five of *The Life and Times of Liberal Democracy*. Citing Marx and Mill, he maintains that 'only through actual involvement in joint political action can people transcend their consciousness of themselves as consumers and appropriators,' and he makes specific reference to participation in social movements. This confronts an apparently vicious circle: 'we cannot achieve more democratic participation without a prior change in social inequality and in consciousness, but we cannot achieve the changes in social inequality and consciousness without a prior increase in democratic participation.' (L&T, 100)

Hope for breaking this circle is at least conceptually possible if one sees their elements as containing potentially upward spirals. Impetus for participatory action is sparked by 'loopholes' in the vicious circle with 'the increasing awareness of the costs of economic growth, the increasing awareness of the costs of political apathy, the increasing doubts about the ability of corporate capitalism to meet consumer expectations while reproducing inequality.' Together these things 'conduce to a decline in consumer consciousness, a reduction of class inequality, and an increase in present political participation.' (*ibid.*, 106 and see DT, 76)

Macpherson returns to this theme in essay eight of *The Rise and Fall of Economic Justice* (reprised from a 1979 publication on pluralism and participation). The main weaknesses of social movements, in addition to the fact that they 'do not usually have many friends in high places,' is that unlike unions they lack the power of the strike. (EJ, 98) However, social-movement involvement can directly affect the consciousness of participants and indirectly affect the thinking of people outside of them:

> To the extent that a developmental group can do this, whether by mass demonstrations, marches, civil disobedience, and other physical action, or more quietly by persistent propaganda, they can be effective. Politicians and governments who depend on reelection must make some concessions to their demands, whether the demands are for pollution controls, day-care centres, protection against racial or sexual discrimination, legalization of marijuana or of abortion, or whatever. All such uses of the electoral sanction can win concessions. (EJ, 98)

This hypothesis goes beyond the 'scribbler' comment to highlight the educative potentials of social-movement activism as a factor in influencing people's consciousness.

SELF-OWNERSHIP

Another theme central to Macpherson's theoretical undertaking is a postulate of the possessive market model that '[e]ach individual's capacity to labour is his own property and is alienable.' (PI, 54) This concept is associated with the notion of self-ownership, often interpreted as the idea that people ought to have proprietary rights over themselves. Robert Nozick makes this principle the cornerstone of his philosophical libertarianism. (1974, e.g., 32) Typical of deployment of the principle by followers of Nozick is that of Lloyd Gerson, who sees self-ownership as essential for someone being a responsible moral agent since it provides a link 'between the metaphysical concept of person and the implicit normativity of ascriptions of personhood.' (2012, 84)

Macpherson does not engage the philosophical literature around this topic but confines himself to tracing what he takes to be the possessive-individualist sustaining consequences of regarding people's talents as private property. In *Democratic Theory* (essay vi) he notes that, strictly speaking, property is not a thing but a right to exclusive use of something.

In *Economic Justice* (ch. 7) he decries a shift in thinking about property as a means, for example, to achieve a good life or as a prerequisite for individual freedom, to regarding possession of property as an end in itself. In criticizing self-proprietorship he is focusing on these aspects of property in relation to the alienation of people's capacities rather than on the ownership of persons or selves (which likely does get one into metaphysical waters). His main point is that if someone's capacities are legally designated their private property, then they have a right to sell or to buy their use. Capitalists are buyers who then get to dictate how the capacities are to be used, and workers lose control over the use of their capacities, thereby laying themselves open to disadvantageous transfers of their powers.

Individuals and Society

In chapter two it was argued that Macpherson's normative individualism is compatible with his recognition of the social origins of individual aspirations and of the conditions that impede or facilitate their realization. This position is well articulated by Macpherson in his rejoinder to the criticisms of Alasdair MacIntyre summarized in that chapter. MacIntyre never responded to this rejoinder, but he could have argued that Macpherson had not gotten to the crux of the communitarian challenge. In the article to which Macpherson reacts, MacIntyre maintains that:

> the essentially human capacities are most significantly manifest not only in the abilities of individuals, but, *above all*, in the formation and maintenance of certain types of relationships between certain types of community. (1976, 179, emphasis added)

Another, more pointed, communitarian-inspired criticism is by Bikhu Parekh, who concludes that Macpherson wishes 'to create a *socialist* society in order to realize *liberal* man.' (1982, 72)

Macpherson certainly argues for the 'maintenance and formation' of a certain type of community, namely, one not built around possessive-individualist principles, but such a community is to be valued just because it serves the development of individuals' essentially human capacities. To this extent, and bearing in mind that for Macpherson 'liberal man' is not an atom in the sense discussed earlier, Parekh's characterization is accurate. A community that worked against this goal, whether capitalistic or otherwise (one thinks of fundamentalist religious communities), is disvalued by Macpherson. He simply is not a communitarian theorist.

Macpherson's individualism does not, however, preclude him from valuing communities that do serve developmental goals. One reason for this is that the development of truly human capacities requires cooperation. A general feature of these capacities is the condition that their exercise by some is not at the expense of attempts by others to exercise theirs. Activities prompted by possessive-individualist values, such as capitalist efforts to keep down wages, unavoidably engender conflict. As some critics of Macpherson note (e.g., Lukes 1979, 148) there can also be conflicts among people pursuing developmental aims, as for example when securing a salary sufficient to afford resources for developing artistic talents means winning out in competition with others for scarce jobs.

But these sorts of conflict derive from conditions that are subject to removal (in the example, by economic policies ensuring full employment), and cooperation is required if such policies are to be democratically implemented. Campaigns for social and economic policies sufficient to facilitate any developmentally compatible aims (artistic, scientific, recreational, etc.) and to negotiate compromises when sufficient resources are not or not yet available again require that the campaigns be undertaken in a spirit of cooperation.

Positive evaluation of communities insofar as they foster cooperation is an instrumental matter. Such communities are to be valued because they serve certain goals striven for by individuals, including, as noted in the earlier chapter, the goal of preserving a community or taking collective action. By implication, could such goals be attained by means other than social cooperation, it might be thought that there is no reason to value the communities. It is in reaction to this sort of reasoning that some, such as Robert Maynell, think Macpherson's individualism either presupposes or requires a philosophical theory to resist an opposition between self-interested individualism and socially minded cooperativism—crudely put, between Hobbes and Rousseau.

Meynell offers up an Hegelian theory of recognition for this purpose (2011, 99–101), a version of which he claims is shared by Macpherson with the later theories of the nature of the human self-developed by Charles Taylor (who explicitly *does* draw on Hegelian philosophy, 1989). Hegelian concepts might have helped Macpherson to justify as coherent his overarching aim to 'bring back a sense of the moral worth of the individual, and combine it again with a sense of the moral value of community.'

(PI, 2) But he, himself, does not avail himself of Hegelian or any alternative philosophical orientations that could support him, for instance, Edmund Husserl's theory of essential human intersubjectivity (1960 [1929], V) and its application by Alfred Schutz (1967 [1932]) or the Symbolic Interactionist theory associated with George Herbert Mead. (1934)

Instead Macpherson advances the considerations reviewed in earlier chapters that temper stark instrumentalism on this topic. He can acknowledge group-based commitments and endorse collective rights. Also, important for him is that some valued capacities, such as for friendship or love, are social of their very natures. Macpherson shares with Dewey the idea that 'democracy is a name for a life of full and free communion.' (Dewey 1984 [1927], 450; Macpherson, EJ, 95) This notion is central to both Macpherson's critique of possessive-individualist values and his enthusiasm for participatory democracy, where securing the latter requires changes in the former, that is, away from people:

> seeing themselves and acting as essentially consumers to seeing themselves and acting as ... enjoyers of the exertion and development of their own capacities. This is requisite not only to the emergence but also to the operation of a participatory democracy. For the latter self-image brings with it a sense of community which the former does not. One can acquire and consume by oneself, for one's own satisfaction or to show one's superiority to others .... Whereas the enjoyment and development of one's capacities is to be done for the most part in conjunction with others, in some relation of community. (L&T, 99)

As in the case of most of the key theoretical theses Macpherson advances he sees tensions or problems not in abstract terms but as tasks for practical solution. A task of the political theorist is to identify the kinds of society where individual development in cooperation with other members of the society is facilitated. (DT, 57) Macpherson's approach to this, as to many other topics, is very much in keeping with the pragmatic one of John Dewey:

> The democratic ideal poses, rather than solves, the great problem: How to harmonize the development of each individual with the maintenance of a social state in which the activities of one will contribute to the good of all the others. It expresses a postulate in the sense of a demand to be realized: That each individual shall have the opportunity for release, expression, fulfillment,

of his distinctive capacities, and that the outcome shall further the establishment of a fund of shared values. Like every true ideal, it signifies something to be done rather than something already given, something ready-made. Because it is something to be accomplished by human planning and arrangement, it involves constant meeting and solving of problems. (Dewey 1985 [1932], 351)

HISTORICISM

In *Possessive Individualism* Macpherson defends the coherence of Hobbes's theory of human nature and the political prescriptions he derives from it by locating both in Hobbes's times:

> [W]hen Hobbes's universal claims are reduced to an historical measure, there is no need to divorce his theory of human nature from his political theory in order to rescue the latter; both theories are seen to have a specific historical validity, and to be consistent with each other. (PI, 13)

Macpherson is here approaching precarious territory. Read one way he is expressing some form of historicism. Starkly put this is the claim, regarding morality, that norms appropriate to one historical epoch are justified ('valid' in Macpherson's terminology) because they perform an essential function in that epoch, but they are not justified in epochs with different needs and possibilities, for which other norms are essential.

This historical relativity extends as well to human nature. If one holds that this is fluid, then, for the historicist, it is allowed that humans may have one nature (e.g., as seekers of infinite appropriation) in one historical epoch and another nature (as striving to develop non-acquisitive talents) in a different epoch. Conjoined with the views that conceptions of human nature are value-laden and that value judgments are neither true nor false, this yields an historical relativism that some may be comfortable with, but others will not. Macpherson's scattered comments about the historical relativity of norms and human proclivities lend themselves to alternative interpretations.

One version of historicism, sometimes attributed to Marxism, is that the exigencies of an historical period's economic structure, including its level of technology and its class relations, permit, require, and therefore prompt dominant values and modes of human comportment. A morally relativistic conclusion of this description of changing popular values is drawn when it is further maintained that the values are not just ones that people can be expected to espouse in some epoch but are also in some ethically-philosophical sense justified during the epoch. For the relativist, when the epoch's economic structure changes, the values cease to be justified and new ones suitable to the new structures are espoused and justified. Some of Macpherson's language lends itself (though not unequivocally) such a viewpoint (e.g., PI, 275, DT, 36–38; L&T, 4–5; EJ, 50).

On an alternative interpretation developmental-democratic self-conceptions, values, and behaviour are always morally superior to possessive-individualist ones, and they exist as trans-historical human *proclivities* such that some historical circumstances are permissive of and conducive to their being pervasive motivations in a society. However, absent such circumstances, people act in possessive-individualist ways and profess, or at least do not challenge, possessive-individualist values and conceptions. They are, so to speak, possessive individualists by default. Macpherson explicitly expresses such a position with respect to the anti-communal dimension of possessive individualism:

> [I]t is only scarcity and the extractive market situations that have made people behave atomistically; and ... in the measure that scarcity and extractive relations are removed, people will cease to behave atomistically. (1979, 199)

And the perspective is also in keeping with Macpherson's often-repeated argument that technological advances have now made it possible realistically to envisage a world beyond possessive-individualist competition and acquisitiveness. (e.g., RWD, 54–55)

An elaboration of this position attends to a distinction between two dimensions of Macpherson's democratic ontology: that the development of truly human capacities is to be favoured from a moral point of view and that the means for such development ought to be equally available to everyone. The first of these has served as a major moral touchstone from ancient times through the middle ages and into modern epochs. But for much of human history its realization has been possible only for a few, and in unchallenged market societies accommodation to life and work in accord with possessive-individualist values is unavoidable though not therefore morally justified.

Of the fully historicistic, relativistic interpretation and the possessive-individualism-by-default interpretation, the latter is most in accord with Macpherson's overall project of exposing conditions conducive to or detractive from a culture of developmental democracy. Capitalism at least undercut ancient aristocratic and feudal inequalities based on hereditary rank, but until recently gender and property requirements for full citizenship were retained, and, as Macpherson argues at length, the extractive powers of capitalists restrict equal full development even absent formal constraints. Also, the nature of the equality that was legitimized in the ascendant capitalism is formal equality of opportunity in market competition; so, absent the prospect of full and substantive equality, this limited what egalitarian morality it was realistic to accept.

The new conditions Macpherson sees as opening up popular-level challenges to this aspect of capitalistic societies are, on the one hand, growing dissatisfaction with restriction of equality to market opportunities made possible, in part by technological advances with the potential to reduce scarcity, and, on the other hand, growing political strength of the working class sufficient to secure a universal franchise. (PI, 271–276) The first condition means that full-blown developmental equality can be valued as more than a purely utopian dream. The second condition holds out the promise of a government that facilitates and enforces full equality.

Given the detail with which he discusses conditions that make possible realistic aspiration for a developmental-democratic future, the non-historicistic, 'default' interpretation may be taken as most consonant with Macpherson's overall views, though it seems he had not thought this matter through. At least the default position can be regarded as his for the purposes of this book, which aims to apply his theories to contemporary problems. Even if Macpherson is taken to have held that in past epochs developmental democracy had no claim to moral superiority, in the present era it is clear that he thought it is only realistically changeable circumstances that prevent people from valuing and embracing a developmental-democratic mode of life.

Foundationalism

Considerations of historicism with respect to Macpherson's theories are related to ones about what has come to be called 'foundationalism' in social and political theory. This is the approach that looks to find principles rationally to anchor theories and prescriptions about something, as opposed to anti-foundationalism, which shuns such principles, and, on one current version, instead seeks, in the manner of post-structuralism, to identify ways that a plurality of people's self-conceptions and normative visions are constructed in their various and changing interactions (summarized in Cunningham 2002, ch. 10, and see Laclau and Mouffe 1985).

Relating this opposition to Macpherson, Carol Gould maintains that he holds to an essentialist interpretation of human capacities but one that lacks 'an adequate philosophical grounding.' (1988, 19). Her alternative is to view individual capacities as not fixed but open to change in light of agents' choices, and she describes this approach as neither 'foundationalist in an essentialist way' nor 'anti-foundationalist in a relativistic way' but as 'quasi-foundationalist.' (27).

Macpherson's approach can also be read as neither philosophically foundationalist nor anti-foundationalist, but while Gould is seeking a way philosophically to ground her view of human capacities that is separate from these two approaches, Macpherson, as argued in the previous chapter, avoids taking a stand on this topic by maintaining agnosticism about foundational philosophy altogether. On the possessive-individualism-by-default interpretation of his intent Macpherson is claiming that as a matter of fact, unless impeded by lack of resources or psychologically manipulated to act in competitive and acquisitive ways people will strive to develop the potentials of which he gives his sample list. A philosopher who concurs will seek an explanation for this tendency in something essential to human nature, drawing, for instance, on Aristotle's metaphysics of human potency and act or on Hegel's phenomenology of personhood.

But Macpherson is not trying to *explain* his view that people will, in the right circumstances, try to develop certain potentials. He is asserting this as a hypothesis borne out by experience and historical example. Those who agree with him will seriously entertain his further claim that a market society is an overriding impediment to the successful development of these potentials. Similarly, on this interpretation Macpherson is not *prescribing*, that people should develop certain potentials, in the manner of the perfectionist philosophers of ethics. Rather, he is *asserting* that a society that enables such development is morally superior to a possessive-individualist society. Those who do not share this sentiment or who think that the conditions required to achieve a developmental-democratic society are never available will be less interested in the other things Macpherson has to say than those who agree with him.

This is a feature of much of Macpherson's writings, and it relates to his abstinence of an effort philosophically to argue people into accepting his theories. For instance, in his notes on the most general social vision he shares with Marx, Macpherson writes that one:

cannot demonstrate that human life and the fullest possible development of everyone's human attributes and potentials are the ultimately desirable things. But fortunately it doesn't need to be demonstrated to people of good will in the liberal tradition: their ultimate goal (ultimate moral value) is virtually the same as Marx's. ... Where they differ from Marx is in what needs to be done to move nearer to the goal. (UTA 1968, 61b–c)

This perspective, combined with Macpherson's displacement, pragmatist-like, of attempted complete theoretical resolution of issues of social and political contention to the domain of problems for practical solution, can be viewed either as a weakness or as a strength. It is a weakness in limiting his work's potentially receptive readership. It is a strength in allowing him to make some theoretical progress for those who share the central values of his vision and agree with at least the main aspects of his political-theoretical theses.

References

Berlin, Isaiah. 1969. Two Concepts of Liberty. In *Four Essays on Liberty*, 118–172. Oxford: Oxford University Press.
Cunningham, Frank. 2002. *Democratic Theory: A Critical Introduction*. London: Routledge.
Dewey, John. 1984 [1927]. *The Public and Its Problems*. In *John Dewey: The Later Works*, vol. 2, 235–372. Carbondale, IL: Southern Illinois Press.
———. 1985 [1932]. *Ethics*. In *John Dewey: The Later Works*, vol. 7. Carbondale, IL: Southern Illinois University Press.
Gerson, Lloyd. 2012. Who Owns What?: Some Reflections on the Foundations of Political Philosophy. In *New Essays in Political and Social Philosophy*, ed. Ellen Frankel et al., 81–105. New York: Cambridge University Press.
Gould, Carol. 1988. *Rethinking Democracy: Freedom and Social Cooperation in Politics, Economy, and Society*. Cambridge: Cambridge University Press.
Hurka, Thomas. 1993. *Perfectionism*. Oxford: Oxford University Press.
Husserl, Edmund. 1960 [1929]. *Cartesian Meditations: An Introduction to Phenomenology*. The Hague: Martinus Nijhoff.
Kontos, Alkis. 1979. Through a Glass Darkly. *Canadian Journal of Political and Social Theory* 3 (1, Winter): 25–45.
Laclau, Ernesto, and Chantal Mouffe. 1985. *Hegemony and Socialist Strategies*. London: Verso.
Lindsay, Peter. 1996. *Creative Individualism: The Democratic Vision of C.B. Macpherson*. Albany: State University of New York Press.

Lukes, Steven. 1979. The Real and Ideal Worlds of Democracy. In *Powers, Possessions and Freedom: Essays in Honour of C.B. Macpherson*, ed. Alkis Kontos, 139–152. Toronto: University of Toronto Press.

MacIntyre, Alasdair. 1976. On "Democratic Theory: Essays in Retrieval" by C.B. Macpherson. *Canadian Journal of Philosophy* 6 (2): 177–181.

Macpherson, Crawford Brough. 1962. [PI] *The Political Theory of Possessive Individualism: Hobbes to Locke*. Oxford: Oxford University Press. Reissued with an Introduction by Frank Cunningham. Toronto: Oxford University Press, 2010.

———. 1965. [RWD] *The Real World of Democracy*. Toronto: Canadian Broadcasting Corporation. Reprints: Oxford: Oxford University Press, 1966; Toronto: House of Anansi Press, 1992.

———. 1968. [UTA] *Marxian Theory*. University of Toronto Archives B1987-0069, Box 2a, file 4.

———. 1973. [DT] *Democratic Theory: Essays in Retrieval*. Oxford: Oxford University Press. Reissued with an Introduction by Frank Cunningham. Toronto: Oxford University Press.

———. 1977a. Needs and Wants: An Ontological or Historical Problem? In *Human Needs and Politics*, ed. Ross Fitzgerald, 26–35. Oxford: Pergamon Press.

———. 1977b. [L&T] *The Life and Times of Liberal Democracy*. Oxford: Oxford University Press. Reissued with an Introduction by Frank Cunningham. Toronto: Oxford University Press, 2012.

———. 1979. Second and Third Thoughts on Needs and Wants. *Canadian Journal of Political and Social Theory* 3 (1, Winter): 46–49.

———. 1984. [EJ] *The Rise and Fall of Economic Justice*. Oxford: Oxford University Press. Reissued with an Introduction by Frank Cunningham. Toronto: Oxford University Press, 2013.

Mead, George Herbert. 1934. *Mind, Self and Society*. Chicago: University of Chicago Press.

Meynell, Robert. 2011. *Canadian Idealism and the Philosophy of Freedom: C.B. Macpherson, George Grant, and Charles Taylor*. Montréal and Kingston: McGill-Queen's University Press.

Nozick, Robert. 1974. *Anarchy, State, and Utopia*. New York: Basic Books.

Nussbaum, Martha. 1999. *Sex and Social Justice*. Oxford: Oxford University Press.

Parek, Bhiku. 1982. *Contemporary Political Thinkers*. Oxford: Martin Robertson.

Schutz, Alfred. 1967 [1932]. *The Phenomenology of the Social World*. Evanston: Northwestern University Press.

Sen, Amartya. 1993. Capability and Well-Being. In *The Quality of Life*, ed. Martha Nussbaum and Amartya Sen, 30–53. Oxford: Clarendon Press.

Taylor, Charles (1989) *Sources of the Self*. Cambridge, Mass.: Harvard University Press.

PART III

Contemporary Challenges

INTRODUCTION TO PART III

The following chapters relate Macpherson's views to a selection of twenty-first-century challenges. None of these except the first—the pervasiveness of neoliberalism—is directly addressed by Macpherson himself. Rather, resources in his works for addressing the challenges are sought. This does not mean that discussions in the preceding chapters are only of intellectual-biographical import. The basic ideas of Macpherson abstractly treated in these chapters have relevance to the contemporary conduct of political theory:

Cross-Disciplinary. Macpherson placed himself in the tradition of political economy, and he lamented its demise as an academic discipline, his own university having been one of its last holdouts. His works are important not only for helping to reinvigorate political economy but also for integrating it with a cultural dimension. Macpherson thus provides a model for political/economic/cultural theory. His deployment of this theory is therefore interdisciplinary drawing on the history of ideas as well as on political science and economics.

Political Theory. Macpherson concerns himself with basic theoretical issues—the nature of democracy, freedom, the individual and the community, human needs and powers, political consciousness—but he does so at the level of political theory rather than by derivation from philosophical principles. If, as is argued in chapter four, he is successful in this endeavour, he demonstrates that fundamental questions of political import can be addressed without commitment to some foundational (or for that matter anti-foundational) theory of philosophy. In addition to avoiding entanglement with philosophical schools and controversies, this approach allows for appreciation and use of Macpherson's political theories from within a variety of philosophical orientations.

Visions. Just as Macpherson chides his fellow political scientists for avoiding 'a grand theory of the state,' so are mainstream political theorists guilty of fallaciously assuming that since 'all utopian (i.e., unscientific) thought is visionary, therefore all visionary thought is utopian (i.e., unscientific).' This conclusion, Macpherson argues, 'is surely false, for scientific thought also is visionary.' (EJ, 120) All of Macpherson's writings, beginning with the publication of *Democratic Theory*, are organized around the vision of a developmental-democratic society and its contrast with possessive individualism.

Liberal-Democratic Socialism. In the articulation of his vision, Macpherson defends what is likely his most important contribution to contemporary political theory, namely, his rejection of an opposition between liberal democracy and socialism. As discussed in chapters two and three, the developmental-democratic vision he offers is at once liberal, democratic, and socialist, thus challenging dominant perspectives on both the left and the right according to which simultaneous pursuit of these things is misguided.

Realism and Radicalness. Macpherson strives to defend a vision that is at once radical and realistic. The radical dimension is one he shares with Marxist and other critics of capitalism who advocate the rejection of a market society, rather than looking to 'third way' accommodations to capitalism. Macpherson does not provide blueprints for the realization of his developmental-democratic vision; instead, he identifies problems and urging working away at them guided by the norms informing his overall vision. Relevant to the realism of his vision are the following considerations.

- Macpherson does not just advocate that people lead less costly or extravagant lives, but he depicts this as a consequence of an attractive mode of life unlike the precarious and fear-ridden possessive-individualist alternative.
- In his deployment of the history of ideas, Macpherson offers reasons to believe that possessive individualism is not an essential part of human nature but has been historically constructed. This is important

for countering the fatalistic belief that one flies in the face of human nature in challenging possessive individualism and policies catering to it.
- The vision Macpherson projects is secular and, in appealing to individual development, individualistic; therefore, it is consistent with these aspects of liberalism. This distinguishes his entreaties from ones that require religious beliefs or that appeal to communitarian standards. At the same time, thanks to the complementarity of 'truly human potentials' his view is individualistic in a way that invites cooperation.
- Finally, in identifying 'loopholes' in the vicious circle whereby possessive individualism creates attitudes that preclude challenging it, Macpherson highlights features of the world (as prominent today as when he was writing) that reflect or prompt questioning the market-society *status quo* in popular consciousness: failure of market societies to deliver on promised economic gains for any but the rich; increasing environmental degradation; inability (or unwillingness) to take advantage of the enormous potentials of modern technology for humanistic purposes; growing gaps in economic equality; dissatisfaction with the quality of a life dedicated to consumption; and social-movement activism responding to these things.

In the following chapters all of these themes in Macpherson's theories are relied upon in constructing 'Macphersonian' reactions to the contemporary challenges they address.

CHAPTER 6

Neoliberalism

Of the contemporary challenges discussed in this part of the book, only that of neoliberalism is directly addressed by Macpherson. Though the term 'neoliberalism' was not yet in vogue when he was writing, Macpherson's criticisms of Milton Friedman, who, with Friedrich von Hayek, is considered a pioneer of neoliberal theory, are appropriate to it, as are his treatments in general of market societies. Macpherson describes Friedman's orientation as a 'pure market theory of liberalism.' (DT, 143) The term 'neoliberalism' as used in the nineteenth century had a meaning unlike its later appropriation where it has become advocacy of an unregulated market and the interpretation of all social relations in economic market terms.

Macpherson almost certainly derived the term 'market society' from Karl Polanyi, and like Polanyi he decried its increasing hold in Western democracies. Polanyi writes:

> This institutional gadget, which became the dominant force in the economy—now justly described as a *market economy*—then gave rise to yet another, even more extreme development, namely a whole society embedded in the mechanisms of its own economy—a *market society*. (1977 [1954], 9)

One difference between Macpherson's conception of a market society and Polanyi's is that while the latter describes labour as 'a fictitious commodity' (1944, ch. 6), for Macpherson the most pernicious feature of a market society is that labour is a real commodity:

If a single criterion of the possessive market society is wanted it is that man's labour is a commodity, i.e., that a man's energy and skill are his own, yet are regarded not as integral parts of his personality, but, as possessions, the use and disposal of which he is free to hand over to others for a price. (PI, 48)

While for Polanyi a society with an economic market can, if properly regulated, be relatively benign, at least for a time, Macpherson is less sanguine. He makes few explicit references to Polanyi's work (e.g., at L&T, 86n15), but in notes prepared for an address given on it, he expresses a misgiving about Polanyi's description of a market society as 'a fully self-regulating market mechanism with no state interference with the flow of prices for labour, capital and land' (Macpherson, UTA 1969). This, Macpherson thinks, lets welfare capitalism—called in a catch phrase of the day 'post-capitalism' or later designated by Macpherson a 'quasi-market society' (DT, 133–134)—off the hook of being complicit in perpetuating a market society.

Such nuanced differences do not pertain to neoliberal theorists, who look with favour on the progression Polanyi describes. Friedman's core thesis is summarized by Macpherson as that: 'competitive capitalism can resolve "the basic problem of social organization," which is "how to co-ordinate the economic activities of large numbers of people" by voluntary co-operation of individuals as opposed to central direction by state coercion.' (DT, 144; Friedman 1962, 12) All neoliberals share Friedman's view that market exchanges unconstrained by government regulation (save to maintain a military and police and to enforce contract compliance) are the most efficient ways of conducting economic affairs. They also share the view that state intervention in an economy is not only inefficient but impedes individual freedom or even, as is argued in von Hayek's *The Road to Serfdom* (2001 [1944]), leads to totalitarianism. Public goods such as health care, education, or transportation should be in the hands of private competitors and subject to economic market interactions

The ancestor of neoliberalism is the constellation of schools of neoclassical economic theory first developed in the late nineteenth century by theorists who wished to supplant the classical economic theories associated with Adam Smith, David Ricardo, and Karl Marx. While classical theorists strove to identify the origins and objective values of goods and services and to map their distributions through a society, the neoclassical theorists attended much more narrowly to the subjective determination of prices in market interactions. One of the first systematic iterations of the neoclassical approach was the theory of general equilibrium set down by French theorist Léon Walras. In the 1950s a version was developed by Kenneth Arrow and Gérard Debreu who laid out formal conditions under which supply and demand across all of a society's interacting markets will reach equilibrium. Such a society's economy is held to be as 'efficient' (in a technical sense of this term) as possible.

Though general equilibrium theory and neoliberalism are both prominent species of neoclassical economics, the former, as modified and conjoined with some aspects of classical economics by MIT economist Paul Samuelson, is broad enough to include the views of John Maynard Keynes and prominent Keynesians whom neoliberals such as Friedman and Hayek criticize for endorsing state regulation of markets. The neoliberal, monetarist approach, by contrast, sets itself against any attempt to control an economy through fiscal policy, and it advocates supply-side economics and cutting government spending. This approach became dominant especially within American academia and was used to justify the economic policies of the Thatcher and Reagan governments. The main aspects of neoclassical theories criticized by Macpherson are those that provide support for this neoliberal variant of neoclassical economics.

It will be seen that neoliberalism plays a role in all the challenges addressed in the remaining chapters of this book. Three aspects of the neoliberal project are especially vulnerable to critique from the point of view of Macpherson's theories: subjectivism, promotion of a version of *pleonexia*, and a propensity to encompass all aspects of a society.

SUBJECTIVISM

For those in the tradition Macpherson is criticizing, people enter into market relations to advance their preferences, the objective values of which do not concern the economist. As Walras puts it:

> Necessary, useful, agreeable, and superfluous, all those conditions amount for us only to degrees of being more or less useful. Furthermore, neither is it necessary to take account here of the morality or immorality of any need to which a useful thing can be applied and that it can satisfy. Whether a substance is sought by a doctor to cure a sick person, or by a murderer to poison his family are very serious matters from some points of view, but a matter totally indifferent from ours (2014 [1899], 20–21).

For some economic purposes subjectivism is innocuous, as when the aim is just to predict prices in the short term. An economic market may approximate equilibrium and still be subject to criticism on moral grounds or for failing to provide important public goods, and economists from Adam Smith through some of the equilibrium theorists were prepared to make such critical judgments. But for neoliberals these judgments are to be avoided since they invite state meddling with markets.

Even in its earliest forms a market-based approach to the distribution of a society's benefits and burdens is subjectivist. Macpherson traces this propensity to Hobbes: 'The death of the concept of economic justice may be said to have been proclaimed by Thomas Hobbes' (EJ, 9), who overturned the earlier notion of a just price on the grounds that, in Hobbes's words, 'the value of all things contracted for is measured by the Appetite of the Contractors' (1968 [1651], 208). Macpherson also cites the famous (or infamous) announcement of Hobbes (referred to in the appendix to chapter one) that 'the Value or Worth of a man is, as of all other things, his Price' (*ibid.*, 151–152). By Macpherson's time thoroughgoing subjectivism for economic theorists in this tradition is orthodoxy: 'Individual utilities on which their system is based are given by the preferences and tastes of individuals as they are. In maximizing utility or welfare, all wants are equal. Whatever is, is right.' (DT, 177)

For the most part Macpherson does not engage these theorists with respect to the narrowly economic matters that mainly occupied them, since he is more concerned with the social and political uses of their approach. For instance, one of Friedman's claims is that unconstrained markets avoid employment coercion, because employees dissatisfied with the terms of work of one employer can seek an alternative one (Friedman 1962, 14–15). This argument is subjectivistic since the employees' choices are supposedly freely made, and the outcome therefore represents their subjective preferences. Whether the terms of employment of one employer are objectively superior to those of another does not enter the picture. Macpherson finds that this argument 'almost despairs of logic' abstracting as it does from the essential existence in a capitalist market in a labour force that is 'without a choice as to whether to put its labour in the market or not.' (DT, 146)

Pleonexia

When John D. Rockefeller was asked, 'How much money is enough?' he is said to have replied, 'Just a bit more.' This is a manifestation of what Aristotle called *pleonexia* or an insatiable desire for possessions (1984 [350 BCE], 1782 [1129a], somewhat misleadingly translated as 'grasping') which in his time was considered inimical to a life of genuine happiness. While Aristotle criticizes people with *pleonexic* habits of life and aspirations, Macpherson addresses the phenomenon of 'infinite consumers.' (e.g., DT, 60)

The similarities are that both the *pleonexic* person and the infinite consumer covet appropriation of indefinite possessions in ways that impede a virtuous and fulfilling life. However, while Aristotle views this disposition in psychological terms as an aberration, for Macpherson '[w]hat was new, from the seventeenth century onwards, was the prevalence of the assumption that unlimited desire was rational and morally acceptable.' (DT, 18) Whatever the driving force behind this assumption (about which Macpherson does not venture an opinion), it was necessary as an incentive to justify increasing productivity which in turn was required 'to make possible the increase of wealth (and power) which a new enterprising class saw in prospect for themselves.' (*ibid.*, 19)

In one of the few places where he addresses neoclassical economic theorists on their own terms, Macpherson identifies as a potential problem for them that the demand for a commodity diminishes as a buyer accumulates more of it—in economic language, its marginal utility approaches being negative, or, as Macpherson summarizes Bentham on this point, 'the richer you became the less satisfaction you could get from each additional lot of wealth.' (DT, 177) The problem according to Macpherson is that '[t]o admit this would be to recognize an order of urgency of wants in every man, ranging from the most basic necessities to pure frivolities,' and this 'would be to cast serious doubts on the ability of the market system, with all its inequalities of income, to maximize the aggregate utility of all members of the society.' For this purpose, wants need to be sorted by some objective criterion into those that must or morally ought to be satisfied and other wants, and this is something the neoliberals wish to avoid. (DT, 177–178)

The problem is supposed to be gotten around with the thesis that as some people acquire wealth others try to emulate them, thus generating an unending cycle of increasing desire for wealth (incorporated in equilibrium theory as a 'non-satiation axiom') and by denying that a distinction between desires, whether created by emulation or not, is relevant to economic behaviour. This is one way that the aspiration to infinite consumption 'may be said both to have produced the capitalist market society and to have been produced by that society.' (*ibid.*) The point is echoed by Bernard Hodgson who notes that under pressure of competition in a capitalist market there is always an impetus to produce more goods. This, in turn, requires commensurate indefinite growth in consumer demand: 'The "possessive individualism" uniting entrepreneurs and consumers is indispensable to the product growth integral to market efficiency.' (2004, 295)

In his challenges to the neoliberal subjectivists' refusal to evaluate wants, Macpherson attends to the fact that 'the market system, based on and demanding competition and emulation, creates the wants which it satisfies.' (DT, 182) Then, referring to Rousseau and to Kenneth Galbraith, he distinguishes between 'natural' and 'artificial' wants. As noted in the last chapter, the latter are wants created in capitalist market activities and serve the profit motives of this market. Macpherson is not sufficiently clear about what he means by natural wants. Negatively regarded, they are not wants that serve needs of a capitalist market and that only exist if they do. Positively, he likely means wants the satisfaction of which promotes or facilitates the development of people's truly human potentials. As described in chapter five, these are potentials for rational understanding, moral judgment, aesthetic creation, and friendship, among others, in an open-ended list, which potentials typically thrive on cooperation.

Macpherson's views on the way markets create wants resonates with a project of Samuel Bowles and Herbert Gintis to explore the effects of preference formation created in—'endogenous to'—market behaviour. 'Market and other economic institutions,' as Bowles puts it, 'do more than allocate goods and services: they also influence the evolution of values, tastes and personalities.' (1998, 75) As economic theorists, one of Bowles's and Gintis's efforts has been to show how endogenously produced economic behaviour poses problems for the predictive powers of equilibrium theory, which typically supposes that preferences are formed and rewards or sanctions are given exogenously to market interactions. Backed by empirical studies, Bowles also identifies values produced in and by a market society. Among these are loss of a sense of the intrinsic worth of one's own activities, amorality in social interactions, and indifference to acquiring a reputation as being socially responsible. (*ibid.*, 90–98) He and Gintis conclude that '[a] Walrasian world undermines a culture supporting social norms like cooperation, truth-telling, and non-aggression.' (1993, 95) Macpherson's historically supported arguments that people are not possessive individualists by nature, but are constructed as such in a market society, bolster these conclusions.

All-Encompassing Marketization

Just as markets have a way of spilling out of economic transactions to influence people's values and interactions with one another, so do they expand, cancer like, to affect all aspects of society. An obvious example is the transformation of what had once been thought of as amenities or social services valuable in themselves into commodities: university students become clients; homes become real estate investments; cities become global competitors; ideas become marketable possessions. Macpherson addresses two other ways that market conceptions extend beyond simple exchange, one at the dawn of capitalism, the other a twentieth-century development.

Self-ownership. The first of these is the notion that among the marketable commodities people possess are themselves, that is, the notion discussed in chapter five of self-ownership. This has its origins in the seventeenth century as part of a justification for the conception of property as a universal right of exclusion. One consequence of belief in self-ownership is to encourage an atomistic picture of humanity. Macpherson sees it as a central component of the culture of possessive individualism: 'The individual is proprietor of his own person, for which he owes nothing to society.' (PI, 269) Bowles notes the affinity of this idea with Hobbes's metaphor of people as 'sprung out of the earth and suddenly (like mushrooms), come to full maturity, without any kind of engagement with each other' (Hobbes 1968 [1642], viii.1), which in the manner of neoclassical economic theory 'abstracts from the ways that society shapes the development of its members in favor of "taking individuals as they are."' (Bowles 1998, 75)

The most far-reaching effect of this self-conception is that people come to see their talents not as abilities the exercise of which is intrinsically rewarding and potentially useful to the societies that produce them but as instruments to serve their self-interest. This displaces an alternative orientation where people see themselves as trustees of their abilities rather than their private owners. This conception represents a shift in how people regard their endeavours. Arguing this case, Bowles maintains that people enjoy the exercise of their talents less when they engage in activities 'as a means toward an extrinsic good, such as being paid' than when they engage in it with no such reward. (*ibid.*, 91) A related effect is that 'the relations of dependence between persons have the appearance of impersonal relations between things,' that is, people as property are subject to what Marx called commodity fetishism. (DT, 241; Marx 1996, 81–93)

Catallaxy. The second main spill over is in the realm of politics. The universal franchise is threatening to a capitalist market since a majority may insist on constraining markets in the interests of promoting social services or imposing regulations on capitalist production and exchange. This danger is averted when the equilibrium-market model is imported into democratic politics: 'The democratic political system is typically presented ... as a mechanism whose function is to reconcile or balance or hold in adjustment a multitude of diverse and conflicting individual interests.' (DT, 187) Macpherson is here referring to the approach to democracy called 'catallaxy,' a term coined by Hayek to describe the application of economic principles to political behaviour (a summary is in Cunningham 2002, ch. 6).

Macpherson describes the adoption of this approach in political science (mainly in the United States) as the 'Schumpter-Dahl axis' (DT, 78 and see L&T, ch. IV) referring to Joseph Schumpeter's description of democracy as 'that institutional arrangement for arriving at political decisions in which individuals acquire the power to decide by means of a competitive struggle for the people's vote' (1962 [1942], 269) and to Robert Dahl's understanding, especially in his earlier works, of politics as power-political interactions among myriad interest groups (1956 and several other books). Others in this camp include Anthony Downs (1957), James Buchanan, and Gordon Tullock. (1962) Politics in this approach just means competition among political parties, which, as Downs puts it, 'are analogous to entrepreneurs in a profit-seeking economy' formulating policies to garner votes 'just as entrepreneurs produce whatever products they believe will gain the most profits.' (Downs 1957, 295)

The marketization of politics is not only an abstract model proposed by catallactic theorists. This model is actually realized in democracy as practised in a market society. One of Macpherson's main objections to the model is that it:

> deliberately empties out the moral content which [earlier liberal-democratic models] had put into the idea of democracy. There is no nonsense about democracy as a vehicle for the improvement of mankind. Participation is not a value in itself, nor even an instrumental value for the achievement of a

higher, more socially conscious set of human beings. The purpose of democracy is to register the desires of people as they are, not to contribute to what they might be or might wish to be. (L&T, 78, and see DT, 187-192)

In addition to flowing from a capitalist market society, this weak form of democracy, once in place, makes getting out of such a society, at least by democratic means, difficult. Democracy limited to voting for political parties or leaders responding to dominant economic forces and dependent on monetary campaign support offers little scope for any but minimal reforms on the part of those segments of a citizenry not immobilized by fatalism about democratic politics or themselves buying into a self-interested, competitive version of it.

* * *

Neoliberals advance several justifications for the subordination of societies to the mandates of an economic market. The major arguments they deploy are a negative one that an alternative, regulated market leads to proto-totalitarian planification and a positive argument that thoroughgoing marketization is economically efficient. We shall turn to these after reviewing some subsidiary arguments.

INDIVIDUAL FREEDOM

In a claim echoed by almost all subsequent neoliberals, Hayek avers that capitalist market competition 'is the only method by which our activities can be adjusted to each other without coercive or arbitrary intervention of authority.' (2001 [1944], 37-38) The irony is lost on champions of neoliberalism that its policies were first tried out in Chile, where Friedman, Buchanan, and Hayek himself served as advisors to the brutal Pinochet regime shortly after the 1973 coup that militarily overthrew a democratic government. Justification of this by the neoliberal advisors was based on the claim that it paved the way for major economic growth. (A negative evaluation of this claim may be found in Ostry et al., 2016.) Aside from this and other such glaring incongruities, the association of liberty and the free market is supposedly evident in the bare notion of a market, as in the definition of 'a market' in the *Dictionary of Free-Market Economics* as 'a process encompassing the totality of voluntary economic acts within some context.' (1998, 200)

Macpherson's criticism of negative liberty provides a basis for countering a freedom-based defence of unbridled markets. As discussed in earlier chapters, he argues that liberty should not be thought of just as the ability of people to do what they wish, abstracting from the generation of their wishes, their content, and the contexts which constrain people's actions. (DT, 103–104) The crucial component of markets is that they involve exchanges among individuals (or corporate individuals). Whether the exchanges are voluntarily entered into or the outcomes are in accord with the wills of participants is a question not of definition but of explanation of why people engage in transactions and what consequences their engagements have. Alternatively, the freedom-in-exchange definition is a trivial implication of the fact that exchanges involve deliberate human actions. (When I deliberately stamp an envelope I may choose not to do this, but if I want the envelope to be mailed I must stamp it.)

Unless one is prepared to believe that in a market society everyone's complete liberty would somehow be ensured, it must be allowed that in a democracy, as in any other form of government, some freedoms will be facilitated and others impeded. Referring specifically to a democratic state, Macpherson argues that while 'the liberty of the individual to use his capital unrestrictedly' was once regarded as essential, this 'must now be given up if we are to retain the liberties essential to equal individual opportunities for self-development.' (1942, 418) No doubt champions of unbridled capitalism disagree, but the decision between these views of which freedoms to privilege is not one that can be made by appeal to definitions.

Focusing on the aspect of market exchanges that they involve choices in the narrow sense of taking deliberate actions and declaring that therefore they promote freedom of choice abstracts from: explanation and evaluation of the motivations for actions; the actions' intended and unintended consequences; realistic if not always perceived or pursued alternatives; and the economic, political, and social contexts within which actions are undertaken. All of these factors are implicated in how coercive or liberating a society's economy is for its inhabitants. They raise questions that concerned Macpherson's academic discipline of political economy, and they are questions he hoped to help put back on the agenda of political and economic science.

INCENTIVES

The often-repeated claim that without market-driven incentives people would not be motivated either as entrepreneurs or as energetic workers is also self-serving and ideological. It no doubt applies to those who have completely internalized the notions that their ability to work or to produce things are their own private property, for which remuneration in the form of wages or profit are due them, but this internalization is seldom complete for all members of a society and does not apply in all times and places. A Macphersonian retort, as argued in chapter five, is that to the extent that people act in possessive-individualist ways, this is often in default of having the opportunities and resources to comport themselves in ways consonant with developmental democracy.

Though many working people may have been more desperate in Britain or the United States under the neoliberal reigns of Thatcher, Reagan, and now Trump than in other epochs, it is dubious that they were more inclined to work, and to work enthusiastically, than before or more motivated than people in countries like Germany, Sweden, Japan, and others when their markets were constrained. Similarly, there is no evidence that entrepreneurs in the neoliberal climates have been especially energetic and inventive. Claims about the indispensability of market incentives are at least of limited application. Moreover, when they do have some application, they call for interrogation of the political and economic circumstances that affect incentives. These will include the availability of meaningful work or the ability of entrepreneurs to produce or sell goods in which they can take pride even if they are costly to produce without fear of being driven out of business.

ACCOMMODATING BAD PEOPLE

Buchanan and Tullock defend the coordination of human affairs exclusively by means of market interactions in part *because* it is premised on self-interest. One cannot assume, they argue, that a free individual agent 'will always follow the moral rules agreed on by the philosophers as being necessary for harmonious life.' So instead of counting on moral behaviour for this purpose it is better that institutions should be structured with the always present possibility of selfish behaviour in mind so that selfishness 'can be channeled in such a direction that it becomes beneficial ... to the interests of all members of the community.' (1962, 303–304) They here echo Hayek, when he defends the market as 'a system under which bad men can do the least harm.' (1948, 11) From the point of view of Macpherson, this argument rests on some shaky premises.

Presumably the harm that 'bad men' can do in a society with a regulated economy is to insinuate themselves into positions of political authority which they selfishly abuse. This argument ignores the opening unbridled markets gives to robber barons and electoral manipulation by moneyed interests, neither of which can be said to be beneficial to 'all members of the community.' It also partakes of the endogenous character of markets discussed by Bowles and Gintis that designing politics for the worst people brings out the worst in people, thus not just accommodating to selfishness but creating it.

Macpherson's conception of robust democracy bears on this perspective. It is easier for the bad people to turn government to their own purposes in a weak democracy, where, without sufficient transparency and accountability between elections and with the ability to buy votes during them, the rich can mould regulations to selfish ends or get around them. A robust democracy for Macpherson is one that permits and encourages direct citizen participation, as in social movements, some of which are directed against the machinations of self-serving corporations. More basically, participation in such movements is one way that people's values and estimations of what is possible are affected such that they will be disposed to support progressive government policies and to reject a fatalistic premise of the 'bad men' argument that there is nothing to be done except to accommodate to them (see L&T, 106).

Democracy

The arguments of Friedman and Hayek that government constraints on markets lead to socialism is not one with which Macpherson entirely disagrees. He sees the importation of an equilibrium view of politics (as the balancing of interests, mainly as represented by political parties) as consonant with support for class-divided societies. The interests to be balanced were initially those internal to factional conflicts within a capitalist class. When the franchise was opened to working people, working-class action, especially in the trade unions, became powerful enough that it needed to be taken into account. A reaction was to limit effective access to government to political parties, where big money dominates and citizen apathy is bred. (L&T, 69–69, 86–91) As noted, Macpherson allows that variants of the equilibrium model accurately describe how what is called democracy functions in a class-divided society. For him this is just what is wrong with it, and supplanting such a society is requisite for a robust democracy. This means some variety of socialism, which is why most of Macpherson's essay on Freidman defends socialism against the charge that it is necessarily destructive of democracy.

Macpherson's basic counter to the argument of Friedman regarding democracy and socialism is the one that occupied the discussions of chapter three that there is nothing in principle to prevent a socialist government from being democratic. Macpherson grants that existing socialist societies have objectionably denied the individual freedoms essential to liberal democracy, and he devotes some attention to the conditions that have facilitated this (backward economies, populations unschooled in liberal-democratic values, militaristic habits bred of armed revolutions, and active obstruction on the part of capitalist powers), noting that these do not apply (at least as severely) to the developed liberal-democratic countries. (DT, 153)

Friedman also claims that if the state is the sole employer in a society it can use its monopoly to intimidate challenges to it. Macpherson holds that this is a possibility as long as a socialist society is dominated by 'a ubiquitous [Communist-like] party hostile to political freedom,' but he does not think that this is inevitable. The sort of society he envisages includes competing political parties as well as constitutional guarantees of individual liberties and effective, direct citizen participation. (L&T, 113–114) Macpherson's pragmatic approach to politics is evident in this discussion.

The problem of achieving socialist democracy for him is not mainly a matter of whether there are possible institutional means to guarantee this, as he thinks there are. Rather, it a matter of whether there is the will to construct appropriate institutions. (DT, 151–153) Socialism for him is a project, in particular the project of achieving a society promoting developmental democracy. Such democracy centrally includes liberal-democratic protection of individual freedoms and avenues for substantial citizen involvement in the affairs of state. It is therefore up to those who would further this project to identify and strive to secure its conditions and institutions.

Efficiency

The term 'efficiency' has a technical meaning in equilibrium theory, 'Pareto optimality,' which refers to allocation of resources being such that no reallocation can be undertaken that makes anyone worse off than before it. This provides the neoliberal with an alternative conception of efficiency to one that sees an economic system as efficient if it is effective in achieving some specified social goals (e.g., full employment or provision of public goods) since this conception invites the sort of social planning neoliberals wish to avoid. Macpherson does not concern himself with criticizing the optimality notion of efficiency, though he easily could have.

Resources in this approach must refer just to those someone actually has, since otherwise some objective standard of desirable or acceptable levels would need to be employed. Billionaires in this scheme remain billionaires, while the homeless remain homeless unless the former choose to make large and ongoing charitable donations or some way can be found for addressing homelessness that does not involve taxation of the rich. If the economy of such a society is deemed efficient, one might conclude that this is so much the worse for 'efficiency' as a criterion for distributing a society's wealth.

Most charges of the inefficiency of state economic planning use 'efficiency' in a non-technical sense. Neglecting the poor track record of trickle down economics, neoliberals claim that privatization and unconstrained markets are effective in generating wealth for the whole of a society. By contrast, government-owned enterprises involve, and necessarily so for the neoliberal, artificially high costs and get mired down in government bureaucracy, patronage, and the like. Further, government regulation of private enterprise is supposed to be excessively time consuming, and to create a class of expensive professionals parasitic on the regulations to navigate through or to find ways to get around them (idiosyncratically called 'rent seekers' in neoliberal parlance). As in the case of socialism and democracy, Macpherson can grant the existence or even prevalence of these things in existing societies that include state ownership and regulation, but observe that just as in the political case, realistic measures to counteract them are not hard to imagine and in some times and places have actually been put in place, so, again, confronting these problems is a matter of political will.

It should not go unnoted that the free market is itself replete with inefficiencies of these sorts: obscenely highly paid senior executives, not all of whom exhibit entrepreneurial acumen; complex corporate structures with opaque decision-making mechanisms; and rent seeking-like legal staffs scheming and plotting in competition among corporations and against unions and other movements that challenge profits. Those in public universities who can compare them before and after they started, in the 1980s and greatly accelerated since, to become like private businesses have seen commensurate increases in administrative, legal, and fund raising staffs and expenditures.

* * *

Confronting Neoliberalism

To the extent that neoliberalism has insinuated itself into actual economic policies, confronting it is primarily a matter of political practice. To the extent that it is a theory rationalizing these policies and that has a certain traction in popular political attitudes, resistance at the level of political culture is called for. It is in this latter respect that Macpherson' views have something to offer. The neoliberal perspective is a 'totalistic' one, embracing all aspects of economic interactions and many social ones as well. As a pure version of possessive individualism neoliberalism is subject to Macpherson's critique of this ontology, and insofar as his articulation of this critique has purchase in popular consciousness, it can play a role in weakening support for neoliberal economic and political policies.

In the course of the summary of neoliberal tenets above, reactions from the point of view of Macpherson have already been indicated: neoliberal subjectivism and its narrow concept of freedom ignore oppressive structures; *pleonexic* greed is an endogenous product of market society, not a basic feature of human nature; neoliberal commodification of social life and its catallactic approach to politics are destructive of human community and of robust democracy; its claims to provide incentives for productive labour and to promote economic efficiency are belied by actual economic practices. To these specific criticisms may be added three general aspects of Macpherson's orientation.

Realistic radicalism. The political-theoretical path that Macpherson seeks to take is one that conjoins realism with radicalism. His identification of developmental democracy as a version of liberal democracy, including the core values and many of the institutions associated with it, is the politically realistic side of his project. This aim is shared with neoliberalism, though the neoliberals and Macpherson select different elements of liberal democracy on which to focus. Macpherson's radical aim, diametrically opposed to that of the neoliberals, is to make out a case for conjoining liberal democracy with socialism. If Macpherson's arguments, as reported in this book, are sound, he succeeds in this venture. In particular he provides a radical alternative to conservative versions of liberal democracy, and most strikingly of its neoliberal variety.

There are, of course, non-radical alternatives to neoliberalism, as in 'third way' versions of social democracy or the approaches of those green political parties (such as currently in Canada) that wish to combine a limited number of matters to regulation and public-private ownership with subjection of other matters to free markets. But unless these alternatives actively reject the core tenets of neoliberals, they leave in place the claims of the later that what constraints on unfettered markets they allow are at the expense of efficiency and liberty. By contrast, a radical alternative to neoliberalism adopts the viewpoint of the Pentagon computer in the movie *War Games*, which, charged with winning the game of thermonuclear war, concludes that 'the only winning move is not to play.'

Not playing the game of free marketization means rejecting the perspective that sees subjection to markets as a base-line presumption exceptions to which must be justified case by case. Rather, social goals are identified, best in democratic deliberation, and it is market measures that need to be justified by demonstrating that they play an indispensable role in attaining the goals. Moreover, in keeping with the allowances Macpherson makes for market interactions referred to in chapter three, market-driven distribution of goods or services can and should be constrained by such regulations as price and quality control. Or, to return to the point argued for there, Macpherson could, and at one point did, agree that markets play a role in providing information about many consumer preferences without endorsing full and unqualified marketization for this purpose.

Anti-fatalism. The propensity of economic and political practices in accord with neoliberalism to create the values that sustain them and to absorb all aspects of human interactions, along with neoliberal promotion of a Hobbesist view of human nature, combine to promote an assumption in popular culture that, for better (i.e., for the wealthy) or for worse (for everyone else), accommodation to market society is something people have no choice but to accept. Like Karl Polanyi, Macpherson challenges the naturalness of a market society. His view is entirely in keeping with that of Michael Jacobs and Mariana Mazzucato:

> It is not helpful to think of markets as pre-existing, abstract institutions which economic actors (firms, investors and households) 'enter' to do business, and which require them, once there, to behave in particular ways. Markets are better understood as the outcomes of interactions between economic actors and institutions, both private and public. ... Markets are 'embedded' in these wider institutional structures and social, legal and cultural conditions. In the modern world, as Polanyi pointed out, the concept of a 'free' market is a construct of economic theory, not an empirical observation. Indeed, he observed that the national capitalist market was effectively forced into existence through public policy—there was nothing 'natural' or universal about it. (Jacobs and Mazzucato 2016, 38–39)

Some features of Macpherson's approach are relevant to the sources of fatalism.

There is a difference, and a tension, between the thesis that neoliberalism is inevitable due to its self-perpetuating nature and the claim that neoliberalism is grounded in human nature. The former thesis involves a process perspective where some self-regarding market behaviour prompts values in support of more such behaviour. The latter is a static matter. If possessive individualism is indelibly written into the nature of humanity, it is futile to resist economic and political policies in accord with it. Much of Macpherson's scholarly work is devoted to contesting this conclusion. If people are possessive individualists by default, then given the right circumstances they will opt for behaviour inconsistent with that portrayed by neoliberals as the natural human condition. But even setting this claim aside, Macpherson's historical analyses in *Possessive Individualism* are largely devoted to showing that the view of people as naturally acquisitive private appropriators is an 'historical novelty brought in by the needs of the capitalist market society' and part of a 'perverse, artificial, and temporary concept of man.' (DT, 20)

The self-perpetuation support for fatalism involves a spiral, where, for instance, a student who would prefer to pursue education in the humanities looks to future employment possibilities and instead pursues a degree in commerce, but then the original values change in response first to the culture of a business school and then (should anticipated employment materialize) to the rewards of successful practice in a capitalist environment. No doubt such spirals exist, but, unless competitive-market endogenous preference formation comes to dominate all of one's personality (as in the psychopathological lead character, to cite another must-watch movie, *The Wolf of Wall Street*), spirals are subject to reversal. From the point of view of Macpherson, this is what is sparked when the promises of an unconstrained market are disappointed.

Spirals in a developmental-democratic direction are possible when there is space for and encouragement of behaviour in accord with it, and whether or how such spaces and encouragement exist is not a matter of luck, but can be actively promoted. This brings us to another feature of Macpherson's orientation relevant to neoliberal fatalism. Just as in the cases of protecting government regulation and ownership from bureaucratization, provision of the grounds for developmental-democratic spirals, even if arduous, even if undertaken in the face of opposition, and even at local and initially modest levels, is still, in Macpherson's perspective, a matter subject to human will and effort.

Humanism. In one respect Macpherson's approach and that of the neoliberals are on the same terrain, namely, that of liberal individualism. However, they have very different views about the nature of the human individual: the neoliberals' amoral and atomistic, Macpherson's value-infused and social. Following Hobbes, and in keeping with contemporary rational choice theory (sometimes explicitly employed by defenders of neoliberalism), theorists of neoliberalism typically see the rational individual as approaching any situation that calls for a decision as choosing the course of action most likely to realize his or her highly ranked preferences. Rationality in this approach has only to do with whether appropriate means to a preferred end are pursued. Ends themselves are not evaluated. Nor are the causes, social or otherwise, for people having the preferences they do taken into account.

This orientation is convenient to the neoliberal focus on market efficiency rather than effectiveness in the service of worthwhile goals and in general to its alternative to the broad economic and social problems and issues that have traditionally concerned the field of political economy. In Macpherson's view the neoliberal orientation is anti-humanistic. It denies or abstracts from any but the most anaemic conception of what it means to be a human. It supposes an atomistic picture of people and sees them in their interactions with others primarily in market terms. Macpherson instead views humans, embedded in their social settings, as addressing problems with others and striving to resolve them in ways that are consonant with or advance their overarching goals, and these goals are subject to moral evaluation. For him, the historically longest-standing goal of humans has not been to succeed in self-interested competition with others, but 'to expend our energy in truly human activities—laughing, playing, loving, learning, creating, arranging our lives in ways that give us aesthetic and emotional satisfaction.' (RWD, 38)

There is another aspect of Macpherson's humanistic alternative to neoliberalism that should be noted. Not everyone who endorses neoliberal economic policies also adheres to its concept of the individual as a rational calculator. Most prominently in the United States, but not exclusive to it, *social* conservatives almost always politically line up with neoliberal economic conservatives, though viewed abstractly they ought to recoil from a Hobbesist picture of human nature and from neoliberal economic policies. Except for the wealthy, family life is threatened by the effects of neoliberal economic policies: unemployment of bread winners, unaffordable quality family housing, inadequate health care for children and the aged, and so on. Though Hobbes himself saw value in religion, albeit mainly for the purpose of social cohesion (1968, part three), neo-Hobbesist psychology and values do not sit well with the core tenets of any religion, save, perhaps, for the most austere Puritanism.

What people attracted to social conservatism have in common with those who embrace economic conservatism is the desire to be left alone to pursue their lives privately. Neoliberals do not want anything, and especially the state, to interfere with people's profit-seeking activities. Social conservatives highly value the wellbeing of the communities with which they identify, such as their family, religious affiliations, or networks of like-minded folk (sometimes bound by shared disparagement of others), and they even put preservation of their communities above the self-interest of individuals. However, like the neoliberals, they vigorously resist any intrusion on their communal worlds, and they are at best indifferent and at worst hostile to those who are not parts of them.

The element of Macpherson's orientation most at odds with social conservatism is his egalitarianism. As often noted above, he avers that a feature of truly human potentials is that their development by some need not be at the expense of their development by others, and when this does happen it is not due to essential human competitiveness, jealously, or the like but to potentially changeable circumstances, such as real or artificial scarcity or the promotion in market societies of a culture of possessive individualism. There is no evidence that Macpherson was disrespectful of or hostile to people having communal attachments, unless these attachments are such as to impede the general project of securing circumstances conducive to full development in all human communities. Local attachments and values are not necessarily at odds with this project and in fact can be enriched by them.

Macpherson's conclusion to *The Real World of Democracy* that 'Nothing less than massive aid, which will enable the poor nations to lift themselves to recognizable human equality, will now conserve the moral stature and the power of the liberal democracies' (RWD, 67), refers to a mandate he sees it essential for the Western liberal democracies to take on. It also reflects his own identification with this community.

REFERENCES

Aristotle. 1984, [c350BCE]. *Nichomachean Ethics*. In *The Complete Works of Aristotle*, vol. 2. Princeton: Princeton University Press, 1729–1867.
Bowles, Samuel. 1998. Endogenous Preferences: The Cultural Consequences of Markets and Other Economic Institutions. *Journal of Economic Literature* 36 (March): 75–111.
Bowels, Samuel, and Herbert Gintis. 1993. The Revenge of Homo Economicus: Contested Exchange and the Revival of Political Economy. *Journal of Economic Perspectives* 7 (1, Winter): 83–102.
Buchanan, James, and Gordon Tullock. 1962. *The Calculus of Consent: Logical Foundations of Constitutional Democracy*. Ann Arbor: University of Michigan Press.
Cunningham, Frank. 2002. *Democratic Theory: A Critical Introduction*. London: Routledge.
Dahl, Robert. 1956. *A Preface to Democratic Theory*. Chicago: University of Chicago Press.
Dictionary of Free-Market Economics. 1998. Cheltenham: Edward Elgar.
Downs, Anthony. 1957. *An Economic Theory of Democracy*. New York: Harper & Row.
Friedman, Milton. 1962. *Capitalism and Freedom*. Chicago: University of Chicago Press.
Hayek, Friedrich von. 1948. *Individualism and Economic Order*. Chicago: University of Chicago Press.
———. 2001 [1944]. *The Road to Serfdom*. London: Routledge.
Hobbes, Thomas. 1968 [1651]. *Leviathan*. Harmondsworth, UK: Penguin Books.
Hodgson, Bernard. 2004. On Economic Men Bearing Gifts and Playing Fair. In *The Invisible Hand and the Common Good*, ed. Bernard Hodgson, 279–298. Berlin: Springer.
Jacobs, Michael, and Mariana Mazzucato. 2016. Rethinking Capitalism: An Introduction. In *Rethinking Capitalism: Economics and Policy for Sustainable and Inclusive Growth*, ed. Michael Jacobs and Mariana Mazzucato, 1–27. Oxford: Wiley-Blackwell.
Macpherson, Crawford Brough. 1942. The Meaning of Economic Democracy. *University of Toronto Quarterly* 11 (4): 403–420.
———. 1962. [PI] *The Political Theory of Possessive Individualism: Hobbes to Locke*. Oxford: Oxford University Press. Reissued with an Introduction by Frank Cunningham. Toronto: Oxford University Press, 2010.
———. 1965. [RWD] *The Real World of Democracy*. Toronto: Canadian Broadcasting Corporation Reprints: Oxford: Oxford University Press, 1966; Toronto: House of Anansi Press, 1992.

———. 1969. [UTA] Notes on Polanyi. University of Toronto Archives Box 7 B87 0069/002.

———. 1973. [DT] *Democratic Theory: Essays in Retrieval*. Oxford: Oxford University Press. Reissued with an Introduction by Frank Cunningham. Toronto: Oxford University Press, 2012.

———. 1977. [L&T] *The Life and Times of Liberal Democracy*. Oxford: Oxford University Press. Reissued with an Introduction by Frank Cunningham. Toronto: Oxford University Press, 2012.

———. 1984. [EJ] *The Rise and Fall of Economic Justice*. Oxford: Oxford University Press. Reissued with an Introduction by Frank Cunningham. Toronto: Oxford University Press, 2013.

Marx, Karl. 1996 [1867]. *Capital: A Critique of Political Economy*, vol. 1. In *Karl Marx Frederick Engels Collected Works*, vol. 35. London: Lawrence & Wishart.

Ostry, Johnathan, et al. 2016. Neoliberalism: Oversold? *Finance and Development* 53 (2): 38–41.

Polanyi, Karl. 1944. *The Great Transformation*. Boston: Beacon Press.

———. 1977 [1954–1964]. *The Livelihood of Man*. New York: Academic Press.

Schumpeter, Joseph. 1962 [1942]. *Capitalism, Socialism and Democracy*. New York: Harper & Row.

Walras, Léon. 2014 [1899]. *Elements of Theoretical Economics or the Theory of Social Wealth*. Cambridge: Cambridge University Press.

CHAPTER 7

Global Problems

The problems to which Macpherson's theories are applied in this chapter are globalization and environmental degradation. Regarding globalization, two basic positions will be distinguished: one, where it is seen as important to preserve national autonomy and two approaches (neoliberal and cosmopolitan) that do not share a pro-national autonomy perspective. Whether or how globalization is regarded as problematic partly depends upon one's attitude towards its impact on the autonomy of nations.[1] The position constructed out of Macpherson's theories places it in the national autonomy category and focuses on the potentials in his orientation toward social and political culture within nations to address the negative sides of globalization. Regarding the environment, both those who welcome and those who lament incursions on national autonomy see environmental threats as affecting entire global regions (indeed, the planet as a whole), so no one state can address them alone, and effective coordination among states remains elusive.

---

[1] In this chapter, as in virtually all literature on the topic, the terms 'state' and 'nation' are used interchangeably in abstraction from the phenomena of bi- or multi-national states—for example, Belgium, Canada, and Spain—where sometimes there are differences among attitudes towards globalism between the nations of a single state.

© The Author(s) 2019
F. Cunningham, *The Political Thought of C.B. Macpherson*,
Critical Political Theory and Radical Practice,
https://doi.org/10.1007/978-3-319-94920-8_7

Globalization

In its most general sense, globalization refers to ways that the economic, political, and cultural aspects of each of the world's states are importantly and increasingly affected by similar aspects in other states and by supernational agencies or global economic and cultural forces. As Ulrich Beck puts it:

> No country or group can shut itself off from others. Various economic, cultural and political forms therefore collide with one another, and things that used to be taken for granted (including in the Western model) will have to be justified anew. 'World society,' then, denotes the totality of social relationships which are not integrated into or determined (or determinable) by national-state politics. (2000, 10)

Beck uses the term 'globality' to describe this phenomenon (reserving 'globalization' to refer to global interactions and forces that negatively impact individual states), and Amartya Sen employs 'globalism' in the way Beck does 'globality.' (2014) Each of these authors addresses not just the formal or legal dimensions of national sovereignty, that is, declarations by states that possess or at least aspire to international recognition, of exclusive jurisdiction over all internal matters, but the *de facto* ability of states to comport themselves as they (or their leaders) wish. They are therefore addressing national autonomy rather than national sovereignty. A brief digression is in order to explain the difference between these things.

The contested and complex, theory-laden notion of 'sovereignty' leads many theorists to agree with the conclusion of Michael Newman that the concept 'is so ambiguous and distorted that it is now a barrier to analysis.' (1996, 14–15, and see Étienne Balibar 2004, ch. 8) In agreement with this opinion, this chapter will, as recommended by Charles Beitz (1991, 242), employ the term 'autonomy' to refer to the *de facto* as well as the formal powers of a state to act on goals that it sets for itself. Anthony Giddens's description of what he calls national sovereignty is thus better used to characterize a fully autonomous state as:

> a political organization that has the capacity, within a delimited territory or territories, to make laws and effectively sanction their up-keep; exert a monopoly over the disposal of the means of violence; control basic policies relating to the internal political or administrative form of government; and dispose of the fruits of a national economy that are the basis of its revenue. (1985, 282)

Focusing on autonomy allows one to take account of constraints on a state's ability to comport itself in the ways Giddens describes even when it is nationally and internationally recognized as 'sovereign' in a formal sense. Also, while the concept of sovereignty lends itself to being thought of as an all-or-nothing matter, it is appropriate to regard a state lacking some aspects or degree of autonomy as still being on balance autonomous. This is possible if the powers most important to it are retained or can be regained, and if, in the case of a state that cedes some autonomy, decisions about just what is relinquished are made from within the nation itself and not forced upon it.

Cosmopolitanism. While recognizing some down sides of constraints on national autonomy, Beck, Sen, and several other theorists of international relations see the weakening of state autonomy positively, as offering opportunities for beneficial global cooperation. This is the stance of cosmopolitans like David Held, who holds that: 'the cosmopolitan model creates the possibility of an expanding institutional framework for the democratic regulation of states and society' where states 'would no longer be regarded as sole centres of legitimate power within their own borders.' (1995, 13–14, and see Habermas 2001) Cosmopolitanism in this sense is consonant with Thomas Pogge's conception of citizenship, where 'persons should be citizens of, and govern themselves through, a number of political units of various sizes without any one political unit being dominant and thus occupying the role of the state.'

Cosmopolitan political theorists often uphold regional associations, often referring to the European Union, as models, and there are other variations as well, for example, proposals for a world parliament. (Archibugi 1998, 21–22) These variations are well summarized by Carol Gould (2004, 166–173), who herself favours a model mixing 'international,' 'transnational,' and 'global' political arrangements. (*ibid.*, 173) A main challenge taken on by advocates of any form of cosmopolitanism is to recommend ways to democratize the extra-national institutions they favour. They confront the problem that channels for democratic decision making are confined within states. Held and Archibugi propose transnational political structures to confront this problem. Others take up a more popular-level, activist stance. An example is Richard Falk, who looks to progressive 'globalization from below': 'the main antagonists and sites of struggle can no longer be accurately comprehended by reliance on a statist view of the world. The major antagonists are market forces and their allies on the one side and an array of civil society actors, on the other' (2014, 153–154, and see Cox 2002 and Walker 1990 for expressions of a similar perspective).

Neoliberalism. The opportunities these cosmopolitans see in globalization are entirely different from those of another category of enthusiasts for it, namely, neoliberals. For them the weakening of national autonomy removes strictures on free market exchanges that they decry: public ownership; regulation of markets; state support for nation-based enterprises; and so on. Their claim is that just as a free market in an individual nation will ultimately benefit all its citizens, so free trade and in general removal of restrictions on market interactions across state boundaries will benefit the world as a whole. Susan Strange understands this globalization in practice to mean that:

> [T]he impersonal forces of world markets, integrated over the postwar period more by private enterprise in finance, industry and trade than by the cooperative decisions of government, are now more powerful than the states to whom ultimate political authority over society and economy is supposed to belong (1996, 4, and pt. 11 and see Stiglitz 2017 and Streeck 2016)

While globalization in this sense is deplored by Strange and others, it is *applauded* by the neoliberals precisely for exhibiting these characteristics.

National/Super-national stances. Considering the question of how, or more precisely where, neoliberalism may be combatted by those who oppose it throws into relief yet another distinction, now among those on the political left (broadly conceived), between cosmopolitans and left defenders of national autonomy. The latter differ from right-wing nationalists such as Le Pen and Trump in their egalitarian and anti-neoliberal economic policies. As well, they reject national chauvinism, isolationism, and a conception of democracy in which obedience to a political leader self-proposed as embodying the 'true values' of the nation displaces rule-governed political processes and pluralistic recognition of legitimate differences within a state.

The opposing stances below (explicitly or implicitly regarding the European Union) illustrate the difference between pro- and anti-nationalist orientations:

> [T]here is a growing body of opinion which implies that the EU level [of political action] now has primary importance in the establishment of an advanced socially regulated economy. As one proponent of this viewpoint puts it, 'The theory of national roads is bankrupt ... the epoch of construction of social democracy in one country has come to a close (Michael Newman 1996, 60, quoting Donald Sassoon, 1992)

[A]ny struggle to preserve social democracy as it exists today is a struggle to defend national institutions. And do we ever, today, see national governments compelled by international agreements or by the pressure of international trade and finance to nationalize private industries, strengthen labor protections, or increase the generosity of social insurance? Or is the pressure invariably in the other direction? (J.W. Mason 2017, 32)

At a more theoretically abstract level, Robert Dahl challenges the realism of global governance in a world where even the foreign policies of individual states are largely beyond the control of their own citizens. (Dahl 1999) Will Kymlicka is more optimistic than Dahl on this point and argues against the cosmopolitans that international institutions and practices can and should be made indirectly accountable by 'debating at the national level how we want our national governments to act in intergovernmental contexts.' (Kymlicka 1999, 123)

Macpherson's Theories and Globalization

Some of the specific negative effects of globalization insofar as it is largely dominated by neoliberal policies are discussed in subsequent chapters. Especially alarming are neoliberalism's effects on democracy. '[I]t is now quite clear,' as Wolfgang Streeck puts it, 'that the democratic states of the capitalist world have not one sovereign, but two: their people, below, and the international "markets" above. Globalization, financialization and European integration have weakened the former and strengthened the latter.' (Streeck 2016, 144) Macpherson's criticisms of neoliberalism were summarized in the last chapter: subjectivist calculation of self-interest displacing moral, normative considerations; indefinite accumulation of goods motivated by an ethic of acquisitiveness (*pleonexia*); reliance on markets instead of collective deliberation to determine policies; and, when democratic decision making is allowed, it is through competition among elite-supported political parties (*catallaxy*).

These criticisms culminate in the articulation of an alternative vision to the one informed by possessive individualism. This is the vision of developmental democracy, where everyone is provided with the resources and opportunities to develop and exert his or her 'truly human' potentials to the fullest. The developmental vision is a radical alternative to neoliberal possessive individualism. Rather than proposing an alternative that is better at achieving goals shared with the neoliberals, a developmental-democratic alternative aims at entirely different goals.

An example is the promise of neoliberalism continually to increase a country's (or a region's or the world's) economic productivity. The aspiration to achieve unlimited growth is shared by those critics of neoliberalism who claim that some version of regulated capitalism can deliver better on this promise than can free markets. By contrast, Macpherson's vision rejects the idea 'that an increase in the Gross National Product [is] the supreme goal of national policy' (1971, 34), and he substitutes for a dream of indefinite consumption an ethic where 'consuming in order to act' replaces 'acting in order to consume.' (*ibid.*, 29) His critique of and alternative to neoliberalism exhibit or suppose two focuses pertinent to an approach to globalization generally: on culture and on nations.

Culture. As in the case of nearly all his work, an approach inspired by Macpherson will focus on social and political culture. J.W. Mason observes that 'much of the classic arguments for free trade—from James Mill to Milton Friedman—depend as much on the cultural and political benefits of internationalism as they do on its economic benefits.' (2017, 25) And some critics of neoliberal versions of globalization, like Hedley Bull, argue that a cosmopolitan political structure requires a culture valuing peace, justice, and environmental protection. (1995, 284–285, 303–305) Neoliberals avoid cultural questions, and most cosmopolitan theorists also focus just on political and economic institutions.

Macpherson does not ignore macro-structural matters. He would agree with the characterization of globalization by Susan Strange quoted earlier or that of Claude Ake: 'globalization is driven by a vigorous, triumphant capitalism which is aggressively consolidating its global hegemony.' (1997, 282) But Macpherson's attention to capitalism is, from the beginning of his writings, on: the culture it bred and that sustains it; how a market society creates the desires consistent with possessive individualism; and what prospects there are for transcending these values and conceptions. Similarly, the main focus of his alternative, developmental-democratic vision is on the values of self-development, egalitarianism, and robust democracy. Macpherson's theories are useful for illustrating how neoliberal and in general capitalist-serving globalization embodies and reinforces a culture of possessive individualism and for seeking weaknesses of the grip of this culture on popular consciousness.

That this task may be easier in the case of globalization than of national market societies is suggested by the relative weakness of a popular culture of globalization by comparison to that of a market society. State-based capitalism has been able to associate itself (albeit hypocritically) with nation building, thus drawing on nationalist sentiments. It is the success of this hegemonic effort that has made possible contemporary right-wing nationalist political movements. Champions of globalization (left and right) have not had time to achieve a similar association, and it is hard to see on what bases they could do so. Meanwhile, cosmopolitan theorists such as Bull or Pogge advocate dissemination of a culture where people see themselves primarily as global citizens, but to their disappointment there seems little evidence that such a culture is taking hold in the way that possessive individualism did or that elements of developmental democracy, as Macpherson argues in *Democratic Theory*, have a history capable of being retrieved.

Most cosmopolitans aim to replace national identifications with regional ones, but this is still not global identification, and it is questionable how far it has reached outside some political and academic circles. Perhaps the only specifically cultural 'achievement' of globalization has been to foment an opinion in popular consciousness that opposition to its negative effects is futile and people have no choice except, as Dani Rodrik puts it, 'to buy into a narrative that gives predominance to the needs of multinational enterprises, big banks, and investment houses over other social and economic objectives.' (2011, 206) To see how a campaign to combat such fatalism and to encourage a widespread developmental-democratic culture is best pursued a presupposition of a Macphersonian approach to this challenge needs to be underscored, namely, that it must be based in individual nations.

Nation centrism. Aside from advocating entrenchment of a charter of rights in the Canadian constitution and his book on the Social Credit party in Alberta, Macpherson was silent on national issues in his country, even though he lived through a time of turbulent debate over whether or how Canada could protect itself from economic and cultural domination by the United States and over Quebec separatism. As President of the Canadian Political Science Association, he was an ex officio co-editor with his Quebec counterpart of a collection of papers on Canadian federalism commissioned by the Association (1965), but the editors' introduction to this book carefully avoids taking any stands on the contested issues expressed in it. Still, if Macpherson's theories are to have anything to offer to global problematics, they require a nation-centric orientation.

The super-national institutions that constrain state autonomy with negative effects on their citizens are not easily or at all changed at their own, global level. Rather, as Richard Sandbrook puts it:

The global governance institutions that define and enforce the rules of the game, principally the IMF, the World Bank, and the WTO, are, after all, creatures of national governments. Hence, a major policy shift in national governments is virtually a precondition for a shift in the global regime. (2014, 339)

A cosmopolitan project of democratizing new or existing international institutions, such as economic forums, regional governments, or a strengthened United Nations, cannot be pursued from the top down if for no other reason than that a recalcitrant and sufficiently powerful member state can subvert such efforts or simply withdraw. Bottom-up cross-border initiatives of the kind Falk and others advocate also require national bases.

In recent years the pernicious effects of globalization have sparked ground-level popular actions cutting across state boundaries, such as multi-national protests at meetings of the G20 or in gatherings of the World Social Forum. It is doubtful that these actions could be sustained or attain their magnitude without drawing on the leadership and enthusiasm of protests against gross inequality at national levels. Leslie Sklair calls for 'transnational' social-movement activism to lay the basis for 'socialist globalization.' (2002, 305) Noteworthy is that in illustrating such activism, he refers only to nation-based examples: participatory budgeting in Brazil, self-help networks for women in India, and rural women's co-ops in China. A nation-centric approach need not and should not shun cross-border coalition efforts, but the ground work for these needs to be laid in member countries. For example, cooperation in opposing the North American Free Trade Agreement among Canadian, Mexican, and US trade unions was preceded by protracted and sometimes difficult campaigns in the unions within these states (see Dreiling and Robinson 1998).

For these reasons and if, inspired by Macpherson's orientation, an approach to globalization is focused on social and political culture, it requires anchors in nations, taking the side identified earlier of Kymlicka or Mason against Held or Newman. Even though national powers are diminished, not least by global forces themselves, states have more resources to resist these forces than individuals or, in today's world, cross-border associations of individuals, such as international unions or social movements, alone. Institutions that affect culture, such as schools, are located and administered within nations, as are, at least potentially, news and entertainment media. State leaders and social-movement activists are better placed to advocate for and help to organize international cooperation when they have the backing of people in their own national constituencies than otherwise.

A nation-centric approach can also appeal to citizens' national loyalties. Such appeal is effectively employed by right-wing populists, but contrary to those who find any form of nationalism objectionable, valuing the protection of one's national autonomy is compatible with wishing it to relate in positive ways to other nations, for instance, in cross-border trade or cultural exchanges and by taking joint actions regarding the environment, natural disasters, or poverty. In opposition to the my-country-right-or-wrong version of nationalism to which the populists appeal, national identifications and loyalties can include feeling pride when one's compatriots or government make admirable contributions in world forums but also feeling shame when they comport themselves badly. While national citizenship on this perspective involves taking on responsibility for the wellbeing of fellow nationals, in part by protecting national autonomy, it also recognizes responsibilities to people of other nations. So an attitude of global citizenship can be a *component* of national citizenship rather than being at odds with it.

Extortion. The task of defending (or regaining) national autonomy is indeed challenging. Confronting global forces destructive of national autonomy requires, in the first place, that some gains are made to alleviate the insecurity of low incomes, unemployment, costs associated with ageing and health problems, and the like. The reason for this, as argued in chapter three, is that these insecurities deny people the time to engage in political action, and they contribute to attitudes of fatalism and individualistic competitiveness. Required, therefore, are a politics and attendant institutions that go beyond the forms of welfarism that Macpherson criticizes or Blairite and other forms of right-wing social democracy. (This topic is examined in more detail in Cunningham 2008.)

Hard enough to solve absent globalization, the problems of making progress towards securing egalitarian and regulator measures are even more severe given the extraordinary abilities afforded to capitalist firms and organizations by globalization. Deployment of these abilities may be seen as a form of blackmail or extortion. To threaten to outsource jobs unless significant wage cuts are accepted, to relocate in another part of the world unless freed from taxation pressures, to call on transnational financial agencies to lower a country's credit rating if it tries to implement confining regulations, to challenge in international trade tribunals measures aimed at protecting local manufacturing, imposing price controls, enacting laws to protect the environment, or enhancing state provision of social services—all these things are on a par with ordinary extortion: agree to our terms or we'll see to it that bad things happen to you.

As the example of bailouts for finance capital enterprises in the wake of their precipitation of the 2008 world economic crash illustrates, seeking accord with the most powerful economic agents does not elicit concessions from them. An alternative reaction is for states to pursue egalitarian policies against the wishes of big business, thus calling the bluff of the extortionists by daring them to carry through with their threats. The difficulty for this strategy is that the largest firms and agencies supporting them are not bluffing, but are willing to carry out their threats. So a country will have to be prepared to live with the economic consequences. As in the Battle of Britain during World War II when the German military was surprised at the determination of British people to endure large-scale bombing destruction rather than surrender, a population will have to be prepared to reduce its living standards rather than give in to internal and external economic threats.

The question then becomes one of how realistic it is to expect this. As suggested earlier, national loyalties might provide a motive, but how effective this can be in the long run depends upon the content of a nationalist appeal. The nationalism of right-wing populism, such as that at work in the Brexit campaign in the UK or in Trump's advocacy of US isolationism, is integrated with a possessive-individualist stance in claiming that protectionism and isolationism will garner substantial individual economic advantages. When these advantages are not forthcoming (and globalization contributes in no small measure to this result) the force of such a nationalist appeal is lost. From a Macphersonian point of view, nation-based resistance should, instead, be linked with values favouring developmental democracy and with state efforts towards realizing them.

In chapter five it was suggested that, for Macpherson, to the extent that people adopt possessive-individualist life styles this is by default due to lacking opportunities for leading meaningful lives in the sense he tried to retrieve from dimensions of liberal-democratic traditions. Unlike a life guided by consumerist and other possessive-individualist aspirations, one consonant with developmental democracy is not expensive, and its rewards are intrinsic to the talent-developing activities themselves rather than residing in the wealth one may accumulate.

The promise of developmental democracy is to enhance the quality of people's lives rather than to quince a thirst for unlimited consumption. Hence, a society geared to realization of the values of developmental democracy has the potential to reduce costs of living without people having to make undue sacrifices, and indeed leading more satisfying lives than those associated with self-centred consumerism and greed. These considerations offer part of a solution to the chicken-and-egg problem that standing up to extortionist threats requires a populace that at least enjoys the security in terms of jobs and income provided by progressive (i.e., pro-equality) governments that the threats are meant to curtail.

Of course, for neoliberals there is no problem to be addressed. Utopian neoliberals see the invisible hand of the market resolving any problems, and Social-Darwinist neoliberals are not distressed if those who cannot triumph in an economic market suffer for it. Or, from another direction, optimistic cosmopolitans might think that the need for international regulation of global markets will somehow call into being trans-state organizations whose leaders are committed to taming markets for the betterment of humanity in general and who will instigate policies to this end internationally as well as encouraging them in individual states. The record of neoliberalism has not been such as to engender enthusiasm by any except the few who profit from its policies. As to actions by transnational organizations, these can, of course, be helpful. Subsidization of social programmes and infrastructure development in member states by the European Union provide examples. But these require willing and proactive compliance by its individual states to be effective.

Chicken-and-egg problems where solutions are required as means to themselves are usually easier to confront in practice than in theory. This is because most social processes are of a spiral nature such that small changes at the beginning can lead to larger ones in a self-building way. Thus one can imagine initially modest, and hence affordable, ventures on the part of national and local governments, businesses, unions, schools, citizen groups, and so on, aimed at providing and expanding opportunities for people to develop the potentials Macpherson wrote about with the aim of gradually building popular attraction for such non-possessive-individualist pursuits, thus making it possible for political leaders to stand up to intimidation. The prospect of such spirals does not exist just in the realm of ideas. They can be encouraged by institutional and civil-societal initiatives within existing states. (L&T, 101–102) There are ways increasingly to make a society safe for developmental democracy.

Guarantee of a living wages, price controls, policies for full employment, shortening of the work week, making available child care and affordable housing, and other such measures clear the time and provide the financial resources for people to undertake activities beyond just making a living. Also possible are government-sponsored programmes for youth activities, free or substantially subsidized education at all levels, providing quality sports and arts training and facilities not requiring wealth to access and not mainly dedicated to producing a few stars, and supporting worker cooperatives. These are examples of measures in a category relating to the aspirations and life styles people are assumed by Macpherson to favour given the opportunities to pursue them but denied in a market society.

Another category of measures comprises those that can directly impact people's values and understanding of alternatives. At all levels of education, curricula and teaching methods can be geared, in ways urged by John Dewey and Paulo Freire and in opposition to narrowly technocratic education, towards fostering critical thinking about alternative life goals, cooperation in potential-developing activities, and relating aspects of any one subject of enquiry to other subjects and to societal problems. Public broadcasting and provision of spaces for deliberation and exchange of information not dependent on corporate advertising can help to provide information and expose the self-serving nature of claims that support fatalistic acquiescence to market forces.

Some of the measures described above, like encouraging worker cooperatives in the first category and providing information, for instance, in social media, can be undertaken by direct citizen action, but all of them require government support. This in turn requires that people dedicated to such measures are elected to public office and that governing structures are both publically responsive and free of manipulation by moneyed interests. As noted in earlier chapters, Macpherson was acutely aware of the problem posed by democratic deficiencies in these matters. While endorsing Dewey's recommendations for education, he notes that Dewey suffered from failure to see how the 'actual democratic system' precluded their implementation. (L&T, 74–76) So we confront another aspect of the chicken-and-egg problem, or what Macpherson called a vicious circle for which he sought 'loopholes.' (e.g., *ibid.*, 100–106)

That there must be some loopholes is evidenced by the fact that all of the measures in both the categories just described have, to varying degrees, existed in several countries, and some persist at local levels and still in some states (though less prominently after the triumph of neoliberalism beginning with Thatcher and Reagan). Hence, the requisite policies, institutions, and civic activities are not utopian schemes, but actual practices and models to build on. In the case of participatory civic action, Macpherson saw social-movement activism as potentially opening other loopholes to the extent that they are too strong to be politically ignored (EJ, 98) and that can be built on in an incremental way to generate an upward spiral.

One might imagine that some country adopts developmental-democratic policies at home, but does not then act to strengthen democracy internationally. Such a scenario is out of accord with Macpherson's conception of developmental democracy. Recall that the truly human potentials nurtured in such a democracy are ones that do not entail denial of opportunities for other people but on the contrary require and are enhanced by cooperation with others. There is no reason to suppose that such others are only from one's own country. Indeed, a potential benefit of globalism in the benign sense of bringing into interaction the cultures, knowledge, technological achievements, and so on, of different parts of the globe, is that it offers people more and more varied opportunities to lead fulfilling lives. This potential, however, can be realized only in a world of mutual respect and cooperation. Such a world would constitute globalization in a sense Macpherson would surely have welcomed.

Environmental Degradation

The potentials in Macpherson's theories regarding global environmental threats are similar to those pertaining to globalization. Predominance of a developmental-democratic culture in a society facilitates environmentally sustainable life styles, as opposed to consumerism and wasteful consumption. It marshals support for shifting a nation's priorities from economic growth to environmental sustainability and for standing up to corporate opposition to environmental regulations and to massive shifts to green industries and sources of energy. Also as in the case of combatting globalization, the evidently crucial need for international coordination requires strong endorsement on the part of citizens in individual nations for international cooperation in environmental protection as well as encouraging cross-border popular-movement environmental activism. So several of the points made in constructing an approach on the part of Macpherson to globalization apply as well to environmental challenges.

Neoliberalism again. Amazingly in the wake of the major environmental damage inflicted on the world by private corporations—deforestation, fracking, dangerous levels of carbon emission, water poisoning, and so on—the neoliberal economic 'solution' to environmental threats still has its proponents:

> Free market environmentalism connects self-interest to resource stewardship by establishing private property rights to environmental resources. Property rights compel owners to account for the costs and benefits of their actions and facilitate market transactions that create efficiency-enhancing gains from trade. ... To entrepreneurs there are no environmental problems caused by market failure, but environmental opportunities enhanced by property rights and markets. (Anderson and Leal 2015, 3 and see 13)

All the criticisms of neoliberalism from the perspective of Macpherson explicated in chapter six apply to this orientation.

Macpherson's views are also apt regarding some economic approaches to the environment that are more friendly to government intervention than is neoliberalism, such as the use of cost-benefit analysis in the aid of formulating regulatory policy including setting pollution taxes or implementing tax and trade policies (see, e.g., Joeres and David 1983). Macpherson would have agreed with critics of these approaches, not just because the results they might yield are too slight, but because they reinforce attitudes that commodify the environment (Ackerman and Heinzerling 2004). And in terms of value priorities, Macpherson would also agree with Mark Sagoff: 'on ethical and aesthetical grounds ... self-respecting and dignified societies do not trade a magnificent natural heritage for a bowl of consumer porridge.' (1984, 170, and see Avner de-Shalit's variation on this theme 2000, 89–92)

Developmental culture. In many places Macpherson extols the potential value of technology for relieving the constraints of scarcity, and this has led some to fault him for having an uncritical attitude towards technology (e.g., Hwa Yol Jung 1978). Were this an accurate criticism, it would align Macpherson with advocates of a 'technological fix,' a recent example of which is expressed by the World Resources Institute (a private research centre supported by the UN and several green energy enterprises):

> Conservation efforts are now strongly focused on introducing new technologies for producing and using energy more efficiently. ... By increasing energy efficiency demand can be reduced without affecting personal lifestyles or a country's economic growth. (quoted in Michael Goldman 1998, 37)

This perspective is at odds with Macpherson's entire project, which is to argue for the importance of changes in personal life styles and countries' economic policies in directions away from possessive individualism and towards developmental democracy.

Technological advance can help to make such a transformation feasible, but it is by no means Macpherson's main focus, which is cultural. His views about the values, personal aspirations, and social visions of developmental democracy support environmentalists insofar as they see life style changes as essential if environmental crises are to be averted and environmental sustainability achieved. The most important features of developmental democracy from an environmental point of view are, on the one hand, rejection of consumerism and aspirations for indefinite consumption with their accompanying cult at national levels of economic growth (UTA 1971, 35) and replacement of the notion of people's possessions as their private property with one where they are trustees of things over which they have control, on the other.

From an environmental point of view, the key feature of the comportment of individuals and of societies consistent with developmental democracy is that it does not depend upon indefinite accumulation of commodities or, on a national scale, unending economic growth. Activities detrimental to the preservation of the environment fail Macpherson's test for truly human potentials that their exercise by some not be at the expense of their exercise by others. Hence, to the extent that a culture of developmental democracy comes to prevail in a society its populace could support policies as well as adopting personal life styles protective of the environment. Considerations advanced above about preconditions for confronting challenges of globalization pertain as well to securing environmental sustainability, as do the hypotheses about how realistic it is to expect such a culture to take hold.

Democracy. Also as in the case of globalization, a nation's participation in global or regional environmental agreements and joint actions requires support from its population. Here the democratic dimension of Macpherson's orientation is at odds with William Ophuls, who maintains that environmental degradation will foment hyper-scarcity and unavoidably undermine democracy: 'return of scarcity portends the revival of age-old political evils, for our descendants if not for ourselves. In short, the golden age of individualism, liberty and democracy is all but over.' (1977, 145) A reaction from the point of view of Macpherson could start with Robert Paehlke's response to Ophuls:

> [S]ome nations may find an answer to future economic, environmental, and resource problems in more rather than less democracy. Democracy, participation, and open administration carry not only a danger of division and conflict, but are as well perhaps the best means of mobilizing educated and prosperous populations in difficult times. (1988, 294–295)

Further, Macpherson's views on democracy can help to make precise just what *kind* of democracy is compatible with environmentalism.

Robyn Eckersley's perspective is, like Paehlke's, at odds with the anti-democratic stance of Ophuls, but for her the kind of democracy required is not liberal democracy but 'ecological democracy.' This variety of democracy rejects what Eckersley perceives as an 'atomistic ontology of the self,' a short-sighted and uncritical focus on self-interest, abstraction from social, biological, and environmental structures, and other 'dogmas' of liberalism. As an alternative she calls for a 'postliberal democracy' that rejects these dogmas. (2004, 242)

Eckersley's arguments against the compatibility of environmentalism and liberal democracy are forceful with respect to the anaemic version of the latter to which Macpherson offers a robust alternative. Her view that ecological democracy has among its aims to lay down 'sustainability parameters ... that should primarily belong to people acting publicly and democratically as citizens, rather than as consumers' (*ibid.*, 95) is central to the developmental-democratic understanding of liberal democracy Macpherson wishes to retrieve. So to the extent that he succeeds in defending this robust conception one need not reject liberal democracy to champion environmentalism.

Another defence of the anti-democratic recommendation, alluded to by Ophuls and advanced by some environmentalists, is that the emergency nature of current environmental crises does not allow the time necessary to mount effective democratic pressure against them. This could, unfortunately, be accurate, but then it would also take time for an eco-dictator not only to marshal sufficient forces within a country to react to the crises, but somehow to mobilize an international consortium of fellow eco-dictators and coordinate their efforts. Also relevant is Macpherson's view that environmental crises can themselves spark cultural changes conducive to developmental democracy. Along with threats to neighbourhoods, Macpherson gives the examples of growing public awareness of the extent of air and water pollution as 'engendering a new demand for meaningful community.' (EJ, 48)

The no-time-but-for-dictatorship claim would have more force in a society thoroughly infused with a possessive-individualist culture that needed to be undone and replaced with a new alternative by means of cultural-political campaigns. On this perspective, Macpherson's prognosis for eventually realizing a general developmental-democratic culture would be utopian. Such is the view of William Leiss in his claim that many of the goals favoured by Macpherson can realistically be achieved by regulated capitalism, the culture of which is at odds with Macpherson's vision: 'Macpherson apparently never considered that consumption activity is in itself a significant domain of human activity and satisfaction—as an expression of individuality, as a source of diverse and genuine satisfaction, and even as an end in itself.' (2009 [1988], 102)

If the culture Leiss describes is in fact overwhelmingly embraced in modern culture, then popular support for environmental policies would indeed be elusive, and there likely would not be enough time for such embrace to wane. On this perspective, as Leiss puts it, one must wait for people to 'eventually become jaded with the consumptive images and give greater priority to other sources of satisfaction' when 'the utopian theorists like Macpherson will have their day.' (*ibid.*, 142) While Macpherson recognizes that the stances Leiss describes motivate many people, he also maintains that possessive-individualist values and visions are alloyed with contrary aspirations. Increasing popular expressions of an anti-consumptionist and pro-environmental attitude, sometimes with political expression, such as the rise of green political parties and activist environmental social movements, are optimistic evidence on the side of Macpherson.

Environmental philosophy. Lacking in Macpherson's theories is a claim that people are essentially developmental democrats as a matter of philosophical anthropology. Jung and Leiss, however, see in Macpherson's theories flawed philosophical assumptions (see Jules Townshend's rejoinders to them, 2000, 128–129). Leiss criticizes Macpherson for holding on to a now-superseded Marxist orientation pitting human against human instead of combatting 'the attempt to assert humanity's unchallenged mastery over nature' and 'to transform the planet for nothing but a supplier of wants for ... and abundant, unlimited, never-ending variety of goods.' (1993, 272) (Leiss does not try to square his rejection of this perspective with his sanguine depiction referred to above about human consumptive activity.) Drawing on views of Heidegger and Hannah Arendt, Jung criticizes Macpherson for failing 'to come to grips with the destructive, anti-humanistic tendencies of technology as the main driving force of contemporary thought' (1978, 268) or to attend to the ill effects of scarcity, thereby taking 'the "banality of evil" inherent in technology too lightly.' (*ibid.*, 265)

It is true that Macpherson does not develop or substantiate his views on the effects of scarcity on people's values and aspirations by means of a philosophical theory about the domination of nature or the evils of technology.

Nor does he invoke other similarly abstract theories, such as those of eco-feminism (as in contributions to Warren 1997, part iv), or Aldo Leopold's 'land ethic' (1977 [1949]), or in either of the anthrocentric or the biocentric positions sometimes depicted at the basic opposition in environmental philosophy and as exemplified in the works, respectively, of Murray Bookchin (1990) and Arne Naess (1989). Macpherson's orientation is akin to the environmental pragmatism of Andrew Light in being compatible with a variety of philosophical perspectives, though, unlike Light, his approach does not lend itself to trying to establish 'metaphilosophical compatibility' among them (Light 1996, 172–180). For some this is no doubt regarded as a deficiency. Alternatively, as argued in chapter four, philosophical abstinence can be seen as advantageous.

For Jung, adopting an anti-technology philosophical perspective throws in relief certain key questions:

> The economics of a finite planet requires a definition of the quality of life in terms of *what* human basic needs are, *how* they can be fulfilled, and what is a just or fair allocation of scarce resources within a nation or among nations. (1978, 265–266)

In fact, Macpherson proffers answers to these questions: basic needs are for the development of individuals' truly human potentials; this requires dismantling the constraints and culture of a market society; and a just distribution of resources and opportunities is one where nobody's enjoyment of them is at the expense of others. Environmentalists, whether informed by philosophical theories or not, may wish to add to these components, for instance, to specify that overcoming patriarchy is a necessary means to attaining environmental goals or that a just distribution must take account of the needs of non-humans, but it is hard to see how any environmentalist could disagree with Macpherson as far as he goes.

An advantage to a Macphersonian approach is that it supports programmes of political action by people who may be motivated by a variety of philosophical perspectives or who may not entertain such at all. Realization of Macpherson's aims would take one no small distance in garnering support for basic changes in a nation's environmental comportment and for extending such support globally.

References

Ackerman, Frank, and Lisa Heinzerling. 2004. *Priceless: On Knowing the Price of Everything and the Value of Nothing*. New York: W.W. Norton.
Ake, Claude. 1997. Dangerous Liaisons: The Interface of Globalization and Democracy. In *Democracy's Victory and Crisis*, ed. Alex Hadenius, 282–296. Cambridge: Cambridge University Press.
Anderson, Terry L., and Donald R. Leal. 2015. *Free Market Environmentalism for the Next Generation*. New York: Palgrave Macmillan.
Archibugi, Daniele. 1998. Principles of Cosmopolitan Democracy. In *Re-imagining Political Community: Studies in Cosmopolitan Democracy*, ed. Daniele Archibugi et al., 19–228. Stanford: Stanford University Press.
Balibar, Étienne. 2004. *We, the People of Europe?: Reflections on Transnational Citizenship*. Princeton: Princeton University Press.
Beck, Ulrich. 2000. *What is Globalization?* Cambridge: Cambridge University Press.
Beitz, Charles R. 1991. Sovereignty and Morality in International Affairs. In *Political Theory Today*, ed. David Held, 236–254. Cambridge: Polity Press.
Bookchin, Murray. 1990. *The Philosophy of Social Ecology*. Montréal: Black Rose Books.
Bull, Hedley. 1995. *The Anarchical Society: A Study of Order in World Politics*. 2nd ed. New York: Columbia University Press.
Cox, Robert W. 2002. *The Political Economy of a Plural World: Critical Reflections on Power, Morals and Civilization*. London: Routledge.
Cunningham, Frank. 2008. Globalization and Developmental Democracy. *Ethical Perspectives* 15 (4): 487–505.
Dahl, Robert. 1999. Can International Organizations Be Democratic? In *Democracy's Edges*, ed. Casiano Hacker-Cordon and Ian Shapiro, 17–40. Cambridge: Cambridge University Press.
Dreiling, Michael, and Ian Robinson. 1998. Union Responses to NAFTA in the US and Canada: Explaining Intra- and International Variation. *Mobilization: An International Journal* 3 (2): 163–184.
Eckersley, Robyn. 2004. *The Green State: Rethinking Democracy and Sovereignty*. Cambridge, MA: MIT Press.
Falk, Richard. 2014. Globalization-from-Below: An Innovative Politics of Resistance. In *Civilizing Globalization: A Survival Guide*, ed. Richard Sandbrook and Ali Burak Güven, Rev. ed., 151–169. Albany: State University of New York Press.
Giddens, Anthony. 1985. *The Nation State and Violence*. Berkeley: University of California Press.
Goldman, Michael. 1998. Inventing the Commons: Theories and Practices of the Common's Professional. In *Nature: Political Struggles for the Global Commons*, ed. Michael Goldman, 20–53. London: Pluto Press.

Gould, Carol. 2004. *Globalizing Democracy and Human Rights*. Cambridge: Cambridge University Press.
Habermas, Jürgen. 2001. *The Postnational Constellation*. Cambridge, MA: MIT Press.
Held, David. 1995. *Democracy and the Global Order*. Palo Alto, CA: Stanford University Press.
Joeres, Erhard F., and Martin H. David. 1983. *Buying a Better Environment: Cost-Effective Regulation through Permit Trading*. Madison: University of Wisconsin Press.
Jung, Hwa Yol. 1978. Democratic Ontology and Technology: A Critique of C.B. Macpherson. *Polity* 11 (2, Winter): 247–269.
Kymlicka, Will. 1999. Citizenship in an Era of Globalization: Commentary on Held. In *Democracy's Edges*, ed. Casiano Hacker-Cordon and Ian Shapiro, 112–126. Cambridge: Cambridge University Press.
Leiss, William. 1993. The End of History and Its Beginning Again, or, The Not-Quite-Yet Human Stage of Human History. In *Democracy and Possessive Individualism: The Intellectual Legacy of C.B. Macpherson*, ed. Joseph Carens, 263–274. Albany: State University of New York Press.
———. 2009 [1988]. *C.B. Macpherson: Dilemmas of Liberalism and Socialism*. 2nd ed. Montréal and Kingston: McGill-Queen's University Press.
Leopold, Aldo. 1977 [1949]. *A Sand County Almanac: and Sketches Here and There*. Oxford: Oxford University Press.
Light, Andrew. 1996. Compatibilism in Political Economy. In *Environmental Pragmatism*, ed. Andrew Light and Eric Katz, 161–184. London: Routledge.
Macpherson, Crawford Brough. 1971. The Currency of Values. *Transactions of the Royal Society of Canada*, series 4, vol. 9, 27–35.
———. 1973. [DT] *Democratic Theory: Essays in Retrieval*. Oxford: Oxford University Press. Reissued with an Introduction by Frank Cunningham. Toronto: Oxford University Press, 2012.
———. 1977. [L&T] *The Life and Times of Liberal Democracy*. Oxford: Oxford University Press. Reissued with an Introduction by Frank Cunningham. Toronto: Oxford University Press, 2012.
———. 1984. [EJ] *The Rise and Fall of Economic Justice*. Oxford: Oxford University Press. Reissued with an Introduction by Frank Cunningham. Toronto: Oxford University Press, 2013.
Macpherson, Crawford Brough, and Paul-André Crépeau, eds. 1965. *The Future of Canadian Federalism*. Introduction by Macpherson and Crépeau. Toronto: University of Toronto Press.
Mason, J.W. 2017. A Cautious Case for Economic Nationalism. *Dissent* 64 (2, Spring): 24–32.
Naess, Arne. 1989. *Ecology, Community, and Lifestyle*. Cambridge: Cambridge University Press.

Newman, Michael. 1996. *Democracy, Sovereignty and the European Union*. London: Hurst & Company.
Ophuls, William. 1977. *Ecology and the Politics of Scarcity*. San Francisco: W.H. Freeman and Company.
Paehlke, Robert C. 1988. Democracy, Bureaucracy, and Environmentalism. *Environmental Ethics* 10 (4, Winter): 291–308.
Rodrik, Dani. 2011. *The Globalization Paradox: Democracy and the Future of the World Economy*. New York: W.W. Norton.
Sagoff, Mark. 1984. Ethics in Environmental Law. In *Earthbound: New Introductory Essays in Environmental Ethics*, ed. Tom Regan, 147–148. New York: Random House.
———. 1988. *The Economy of the Earth: Philosophy, Law, and the Environment*. Cambridge: Cambridge University Press.
Sandbrook, Richard. 2014. The Left, Globalization, and the Future. In *Civilizing Globalization: A Survival Guide*, ed. Richard Sandbrook and Ali Burak Güven, Rev. ed., 235–343. Albany: State University of New York Press.
Sassoon, Donald. 1992. A New Political Order?: The Agenda for Social Democracy. In *A More Perfect Union? Britain and the New Europe*, ed. David Miliband. London: IPPR.
Sen, Amartya K. 2014. How to Judge Globalization. In *The Globalization Reader*, ed. John Boli and Frank J. Lehner, 5th ed., 19–24. Oxford: Wiley Blackwell.
de Shalit, Avner. 2000. *The Environment Between Theory and Practice*. Oxford: Oxford University Press.
Sklair, Leslie. 2002. *Globalization, Capitalism, and Its Alternatives*. 3rd ed. Oxford: Oxford University Press.
Stiglitz, Joseph E. 2017. *Globalization and Its Discontents Revisited*. New York: W.W. Norton.
Strange, Susan. 1996. *The Retreat of the State: The Diffusion of Power in the World Economy*. Cambridge: Cambridge University Press.
Streeck, Wolfgang. 2016. *How Will Capitalism End?: Essays on a Failing System*. London: Verso.
Townshend, Jules. 2000. *C.B. Macpherson and the Problem of Liberal Democracy*. Edinburgh: University of Edinburgh Press.
Walker, R.B.J. 1990. Sovereignty, Identity, Community: Reflections on the Horizons of Contemporary Political Practice. In *Contending Sovereignties: Redefining Political Community*, ed. R.B.J. Walker and Saul H. Mendlovitz, 159–185. Boulder: Lynne Rienner.
Warren, Karen, ed. 1997. *Ecofeminism: Women, Culture, Nature*. Bloomington: Indiana University Press.

CHAPTER 8

Intellectual Property

For academics and students in the social sciences and humanities intellectual property has to do with restrictions on the use of articles and books with copyright protection. Intellectual property is also a concern of independent writers and in the world of film, music, and computer system development. These and related dimensions of intellectual property are subjects of ongoing debates about how or how far authors or those with legal rights over their products can or should legitimately restrict use of these products. The debates involve some thorny issues.

Those who depend in part upon 'intellectual' work for their livelihoods are disadvantaged by unrecompensed appropriation of its fruits. But at the same time restrictions defeat an aim of making these fruits available to a broad public. Also, since individuals' intellectual achievements draw upon contributions of previous and contemporary others, identifying what is uniquely one's own is problematic. It will shortly be suggested that Macpherson's theories bear on these questions, but first the much larger context within which issues of intellectual property are currently engaged must be identified.

The Globalization of Intellectual Property

In their *Intellectual Property Rights: A Critical History*, Christopher May and Susan Sell describe two major transformations in the history of approaches to intellectual property. The first of these was in Europe in the early eighteenth century when, appealing in Britain to John Locke on property rights, laws were enacted defending copyright as 'a "just reward" for authorial labor' and as 'stimulation of creativity.' (May and Sell 2006, 93) The second transformation dates from the mid-twentieth century, when, concerned more with patents and trademarks than with copyrights, intellectual property rights became subject to international regulation. This began on a large scale with the founding in 1970 of the World Intellectual Property Organization (WIPO), which four years later affiliated with the United Nations. (In 2001 it declared April 26 to be World Intellectual Property Day.)

This trend was accelerated when the World Trade Organization (the WTO, founded in 1994) expanded and refined principles regarding intellectual property laid down in the earlier General Agreement on Tariffs and Trade by incorporating an Agreement on Trade-Related Aspects of Intellectual Property Rights (TRIPS). In addition to these broad initiatives many bilateral and regional trade agreements have included intellectual property right provisions. An example is the 1994 North American Free Trade Agreement (in its Chapter 17).

Critics of trans-border agreements maintain that they impede dissemination of intellectual products as well as making it difficult for governments to provide support for their own countries' cultural enterprises (see Davidson 1993). While the mandate of the WIPO is to coordinate intellectual property with the broad objectives of the United Nations around education and aid for poorer countries, the TRIPS concerns itself almost exclusively with economic matters of interest to the developed, capitalist countries. In spite of a preamble stating that national policy objectives should retain some weight, this agreement's focus on expansion of ownership rights is, as one critic puts it, 'so important that individual member welfare should not stand in the way of their being protected as an entitlement of the creators' (Kurt Burch, quoted in May and Sell, 163, and see Braithwaite and Drahos 2002).

To this end, the agreement explicitly excludes its members from obligations under a nineteenth-century convention (the 1886 Bern Convention inspired by Victor Hugo) to respect authors' and creators' moral rights. Instead the agreement favours protection of economic entitlements (summarized by May and Sells, 65–66). Copyright law in the earlier convention was motivated by respect for authorship because authors should be acknowledged for their efforts. Subsequent agreements commodified the products of intellectual endeavour, thus limiting general access to them.

May argues, in a way consistent with Macpherson's approach to the history of property rights, that the process by which this transformation took place is one of reification: '[T]he key function of intellectual property (as with any form of commodification) is to bring resources (of whatever form) into the market by establishing ownership rights over them. This function is not "natural," but rather a reified social process.' (2006, 36)

That the TRIPS focus is economic is not surprising, since it issued from a concerted campaign by a group of executives calling itself the 'Intellectual Property Committee' whose founding member corporations were Bristol-Myers, DuPont, FMC Corporation, General Electric, General Motors, Hewlett-Packard, IBM, Johnson & Johnson, Merck, Monsanto, Pfizer, Rockwell International, and Warner Communications (Sell 2003, ch. 5). 'In effect,' as Sell puts it, 'twelve corporations made public law for the world.' (*ibid.*, 96)

It is thus that the expansion of intellectual property to encompass multinational corporate patents and trademarks was simultaneously an exercise in globalization. Like globalization generally it has had negative impacts on the sovereignty of individual states and on access especially for developing countries to vital products, such as pharmaceutical goods. Polemics over intellectual property in this globalized context have little to do with those around intellectual property considered as the protection of ideas on the part of (non-corporate) individuals, but the language used to describe them by the WTO and the WIPO is that of Locke and others in earlier epochs.

Arguments defending private, exclusive possession of patents by international corporate entities are the same as those used to justify the copyrights of individual writers, composers, and the like, as well as private property generally. These are (to adopt a summary by May and Sell, 20–22):

1. Assuming, with neoliberalism, that efficient deployment and transfer of human products requires their being made subject to market forces, they need to be bought and sold by private owners.
2. The prospect of holding property rights is a necessary, or at least the best, way to encourage exertion of effort and innovation.
3. Property rights protect people's moral claims to exclusive disposition of products of their labour (Locke's main justification).
4. A tangent but separate justification is one advanced by Hegel that full human personhood requires the possession of things as private property. (1967 [1821], 40–57)

Justifying rights over things patented or trademarked by private enterprises as regulated and negotiated by international trading organizations brings the rhetoric and public perception associated with works produced by artists and writers into the realm of trademarks and patent law with their myriad of variations, to the extent that, as Richard Stallman (developer of the GNU Free Software project) puts it, 'any statement which purports to be about "intellectual property" is pure confusion.' (2010, 346) It also serves to make denial of, for example, medical or infrastructural resources to those who most badly need them more palatable than if this were seen as a transparent manifestation of corporate greed and monopolization. Many react to this situation just by urging that a basic distinction between individual and international, corporate rights be made. A response inspired by Macpherson's theories is more radical. He challenges the justification of private property *per se*. Success in this challenge would, then, denude the expansion of property rights into international and corporate realms of its persuasive force at its most basic level.

MACPHERSON ON PROPERTY

'All roads,' Macpherson announces in *Democratic Theory*, 'lead to property' (DT, 121), by which he means that the idea that people have exclusive property rights is essential to a possessive-individualist ontology and that an alternative conception of property 'not to be excluded from the use or benefit of the accumulated productive resources of the whole society' (DT, 133) is central to the developmental-democratic ontology he champions. As noted in previous chapters Macpherson's criticisms of the exclusivist conception are that the possession of property is seen as an end in itself (EJ, ch. 7) and that it regards property as things rather than as rights over the use of things. (DT, sec. vi)

Property is thought of as a primary goal by those imbued with market-society culture, for whom the mere private possession of property is of paramount importance—*my* house, *my* car, *my* business. Macpherson's characterization is compatible with this interpretation, but it is somewhat different. For him amassing private property is regarded as a paramount goal:

> [I]n the liberal utilitarian tradition, from Locke to Bentham, the *accumulation* of private property is treated as an end. For them, maximization of utilities is *the* end, and by Bentham the command of utilities is measured by material wealth. Thus maximization of material wealth (property) is indistinguishable from the ethical end: property is virtually an end in itself. (EJ, 87)

This conception of property, which Macpherson saw prefigured in Hobbes, marks a basic break with ancient and medieval conceptions in which property was regarded a means to some valued goal beyond its accumulation. Focusing on property as a means to things other than exclusive power over possessions or other people's labour invites critical thinking about the ends one's property can and ought to serve, such as those in pre-capitalist philosophers. Thus, it was justified as 'a necessary means to the good life of the citizen (Aristotle), or as necessary to counteract the avaricious nature of fallen men (Augustine), or to provide for peaceable and orderly relations between individuals (Aquinas).' (EJ, 88)

These earlier thinkers still regarded property as in one sense private, but, in the other dimension of Macpherson's critique, this need not be the case. Conceiving of property as things rather than rights over things obscures the fact that in being a legal concept it is also a political one. What counts as property worthy of legal protection is a matter of political will which need not be limited to enforcement of exclusionary rights over property:

> The state *creates* the rights, the individuals *have* the rights. Common property is created by the guarantee to each individual that he will not be excluded from the use of benefit of something; private property is created by the guarantee that an individual can exclude others from the use or benefit of something. (Macpherson 1978, 5)

This is a deployment of Macpherson's basic distinction between exclusive and inclusive conceptions of property rights. As noted in chapter three, he allows that in a non-market society some sorts of property may still be held by individuals in the sense that they have privileged discretion over its use. In the case of common property, those who have enacted or support the rights that create it (in a democracy, a majority) may impose restrictions on its uses. In both cases a requirement of inclusive property is that those with direct or indirect discretion see themselves as its *trustees*, responsible for preserving property and making it available to the benefit of contemporary and future others.

This approach is not easily taken by those who, viewing things through possessive-individualist lenses, think that only a promise of self-interested return will motivate taking on trusteeship roles. However, an ethic of trusteeship comes naturally to people motivated by developmental-democratic values, which include facilitating everyone having the opportunities and resources to develop their talents to the fullest. Even neoliberals recognize that there are justifiable constraints on the use of people's capacities, for instance, to prohibit using them for criminal purposes. Like most other liberal democrats, Macpherson goes further to recognize as well positive obligations to help others, as when, to the annoyance of the neoliberals, taxation to finance social services is sanctioned. Treating one's talents and possessions as resources for which someone is a trustee is an extension of this attitude.

Combining Macpherson's anti-atomist stance, discussed in chapter two, that human capacities 'are socially derived, and that their development must also be social' (DT, 57) with his rejection of the notion of self-ownership (as discussed in chapter five) in favour of taking a trusteeship attitude towards one's talents and capacities yields a position on intellectual property. Intellectual achievements do not come into existence in vacuums. Studies in any field of endeavour (as well as against the formative background of social, economic, and political circumstances) are instructive: Plato and the Eleatic Presocratic philosophers; the Presocratics themselves and earlier mythic and religious cosmologies; Descartes and the new science of such as Galileo; Galileo and some of the Paduan philosophers; Boyle and the Iatrochemists and, yet earlier, Paracelsus and the alchemists; and so on. (Examples of pertinent historical studies regarding science are by Mason 1962 and Butterfield 1962, and regarding ancient Greek philosophy by Cornford 1965.) Similar histories are in technology, the visual arts, mathematics, music, and so on.

To be sure, some thinkers make important advances on previous thought. However, these advances still draw upon prior intellectual achievements just as subsequent developments in thought draw upon theirs. Appropriate in this connection is Isaac Newton's famous comment: 'if I have seen further [than Descartes and Robert Hooke regarding the nature of light] it is by standing on the shoulders of Giants.' (1959 [1675], 416) Newton's acknowledgement of intellectual debts is compatible with his taking pride in his own contributions, and it might be thought that this provides another justification for intellectual property rights, namely, to ensure that those who make cultural, scientific, technological, and other achievements are acclaimed for doing so.

Macpherson provides some textual evidence that for Hobbes people seek glory and honour as a manifestation of their power, which in a market economy is in turn valued for its competitive advantages. (PI, 44–45) This suggests that one motive for insisting on intellectual property right protection is economic, which is the case when the main reason someone engages in intellectual production is to realize profit. However, this is not an overriding motivation for many artists, writers, or scientists, for whom the necessity of intellectual property protection derives from working in societies with inadequate provisions to support their creative efforts. So Macpherson's views about the effects, subject to remediation, of inequality and of real or artificial scarcities are relevant.

Still, even those who are not dependent on copyright or similar protections for their livelihood, such as gainfully employed academic researchers, will also want to be appreciated. But why are legally enforced exclusive property rights necessary for this? Achievements can be applauded, plagiarism exposed and shamed, and people publically honoured without such enforcement. There are venues for free dissemination of intellectual work (see, for instance, Heather Morrison 2016), of which many creators of intellectual products make use and in which they are recognized.

Restrictions of the sort that inclusive property legislation impose, in addition to arbitrarily assigning originality to a creator of intellectual products, impede the widespread dissemination of these products and thus constrain progress in their continuing development. Those with talents for contribution to such development who view themselves as trustees of their capacities and of the achievements they have made in virtue of them are aware of their debt to past and contemporary contributors and less likely than immodest peers to take measures to limit the number of those who can make fruitful use of them. The advantage of an inclusivist perspective is illustrated in the case of technological or medical advances that draw not only on past work but are the result of cooperative efforts of research teams and wide networks of collaborators. Privatization of the fruits of their labour not only impacts on continuing progress but restricts the often vitally needed immediate dissemination of these fruits.

Counter-Arguments

Against a non-exclusivist perspective is an argument that copyright or patent restrictions are essential to, or at least enhance, continuing intellectual achievement by providing an incentive for energetic intellectual labour. This is one of the arguments in defence of exclusive intellectual property rights. Reports (or construction) of rejoinders to this and other defences on the part of Macpherson will serve to round out the application of his theories to this issue.

Efficiency. The argument that economically efficient distribution of intellectual property rights requires that intellectual products be privately owned depends on their being regarded as commodities or potential commodities, and the sense of 'efficiency' employed is the narrowly neoclassical one discussed in chapter six. From the point of view of ascertaining the justification of exclusive property rights, therefore, this argument supposes the neoliberal perspective, Macpherson's extensive critique of which is the topic of that chapter.

Incentives. A more widespread opinion is that the prospect of economic profit serves as an incentive for people to devote the time and energy required for intellectual achievements. The strongest version of this argument, that *only* the promise of profit can motivate intellectual labour, is certainly wrong. There are too many examples of people exerting intellectual effort absent this incentive for it to be accurate. As one critic of intellectual property rights, Claire Poster, observes, 'some of the most significant drug-related discoveries of the twentieth century (insulin, penicillin, the polio vaccine) were developed in public, not-for-profit institutional laboratories.' (2016, 34)

A weaker version of the incentive argument is that profit motives prompt concerted intellectual labour on the part of those who would not otherwise engage in it, so privatization of intellectual endeavours could only increase intellectual production. Against this is the counter that privatization of intellectual achievements is not a no-lose addition to other motivations but has detrimental consequences for intellectual labour. Poster thus observes that:

> Open communication and knowledge sharing, long considered the lifeblood of scientific endeavour, are lost in the competitive atmosphere between rival firms. Instead, competition restricts the sharing of results, causes needless repetition and duplication, and leads to concealing and/or delaying publication of findings to protect commercial interests. The driving force is market profitability, not finding solutions to human problems. The impacts are profoundly negative. (*ibid.*, 27)

Questions about how people are motivated to engage in intellectual pursuits are empirical matters. Lacking data about these things, I offer instead the following story (Table 8.1).

I interpret this to be favouring a life of 'happiness' in Aristotle's sense—that is, a life of developing one's proper potentials in accord with virtue as opposed to one of seeking fame, wealth, or power (1984 [350 BCE],

Table 8.1 Short Teaching Story

For several years in the 1970s and 1980s I taught a course to 300 first-year students in my university's engineering faculty as an arts complement to their technical courses. This included a component on 'the meaning of life' in which a selection of philosophical theories were introduced. In class discussion the following question, adapted from Aristotle, was put to the class:

> Suppose that you have a choice between personally developing an ingenious and very popular but trivial play thing, or working with a team of others contributing to solving an important and challenging problem (the example I used was the 'battery problem' of affordably storing solar energy), which will only reach full development after your death. Following the first path, you will make a very large amount of money and be famous. If you follow the second path, you will make enough money for a comfortable life, but by no means acquire the fortune of the alternative and you will not be famous. Which path would you choose?

Almost always the first question from the class was about the comfortable life qualification, to which I replied that they would receive a respectable and secure middle-class income and ongoing employment. Thus assured, the majority choice every year was for the second path—and this even during the Thatcher/Reagan years and by students in a professional faculty who, moreover, had no problem expressing disagreement with their left-wing professors.

1846 [1068b])—and a counter-example to the incentive argument regarding intellectual property. Especially pertinent to Macpherson's view is the exchange regarding a comfortable life. For him, removal of economic insecurity, as in the imaginary example for the students, allows behaviour consonant with developmentalism.

Personal right. Macpherson traces the claim that people have a right to exclusive property to the seventeenth century, prototypically argued for by Locke. This argument rests on the doctrine that people are owners of their own talents and are therefore claimed to be exclusive owners of products of these talents. One could challenge a connection between ownership of talents and ownership of their products. Governments might lack the ability to put legal restrictions on what talents one may seek to develop and exercise (notwithstanding the mechanisms increasingly used by governments to steer people towards perceived national economic goals) while there are still inclusive rights to the use of crucial categories of the fruits of these talents. But this is not the tack Macpherson takes. Instead he casts doubt on the entire package of self-ownership and exclusive rights, especially to land, capital, and other people's labour (though not to individually consumable goods, regarding which exclusive use is appropriate, 1978, 203).

To sustain this perspective, Macpherson argues, in the first place, that there is no conceptual reason why property should only be regarded as private. Attending to the generic characteristics of property or 'property as such,' inclusive property rights have at least as much claim to being enforced as do exclusive ones. The generic characteristics of property are: that property rights are the rights of individuals, derivable from a concept of the human essence; that property is a right, not a thing; and that property is 'the creation of society, i.e., in modern times, the creation of the state.' (*ibid.*, 201–202) Macpherson's notion of property being a right subject to political will was noted above. He emphasizes the fact that property is an individual right, and this includes common property, such as public parks and highways, to which individuals have a right of access, though this right is created as well as enforced by the state. State property, such as a state-owned airline, is classified by Macpherson as a species of corporate property, where the corporation is legally regarded also as an individual. (DT, 123–124)

Recognizing that common property is the property of individuals denies advocates of private property the ability to claim that they alone champion individual rights. As Macpherson puts it, 'a right not to be excluded from something is as much an individual right as is the right to exclude others' (1978, 202). The point about rights being derivable from a notion of the human essence applies both to those who limit rights to exclusive ones and to those who recognize inclusive rights, where these pair, respectively, with possessive and developmental conceptions of human power. Whether the rights actually enforced by a state are mainly inclusive or exclusive is historically relative. In pre-capitalist times, many state-enforced inclusive rights were in place. This changed with the transformation to a capitalist market, centrally including a market in labour:

The concept of property as nothing but an exclusive, alienable, individual right, not only in material things but even in one's own productive capacities was thus a creation of capitalist society: it was only needed, and only brought forth, when the formal equality of the market superseded the formal inequality of pre-capitalist society. (DT, 130 and see 1978, 202–205)

We shall return to the force of Macpherson's arguments on this matter shortly, but first Hegel's view on private property merits attention.

Property and personhood. In his unpublished notes on Hegel's *Philosophy of Right* (UTA 1981), Macpherson pays most of his attention to theses relating to property and in particular to Hegel's assertion that:

A person by distinguishing himself from himself relates himself to another person, and it is only as owners that these two persons really exist for each other. Their implicit identity is realized through the transfer of property from one to the other in conformity with a common will and without detriment to the rights of either. This is *contract*. (Hegel 1967, 38)

Hegel's subsequent philosophical explication of this view is that a full and free person (or 'personality') requires intimately relating oneself to something that is simultaneously external and internal, and this is achieved through the possession of property. (40–41, 235–236)

Hegel's view is not immune to philosophical contestation. It is, for instance, in conflict with Kant's opinion that self-proprietorship is incompatible with the idea of personhood (Kant 1963, 165, and see G. A. Cohen 1995, 211, 238–243). Macpherson, however, does not take note of Hegel's philosophical explication, though in *Possessive Individualism* he remarks on a similar conclusion regarding personhood and property in one's self by the Leveller, Richard Overton: 'everyone as he is himself, so he hath a self propriety, else he could not be himself.' (quoted in PI, 142) In both cases Macpherson is concerned with the conclusion that possession of exclusive property is somehow essential to being a human.

Macpherson's approach to this question is consistent with what was argued in chapter four to be his agnosticism regarding philosophical foundations. He has articulated a conception of the essence of humans as, given the opportunities, developers of their potentials equally and harmoniously with one another. In his views about property he undertakes to demonstrate that this conception is a coherent alternative to a possessive-individualist conception. He also thinks that the moral norms implicated in the developmental conception are 'more morally pleasing' (DT, 34) than those of the possessive conception, and that by his time 'a considerable transformation of the concept of property,' going beyond 'a handful of radicals and socialists,' can be seen in demands such as the organized labour movement's for the right to employment. (DT, 132–133) Macpherson's intended audience is those whose experiences and moral instincts make them at least receptive to these arguments and who will therefore seriously entertain the political implications he sees them as implying.

Concluding Comment

All of these Macphersonian criticisms of exclusive property rights apply to their current extensions in international trade agreements. In fact, some of them constitute overkill. In particular, appeals to the rights of persons or to personal identity pertain to real persons, but the overwhelmingly large number of actors whose protection the recent international agreements are meant to protect are artificial, corporate persons. The corporate heads and shareholders who profit from exclusive property rights have not mixed their labour with the protected products, and those who have played important roles in their production, in addition to 'standing on the shoulders' of many others, are usually research teams, whose members are often not shareholders and who, moreover, derive respectable incomes from universities or other public centres of research.

The same consideration pertains to the Hegelian argument about personhood, but if Hegel's perspective can be applied to corporate individuals, it is with some unpalatable consequences. It may be that a corporation acquires its identity (in some sense of this term) in virtue of entering into contracts with customers and other corporations and thus acquires personality. If so, and if we credit Hegel in this matter, then the corporation, like the human person:

> has as his substantive end the right of putting his will into any and every thing and thereby making it his, because it has no such end in itself and derives its destiny and soul from his [now the corporation's] will. This is the absolute right of appropriation which man has over all things. (Hegel 1967, 41)

Harry Glasbeek, for whom 'The corporation is a legally created predator' (2017, 241, and *passim*), is not the only one who would be wary of affording such personhood to corporations and who would want to resist the power that intellectual and other private property rights gives them.

REFERENCES

Aristotle. 1984 [c350BCE]. *Nichomachean Ethics.* In *The Complete Works of Aristotle,* vol. 2. Princeton: Princeton University Press.
Braithwaite, John, and Peter Drahos. 2002. Intellectual Property, Corporate Strategy and Globalization: TRIPS in Context. *Wisconsin International Law Journal* 20 (3, Summer): 451–480.
Butterfield, Herbert. 1962 [1932]. *The Origins of Modern Science.* New York: Macmillan.
Cohen, G.A. 1995. *Self-Ownership, Freedom, and Equality.* Cambridge: Cambridge University Press.
Cornford, Francis M. 1965. *Principium Sapientiae.* New York: Harper & Rowman & Littlefield.
Davidson, Roy. 1993. Intellectual Property. In *Canada under Free Trade,* ed. Duncan Cameron and Mel Watkins, 214–223. Toronto: Jams Lorimer & Company.
Glasbeek, Harry. 2017. *Class Privilege: How Law Shelters Shareholders and Coddles Capitalism.* Toronto: Between the Lines.
Hegel, G.W.F. 1967 [1821]. *Hegel's Philosophy of Right.* Oxford: The Clarendon Press.
Kant, Immanuel. 1963 [1775–1780]. *Lectures on Ethics.* Indianapolis: Hackett Publishers.
Macpherson, Crawford Brough. 1962. [PI] *The Political Theory of Possessive Individualism: Hobbes to Locke.* Oxford: Oxford University Press. Reissued with an Introduction by Frank Cunningham. Toronto: Oxford University Press, 2010.
———. 1973. [DT] *Democratic Theory: Essays in Retrieval.* Oxford: Oxford University Press. Reissued with an Introduction by Frank Cunningham. Toronto: Oxford University Press, 2012.
———. 1978. The Meaning of Property & Liberal Democracy and Property. Introductory and concluding essays in *Property: Mainstream and Critical Positions,* ed. C.B. Macpherson, 1–13 and 199–207. Toronto: University of Toronto Press.
———. 1981. [UTA] On Hegel. University of Toronto Archives B1987-0069, Box 2, file 3.
———. 1984. [EJ] *The Rise and Fall of Economic Justice.* Oxford: Oxford University Press. Reissued with an Introduction by Frank Cunningham. Toronto: Oxford University Press, 2013.
Mason, Stephen F. 1962. *A History of the Sciences.* New York: Collier.
May, Christopher. 2006. The Denial of History: Reification, Intellectual Property Rights and the Lessons of the Past. *Capital & Class* 30 (1, Spring): 33–56.

May, Christopher, and Susan K. Sell. 2006. *Intellectual Property Rights: A Critical History*. Boulder: Lynne Rienner Publishers.

Morrison, Heather. 2016. Open Access to Scholarly Knowledge: The New Commons. In *Free Knowledge: Confronting the Commodification of Human Discovery*, ed. Patricia W. Elliot and Daryl H. Hepting, 156–267. Regina: University of Regina Press.

Newton, Isaac. 1959 [1675]. *Correspondence of Isaac Newton*, vol. 1, 1661–1675. Cambridge: Cambridge University Press.

Poster, Claire. 2016. The Privatization of Knowledge in Canada's Universities and What We Should Do About It. In *Free Knowledge: Confronting the Commodification of Human Discovery*, ed. Patricia W. Elliot and Daryl H. Hepting, 56–66. Regina: University of Regina Press.

Sell, Susan K. 2003. *Private Power, Pubic Law: The Globalization of Intellectual Property Rights*. Cambridge: Cambridge University Press.

Stallman, Richard M. 2010. *Free Software, Free Society: Selected Essays of Richard M. Stallman*. Boston: GNU Press.

CHAPTER 9

Racism and Sexism

In places where Macpherson writes about the significance of social movements—environmental, student, urban, and so on—he usually includes reference to women's movements (e.g., EJ, 48–49; 1983, 10–11) and once to black power movements. (DT, 50) These references are meant by him to illustrate how participatory activism against other than class oppression and not undertaken exclusively or sometimes not at all by working-class people holds out hope for oppositional, anti-possessive-individualist politics. The only place where Macpherson addresses a substantive theoretical matter regarding the oppression of women is in rejecting the notion advanced by Frederick Engels that women constitute an economic class (L&T, 19–20, Engels 1990 [1884], 173), where he denies that they do (though not referring specifically to Engels).

Of course, Macpherson endorsed the aims of feminist and civil rights movements, but given the pervasiveness of racism and sexism and their implications for the egalitarian and developmental values Macpherson champions, the absence of more than passing references to race and gender in his works must count as a deficiency. Regarding racism, it is not inappropriate to describe Macpherson as suffering from what Charles Mills calls a 'group-based cognitive handicap' (2017, 51) or as partaking in 'an epistemology of ignorance' shared with all too many other white political theorists (1997, 18). The majority of these, including those like Macpherson who were writing during the time of the civil rights movements, either remained at a level of abstraction that avoids considerations of race (mainstream liberal theorists) or focused almost exclusively on class or on gender (the anti-establishment theorists). Macpherson was part of the latter group and hence exhibits the handicap to which Mills refers.

Macpherson's relative silence regarding sexism is even more puzzling. Not only was the women's movement in full force during the entirety of his writing career (from the mid-1960s to the end of the 1980s), but his wife was a leading and high-profile feminist organizer in Canada. Kay Macpherson once allowed (in a personal conversation not long after his death) that, being a very busy activist and not an academic theorist, she had never read her husband's books or articles (and see her comment in 1994, 68). Had she done so, she would most likely have at least corrected his use of (male) gendered pronouns, which use was abandoned by him only from the late 1970s. Though not accusing Macpherson of consciously harbouring sexist sentiments, some feminist theorists criticize aspects of the content of his political theory for being biased in a sexist direction. These criticisms will be noted in due course.

Notwithstanding these gaps, Macpherson's thought has some important things to offer to anti-racist and anti-sexist theories. He, himself, was prepared to incorporate elements of the views of Aristotle and J.S. Mill, though fully aware of serious shortcomings (Aristotle's acceptance of slavery, not to mention the sexism he tried to justify on metaphysical grounds; Mill's refusal to challenge capitalism and his democratic elitism). Marx famously drew on Hegel's philosophy in spite of the latter's class biases and support for private property. Politically progressive post-structuralists are able to incorporate key dimensions of the thought of Heidegger even though he held membership in the National Socialist Party.

Macpherson's potential contributions are in two broad categories: his socialistic interpretation of liberal democracy and his critique of capitalist market societies. His views buttress and supplement certain streams of anti-racist and anti-sexist theories, and they help to focus some key issues.

POTENTIALS IN LIBERAL DEMOCRACY

Zillah Eisenstein expresses one version of feminist criticisms of liberalism:

> feminist politics, rooted in a firm understanding of women's sexual-class oppression within marriage and the market, will cut through the liberal blinders that dichotomize life into male and female, public and private, state

and family, home and work spheres. This perspective undermines the ideology of liberal individualism in feminism because it reveals that woman is part of a sexual class and that this class definition is part of her individual identity. This recognition of the sexual-class character of woman's oppression focuses on the patriarchal roots of liberalism. (1981, 221)

Similarly, David Goldberg, regarding racism:

> Liberalism tends to assume that there are pockets of injustice, in particular of racial injustice, that a liberal or enlightened meliorism will progressively overcome. I am suggesting, by contrast, that racist exclusions, though not exactly everywhere in contemporary racialized social systems, are discursively far more pervasive and diffuse than liberalism is willing or able to acknowledge. (1993, 213)

These criticisms, like virtually all similar ones by anti-sexist and anti-racist theorists, are focused on the liberal dimension of liberal democracy. If, with Macpherson, democracy is added and taken in a robust sense to include full and equal participation in collective self-determination in both public and private spheres, the incompatibility of liberal democracy with racist and sexist exclusions is harder to demonstrate. Still, liberal democracy is a version of individualism; so critiques such as those of Eisenstein and Goldberg remain a challenge to it.

The main endeavour of Mills's *Black Rights/White Wrongs* is to put liberalism to the service of anti-racism: 'contrary to the conventional wisdom prevailing within radical circles, I am going to argue for the heretical thesis that liberalism should not be contemptuously rejected by radicals but retrieved for a radical agenda.' (2017, 10) In a chapter entitled 'Occupy Liberalism!' he reviews nine political-theoretical and one historical argument against the potential of liberalism for this purpose and offers refutations. The central theoretical arguments Mills addresses pertain to the normative and to the descriptive dimensions of individualism, that is, to the charges that liberalism dismisses or ignores social values and lacks a conception of the social constitution of individuals.

Mills's endeavour contrasts with critics of Macpherson such as Virginia Held, who holds that the latter's individualist moral theory is unable to 'appreciate the value of shared, relational activity in itself' central to the communal feminist values she favours. (1993, 149) This claim has already been discussed (in earlier chapters), where it is argued that Macpherson's anti-atomistic version of individualism can and does appreciate this value (and see Townshend's rejoinder to Held 2000, 154–155). From a social-scientific standpoint Macpherson endorses Marx's view that 'the human essence' is the 'ensemble of [one's] social relations' (EJ, 95, Marx 1976, 4), and regarding Held's criticism of his moral theory, it has been noted that some of Macpherson's 'truly human potentials,' such as for love and friendship, are by their nature social and affective and that the participatory democracy he favours, at the core of which is promotion of the development of these potentials, 'brings with it a sense of community.' (L&T, 99) In both cases he sees support in works of John Dewey, J.S. Mill, and some other classic liberal-democratic theorists.

In marshalling historical arguments for his orientation towards liberalism, Mills is on the same retrievalist terrain as Macpherson. Mills draws on the work of Domenico Losurdo (2011) and Rogers Smith (1997), who depressingly illustrate the pervasive and tenacious hold of racism within the history of liberal democracy. However, he counter-poses to Smith's conclusion that this history portrays racism as entirely opposed to liberal democracy a picture of that history as exhibiting a conflict between 'racial liberalism' and 'non-racial liberalism.' (2017, 26) Referring to arguments of Ann Cudd (2006) regarding liberalism and group oppressions, Mills also reiterates a point often made about the history of liberal democracies that, far from their announced ideals supporting group-based oppressions, the latter are in contradiction to these ideals. (2017, 16–18) Mills points out that Losurdo (who criticizes Macpherson for supporting liberalism, 2011, 122) is not in fact a blanket anti-liberal but himself concludes, as Mills summarizes him, that: 'liberalism can be retrieved, but that it will take political struggle to do so.' (Mills 2017, 22 and see Losurdo 344)

A similar position is defended by not a few feminist theorists. They agree with Anne Phillips, who concludes a survey endorsing feminist criticisms of liberal democracy both historically and in its contemporary practice by arguing that liberal democracy has within it elements to counteract its negative aspects:

> [E]stablishing either the historical, or as feminists are well able to do, the contemporary associations between liberal democracy and sexual inequality does not prove a necessary or intrinsic connection. A richer and more equal democracy may still be possible within the broad framework liberal democracy implies. (1992, 81)

Phillips's conclusion is that: 'while liberal democracy has signally failed to deliver on its promises to women, it does not help to address these failings in terms of giving up on liberal democracy' (*ibid.*, 68).

In the course of his historical assessment, Mills makes reference to Macpherson's critique of the possessive-individualist version of liberalism to contrast it with a left-wing version. (2017, 20) Mills's case can be strengthened by attending to Macpherson's argument that a progressive liberal-democratic vision has *always* cohabited with possessive individualism (albeit in the heyday of capitalism largely, if never entirely, eclipsed). Retrieval in Macpherson's sense is not just voiding liberal democracy in practice of its hypocrisies or adding to it new features.

Retrieval involves identifying contests within all the conceptions central to liberal-democratic theory and practice: freedom as negative versus positive, equality as formal opportunity versus substantively, democracy as a voting procedure versus as citizen engagement in governance, property as exclusionary versus as inclusionary. The second of each of these opposing interpretations strengthens anti-racist and anti-sexist orientations and politics and places them broadly within liberal-democratic traditions. To be sure, critics can claim that such orientations and practices are not 'really' liberal democratic, but the anti-oppression theorists will find that in countering such a claim they have support in Macpherson's formidable historical and conceptual arguments.

Market Society Versus Developmental Democracy

Macpherson's views on capitalism and socialism are on the side of socialist feminism (see the touchstone treatment in Alison Jaggar, 1988, chs. 6 and 10). 'Given their understanding of political economy,' Jaggar writes, socialist feminists maintain that 'free sexual and procreative activity requires the abolition of [class] exploitation.' (306) Similarly, in addressing the shortcomings within the liberal-feminist views of Harriet Taylor and John Stuart Mill, Eisenstein argues that their 'notion of liberal individualism is structured tightly in relations to the values of the bourgeois market; the individual *owning his/herself.*' (1981, 126, italics in original)

Feminist discussions and debates around this issue were prominent in the 1980s (during the second wave of feminist theory) when they focused on relations between capitalist class oppression and patriarchal structures of the oppression of women (as exemplified in a key collection of papers debating Heidi Hartmann's thesis on 'The Unhappy Marriage of Marxism and Feminism,' 1981). Macpherson's approach is not anti-structuralist in the sense of denying that there are social, political, and economic dynamics that shape the relations among economic classes, prompt economic and political institutions, and affect people's values and views of themselves. But he does not, in Marxist fashion, try systematically to formulate the laws of such dynamics. His contributions to anti-capitalist opposition to sexism and racism and to socialist alternatives are of a different nature. They are to be found in his democratic-socialist vision and in his critique of market society.

Macpherson's way of conceptualizing socialism is essentially the same for him as of a fully robust democracy. Recall from the discussions in earlier chapters that this vision is of a society that maximizes the development and exertion of truly human potentials, of which Macpherson gives a sample and open-ended list ('the capacity for rational understanding, for moral judgment and action, for aesthetic creation or contemplation, for the emotional activities of friendship and love' as opposed to the potentials for indefinite consumption and competition for profit or jobs). A key feature of these capacities is that their exercise by some need not be at the expense of others and typically requires cooperation. (DT, 4, 53–55)

A major complaint against sexist and racist attitudes, institutions, and policies is that they severely constrain or completely shut off meaningful life opportunities. In addition to being demonstrably false, assumptions that people are incapable of pursuing careers or other endeavours that require levels of rationality that they are supposed to lack in virtue of their gender or race are complicit in shutting off such avenues. Even attribution of outstanding talents to women or visible minorities in sexist or racist societies typically stereotypes entire groups as well as connoting that they lack other talents. Macpherson's developmental-democratic vision provides a worked out and defended vision of a democratic world that can be, should, and already often is integrated with the vision of a sexism- and racism- free world.

Internal/external impediments. Some feminist-inspired criticisms of Macpherson pertain to his appeal to developmental democracy. Held argues that achievement of this democracy, as envisaged by Macpherson, centrally requiring for him removal of 'external,' mainly economic, impediments, 'will be nowhere near enough to enable women to achieve such inner empowerment as provided by a sense of self-worth.' (1993, 142) Macpherson never maintains that overcoming the economic constraints of a market society is sufficient to effect complete changes in attitudes and self-images, including ones supportive of sexist or racist domination. When he writes that the external impediments 'rooted in class, remain basic' (DT, 76) he can be understood as referring to those external impediments that affect specifically economic class consciousness, leaving open the question about what other external impediments and their affects on consciousness there may be.

Nor does Macpherson deny that challenging some 'internal' impediments (i.e., ones pertaining to people's values and opinions about what is possible) is sufficient for effectively confronting the external impediments of a market society. His view instead is that 'breakthroughs' of consciousness can work to undermine acquiescence in a market society and these breakthroughs can include resistance to costs of 'the cult of economic growth' to the environment and to the quality of life. As much feminist and some anti-racist work has shown, overcoming sexist and racist attitudes is also vitally conducive to the upward internal/external spiral Macpherson hopes for. In general, the form of Macpherson's approach—distinguishing between external and internal impediments and interrogating their interactions to identify potential breakthroughs in emancipatory consciousness and action—can be useful for anti-sexist and anti-racist theorists as well as for those concerned with class oppression. Also, though the (external) structures of racism and sexism are not identical to those of class oppression, they importantly include economic dimensions of the sort that Macpherson discusses.

Reform and radical consciousness. Further consideration of this rejoinder to Held's criticism throws into relief some thorny issues to which Macpherson's approach to social action and consciousness applies. Acknowledging the difficulty of directly confronting the internal impediments of what some call false consciousness, Macpherson urges pursuing 'rational analysis of the external impediments ... in the hope of contributing to the break-through of consciousness, and so to a cumulative reciprocal reduction of both kinds of impediment.' (DT, 76.) Not depending exclusively on theoretical argumentation, Macpherson sees the pursuit of political-economic analysis as conjoined with counter-possessive elements in popular attitudes, such as against consumerism. So short of a socialist transformation, constraints on a capitalist market—for example, prohibiting discriminatory hiring and job ghettos, provision of living wages, public child care facilities—make alternatives to subservience realistic possibilities in people's eyes and weaken attitudes that support such subservience.

In this connection Iris Young's discussion of affirmative action programmes is relevant. For her, these programmes 'have only a minor effect in altering the basic structure of group privilege and oppression' (1990, 199). However, this does not mean that they cannot play an important role in people coming to recognize and understand oppressive structures insofar as they 'challenge the primacy of a [legalistic] principle of nondiscrimination and the conviction that people should be treated only as individuals and not a members of groups.' (*ibid.*, 192) Macpherson's orientation can play a role in facilitating ways that affirmative action programmes (or ones for reparation to descendants of slavery or displacement of aboriginal peoples) will occasion such recognition and understanding. This happens when they are integrated with his challenge to possessive-individualist values and market-society structures and practices.

Examples of integrative analyses of the kind Macpherson's theories invite can be found in Theodore Allen's discussion of racism directed against aboriginal peoples. Like many other anti-racist researchers, he sees contemporary racism as originating in the attitudes and values that accompanied colonialism. For example, he cites as a justification for militarily exiling thousands of native people from their traditional lands in Georgia in 1838 that they held common property and, in the words of a general at the time, 'common property and civilization cannot co-exist' (in Allen 1994, 37). A similar opinion reported by Allen is that of a US Indian Commissioner who, writing in the 1890s, condemned 'the degrading communism' of indigenous peoples and looked forward to a time when 'the Indian would be able to say "This is mine" instead of "This is ours."' (*ibid.*, 38)

Also appropriate is the conclusion of Cheryl Harris, in a paper entitled 'Whiteness as Property,' that her article:

> investigates the relationships between concepts of race and property and reflects on how rights in property are contingent on, intertwined with, and conflated with race. Through this entangled relationship between race and property, historical forms of domination have evolved to reproduce subordination in the present racial and economic subordination. Race and property were thus conflated by establishing a form of property contingent on race—only Blacks were subjugated as slaves and treated as property. (1993, 1714–1715)

Citing Macpherson (in his 1978 summary essay on property), Harris relates her view to a 'conception of affirmative action that would dismantle whiteness as property' and would challenge a notion of property 'as the absolute right to exclude.' (*ibid.*, 1789)

These, and similar historically informed studies regarding conceptions of women as property (e.g., by Patricia Crawford 2002), serve to show how Macpherson's views about market societies and a developmental-democratic alternative can (without being reductionistic) strengthen anti-racist or anti-sexist concerns and, moreover, do so in ways that help to exhibit structural dimensions of affirmative action and other reform campaigns, thus going beyond regarding them as only addressing some aspects of individual discrimination.

Extractive power. Macpherson distinguishes between 'developmental power,' which is the ability autonomously to use and develop one's capacities, and 'extractive power' or the ability to make use of other people's capacities. In a market society, the developmental power of working-class people is greatly diminished, and they lack the extractive power of capitalists (DT, 41–42). Lynda Lange criticizes Macpherson for ignoring a respect in which male workers retain and exercise significant extractive power, namely, over women with respect to their reproductive labour. This is a systemic feature of patriarchal society and thus not a matter just of male prejudice any more than is the capitalist extraction of labour from workers only a matter of attitudes (Lange 2014, and see Held 1993, 143 and Ferguson 1989, ch. 4). A similar argument can be made with respect to race, insofar as the white working class to a certain extent benefits from racism—a point made by Mills, though not with reference to Macpherson. (2017, ch. 7)

Referring to pre-capitalist societies Macpherson maintains that in spite of not constituting an economic class women were 'indeed exploited by the male-dominated society, which made most of them perform the function of reproducing the labour force' (L&T, 20), and there is no suggestion that he thought this form of oppression does not persist. All of Macpherson's arguments in favour of a developmental-democratic vision remain intact and, indeed, are strengthened by specifying that the full development of people's truly human capacities requires race and gender as well as economic equality and that overcoming a market society requires confrontation of sexist and racist as well as possessive-individualist values. Conjoining critique of extractive powers, thus broadened, with articulation of an alternative developmental-democratic vision provides a useful framework for theories and practices combatting racism and sexism, as well as market capitalism.

Macpherson's historical treatment of possessive-individualist political-economic theories in the seventeenth century can also serve as a model for similar analyses regarding sexism and racism. Some such studies already exist, though, with the exception of Gordon Schochet's exposition of patriarchal suppositions in the thought of Hobbes (1975), they are less detailed and in-depth than Macpherson's. Mills's *The Racial Contract* treats some of the same authors discussed in *The Political Theory of Possessive Individualism*, exhibiting racist underpinnings analogous to the pro-capitalist ones Macpherson exposes (1997, chs. 1–2). Elements of a similar study are in the work of Goldberg (1993, ch. 2) and of Losurdo (2011, chs. 1–4). Regarding sexism, some feminist theorists (Brennan and Pateman 1979, 184) approvingly cite Schochet's work. The essays in Lorenne Clark and Lynda Lange's *The Sexism of Social and Political Theory* similarly treat a selection of classic authors (1979).

Another criticism by Lange of Macpherson's developmental-democratic vision (raised by her in personal correspondence) is that, freed to develop what Macpherson takes to be their truly human potentials, some women might embrace forms of self-development that perpetuate what many, if not all, feminists regard as objectionable gender roles, for instance, as an earth mother or a stay-at-home wife devoted entirely to parenting. This is one place to underline the point made in chapter three that Macpherson's theories sometimes only lay a groundwork for further examinations. He is able to mark out a field (developmental democracy) for desirable life pursuits, but not to identify and justify exactly what pursuits ought or ought not to be undertaken, which task is referred to ongoing debate. (Alternatively, this question may be left open in the spirit of Engels's remark in opposition to worries of pro-monogamy moralists, that when women are not economically confined in subservient relations 'they will not care a damn about what we today think they should do. They will establish their own practice and their own public opinion,' 1990 [1884], 189).

Developmental powers and Herrenvolk morality. Another concern to be addressed is the prospect that some may wish to develop the potentials Macpherson favours, but be indifferent as to whether others can similarly develop theirs. This is the case of the man of sufficient leisure that he is able to develop and exert his talents but who is not only indifferent about women being able to do likewise but, as described by Lange and others, extracts labour from his wife to facilitate his pursuits. It is found also in the attitudes of members of a privileged group who look to develop their potentials in accord with a developmental vision, but whose racist or sexist biases prevent extending this option to others.

Cornel West charges that just this has happened in the case of those North American Jews who are inattentive to or exhibit anti-black racism (1993). Mills addresses this challenge when he draws on work of the sociologist Pierre van den Berghe (1978) regarding a '*Herrenvolk* ethic.'

This originated in European colonization with differential moral norms between those that the 'civilized' Europeans subscribed to regarding their interactions with each other and those they thought pertinent to people of the colonized world whom they displaced, enslaved, or killed. A patent example internal to a state was in the South African Apartheid regime. Analogues of such differential moral norms persist within present-day societies. (Mills 1997, 96; 2003, 183, 238)

The aspect within Macpherson's vision for confronting this challenge is its democratic dimension. He insists that democracy is not just or primarily a matter of voting, but a social ideal focused on equality. Resources and opportunities for self-development are to be available to everyone. The vision calls for people not just to develop their truly human potentials but to do this in a truly human way. One does not need to appeal to some ethical theory to recognize that there is something morally wrong, something inhuman, about people with sufficient resources to lead a developmental life style ignoring or being complicit in racist or sexist impediments to others leading such a life.

Not depending only on moral suasion, Macpherson maintains that changes in economic constraints facilitate people coming to adopt a fully humanistic stance. The more these changes make universal development realistically possible, the more starkly apparent will become the hypocrisy and arbitrariness of *Herrenvolk* differentiations. As well, pursuing a meaningful life as Macpherson envisages one is impeded by antagonistic conflict; so the *Herrenvölker* depend upon resignation, if not willing acceptance, on the part of those excluded from their comfortable lives, and this is shaken by active resistance as by the social movements to which Macpherson refers.

A market-society matrix. In her *Black Feminist Thought*, Patricia Hill Collins identifies four domains of power: 'structural' (including legal systems, labour markets, housing policies, school systems, etc.); 'disciplinary' as described in Foucault's analyses of bureaucratic and other forms of power and powerlessness; the 'hegemonic' domain of ideology, images, symbols, and the like; and 'interpersonal' domains functioning through day-to-day interactions. (2000, 277–288) Collins usefully describes these domains as each being a 'matrix of domination' (*ibid.*, 275, 287). They are the contexts within which gender, racial, and class exclusions and oppressions are experienced and which must be understood and taken into account if these things are to be combatted.

Macpherson's work suggests that a market society is *also* such a matrix. The specific structures of contemporary societies are all of them affected by market constraints and mandates—obviously in the case of structures of employment, but also in gentrification regarding housing, laws favouring private property, bureaucracies that reify people as clients or commodities, privatization of education, the political culture and ideology of possessive individualism, or the time and other constraints that impede developing and enjoying interpersonal interactions.

Intersectionality. This point can be expanded on by referring to a more recent book of Collins, co-authored with Sirma Bilge, explicating and defending an intersectional approach to different categories of oppression (2016). This approach was prefigured in some earlier feminist theorizing, for example, by Young (1990), and it has more recently been extensively deployed largely by black feminists (e.g., by Kimberlé Crenshaw 2008, who coined the term, and see Mills's survey 2007, ch. 6). In their recent book, a version of the domains discussion is returned to and, giving the example of the garment industry in SE Asia, Collins and Bilge argue that this industry:

> contains a highly feminized workforce, relies on child labor in some countries, uses race and ethnicity as markers for the kinds of people it hires, and favors undocumented migrant workers. This means that workers are drawn from populations who are disadvantaged within intersecting systems of oppression. Their poverty, illiteracy, gender, age, immigration status, race, caste, or ethnicity makes them more vulnerable to capitalist exploitation and violence. (2016, 145)

They continue that paying attention to 'how intersecting power relations have shaped this particular industry provides a more nuanced argument' about how its workers are controlled and exploited, and other such work-related matters. (*ibid.*, 146)

It is surely right that the ways people are exploited in a capitalist market society cannot be fully understood (and hence combatted) without attending to the unique features—the matrices—of racist, sexist, and other relations of power. From Macpherson's point of view it is as well the case that specific forms of oppression within these domains cannot be fully understood without attending to the features of a market society within which they are to be found: the relative importance of different kinds of markets (financial, industrial, service, agricultural); the nature and degree of government economic, employment, and other regulations (if any); the presence or absence of union and other movement oppositions; the nature and amenability to challenges of property laws; the balance among public, private, and melded market enterprises; the interactions of a national market with transnational ones; and so on.

Situating sexist and racist oppression within a market-society matrix does not mean that this is the only context that needs to be taken into account or that it is a privileged context. An example of a treatment that, while addressing a broad range of racism's features and causes, also highlights ways it has been sustained by capitalism is Robyn Maynard's study of racism in Canada. (2017, 57–71) Her analysis illustrates how a market-society matrix interracts with other matrices to sustain the continuing oppression of women.

Mills observes that a 'crucial difference between class and racial exploitation is that the latter takes place much more broadly than at the point of production' and that 'racial exploitation can pervade the whole economic order.' (2017, 125–126) This is accurate regarding the extraction of surplus value from industrial workers, but the elements of a market society in general—commodification, fixation on property, acquisitiveness—are also pervasive. From a point of view informed by Macpherson, that anti-racist or anti-sexist theory and practice today take place within the confines a market society means that this context cannot be ignored.

Property. Because sexist and racist deprivations include limitations on the kinds and extent of property people subject to them can own and because in sexist cultures women have been treated as the property of their husbands and under slavery blacks were literally property, it might be thought that private property rights and the notion that people are owners of themselves should not be included in the pejoratively regarded matrix of market society, at least for the purpose of appealing to this matrix in combatting sexism and racism. This would denude Macpherson's conception of a market society of two of its linchpin elements. Against such a temptation are his arguments in favour of an inclusive meaning of property as a right not to be excluded from the means for developing one's talents and his rejection of the notion that people own themselves in favour of thinking of them as trustees of their talents, which they should put to socially beneficial use.

Endorsing an inclusive notion of property does put constraints on how people can make use of their possessions, but it does not mean that they have no possessions. On the contrary, it means that the resources required for the development and use of their most important potentials may not be denied them in the name of protecting other people's exclusive property rights. Similarly, lack of self-ownership (as argued in chapter five) does not mean that people forgo the ability to be in control of their own futures. It does mean that they cannot exchange legal slavery for wage slavery, and that, to the extent that a developmental-democratic society displaces a possessive-individualist one, everyone would benefit from each other's trusteeship stances in exercising their talents.

Black capitalism/bourgeois feminism. Just as a perspective in keeping with Macpherson's theories can condone reform measures that fall short of dismantling a market society, such as affirmative action, so this perspective need not be hostile to such things as removing obstacles for blacks getting into a professional class or for women breaking through glass ceilings in business and politics. As argued above, Macpherson can welcome such measures to the extent that they are proposed and executed in ways that do not buy into or support possessive-individualist culture and practices. This means conjoining programmes for individuals' professional advancements in business and government with proposals for reforming these venues in ways consonant with developmental democracy and encouraging beneficiaries of these programmes to comport themselves accordingly.

In a fully hegemonic possessive-individualist culture such a task is unrealistic. But Macpherson argues that anti-possessive-individualist attitudes coexist with contrary ones. Evidence is that successful people from discriminated-against groups who use their success to serve publicly worthwhile ends, including to help others in their groups, are more highly respected than those who simply join the club of the self-interested rich. Still, retrieving an inclusive conception of property and rejecting self-ownership is out of keeping with a capitalist dominated market, and so flat-out support for bourgeois feminism and black capitalism is incompatible with Macpherson's developmental-democratic vision. Therefore, how useful a social-market matrix is for anti-sexist and anti-racist politics in part depends on one's views on the desirability or inevitability of a capitalist market society.

One might deplore the effects of a market society, but still support advancement within it by women or visible minorities on a fatalistic 'if you can't fight them, join them' stance. Acknowledging that 'commodification has spread everywhere,' Mills asks whether it is nonetheless 'better in a market, property-dominated society to have property not distributed in …

a racially inequitable way?' (2007, 32) This opinion is strengthened in his subsequent view that since 'racial exploitation is at least in theory eliminable within a capitalist framework ... it is possible to have a non-racial capitalism,' and he goes on to see support for this prospect in the absence of any realistic alternative communist model (though qualifying this to note that the compatibility in question is elusive due to the thoroughgoing racialization of capitalism as it now exists, 2017, 126). To evaluate the strengths and the weaknesses both of challenging the racialization or genderization of capitalism and of estimating prospects for supplanting capitalism with some kind of socialistic alternative, the features of a specific market society, including potentials within one to weaken and finally dismantle it, need to be attended to.

Short of such a full analysis and further to the question about only removing racial or gender inequality from a market society, one might observe that the number of people, men or women, black or white, who can do more than to join the currently economically threatened group of petty capitalists let alone the *grande bourgoisie*, is quite limited; so this prospect is more like a dream of winning the lottery than a realistic goal for most people of colour or women, just as it is for most white men. Even when a minority of women or blacks manage at least to get into the middle class, they continue to suffer economic as well as other forms of discrimination (see Mills's summary of empirical research confirming this regarding blacks, 2003, 135–137).

Also, in an imagined capitalist society absent sexist and racist discrimination, though the standard of living for women or non-whites who become owners of significant productive forces would rise, such a capitalism would still be infused with the competitive and consumerist practices and culture of a market society. So for Macpherson, who sees these things are part of demeaning and limiting styles of life, getting out of gender or race ghettos and into the capitalist class would be an instance of jumping from the fire into the frying pan.

* * *

As well illustrated in the current intersectional attention to relations among gender, class, and race, the nest of oppressions they involve is a tangled web:

> Fundamentally, race, class and gender are intersecting categories of experience that affect all aspects of human life; thus, they simultaneously structure the experiences of all people in this society. At any moment, race, class or gender may feel more salient or meaningful in a given person's life, but they are overlapping and cumulative in their effects. (Anderson and Collins 2014, 4)

Macpherson's views on the potentials for and obstacles to developmental democracy address part of this web, and they do so in a way that goes beyond narrow class analysis to throw into relief the aspects of market societies that adversely affect all their segments. His views also include systemic, structural matters as well as cultural ones and thus escape criticisms, expressed by Bilge (2013), of some forms of intersectional theorizing that ignore structures.

Macpherson's accomplishment is in explicating and defending in detail a conception of democratic socialism melded with anti-atomistic individualism, including participation, and supported by an historically informed critique of anti-socialist, possessive-individualist culture. Subsequent theorists, taking into account more obstacles to full human development than did Macpherson, have this accomplishment at their disposal.

References

Allen, Theodore. 1994. *The Invention of the White Race*. New York: Verso.

Anderson, Margaret, and Patricia Hill Collins. 2014. Why Race, Class, and Gender Still Matters. In *Race, Class, and Gender: An Anthology*, ed. Margaret Anderson and Patricia Hill Collins, 1–14. Boston: Cengage Learning.

Bilge, Sirma. 2013. Intersectionality Undone. *Du Bois Review: Social Science Research on Race* 10 (2): 405–424.

Brennan, Teresa, and Carole Pateman. 1979. "Mere Auxiliaries to the Commonwealth": Women and the Origins of Liberalism. *Political Studies* 27 (2): 182–200.

Clark, Lorenne M.G., and Lynda Lange, eds. 1979. *The Sexism of Social and Political Theory: Women and Reproduction from Plato to Nietzsche*. Toronto: University of Toronto Press.

Collins, Patricia Hill. 2000. *Black Feminist Thought: Knowledge, Consciousness and the Political of Empowerment*. New York: Routledge.

Collins, Patricia Hill, and Sirma Bilge. 2016. *Intersectionality*. Cambridge: Polity Press.

Crawford, Patricia. 2002. Women and Property: Women as Property. *Parergon* 19 (1): 151–171.

Crenshaw, Kimberlé Williams. 2008. Mapping the Margins: Intersectionality, Identity Politics, and Violence Against Women of Color. In *The Feminist Philosophy Reader*, ed. Alison Bailey and Chris Cuomo, 279–309. New York: McGraw-Hill.

Cudd, Ann E. 2006. *Analyzing Oppression*. New York: Oxford University Press.

Eisenstein, Zillah. 1981. *The Radical Future of Liberal Feminism*. New York: Longman.

Engels, Frederick. 1990 [1884]. *The Origin of the Family, Private Property and the State*. In *Karl Marx Frederick Engels Collected Works*, vol. 26, 129–276. London: Lawrence & Wishart.

Ferguson, Ann. 1989. *Blood at the Root*. London: Pandora.

Goldberg, David Theo. 1993. *Racist Culture: Philosophy and the Politics of Meaning*. Oxford: Blackwell.

Harris, Cheryl I. 1993. Whiteness as Property. *Harvard Law Review* 6 (8): 1707–1791.

Hartmann, Heidi. 1981. The Unhappy Marriage of Marxism and Feminism: Towards a More Progressive Union. In *Women and Revolution: A Discussion of the Unhappy Marriage of Marxism and Feminism*, ed. Lydia Sargent, 1–41. Montréal: Black Rose Books.

Held, Virginia. 1993. Freedom and Feminism. In *Democracy and Possessive Individualism: The Intellectual Legacy of C.B. Macpherson*, ed. Joseph Carens, 137–154. Albany: State University of New York Press.

Jaggar, Alison M. 1988. *Feminist Politics and Human Nature*. Totowa, NJ: Roman & Littlefield.

Lange, Lynda. 2014. Contribution to a Panel on Macpherson's Thought, Society for Socialist Studies Annual Conference. Toronto: Ryerson University.

Losurdo, Domenico. 2011. *Liberalism: A Counter-History*. London: Verso.

Macpherson, Crawford Brough. 1973. [DT] *Democratic Theory: Essays in Retrieval*. Oxford: Oxford University Press. Reissued with an Introduction by Frank Cunningham. Toronto: Oxford University Press, 2012.

———. 1977. [L&T] *The Life and Times of Liberal Democracy*. Oxford: Oxford University Press. Reissued with an Introduction by Frank Cunningham. Toronto: Oxford University Press, 2012.

———. 1978. The Meaning of Property & Liberal Democracy and Property. Introductory and concluding essays in *Property: Mainstream and Critical Positions*, ed. C.B. Macpherson, 1–13 and 199–207. Toronto: University of Toronto Press.

———. 1983. Interview on the Centenary of Marx's Death. *Socialist Studies Annual '83*. Winnipeg: University of Manitoba Publication, 7–12. Reproduced in Frank Cunningham, *The Real World of Democracy Revisited* (1994). Atlantic Highlands, NJ: Humanities Press, 14–21.

———. 1984. [EJ] *The Rise and Fall of Economic Justice*. Oxford: Oxford University Press. Reissued with an Introduction by Frank Cunningham. Toronto: Oxford University Press, 2013.

Macpherson, Kay. 1994. *When in Doubt Do Both: The Times of My Life*. Toronto: University of Toronto Press.

Marx, Karl. 1976 [1845]. Theses on Feuerbach. In *Karl Marx Frederick Engels Collected Works*, vol. 3, 3–5. London: Lawrence & Wishart.

Maynard, Robyn. 2017. *Policing Black Lives: State Violence in Canada from Slavery to the Present*. Winnipeg: Fernwood Books.

Mills, Charles. 1997. *The Racial Contract*. Ithaca: Cornell University Press.

———. 2003. *From Class to Race: Essays in White Marxism and Black Radicalism*. New York: Rowman & Littlefield Publishers.

———. 2017. *Black Rights/White Wrongs: The Critique of Racial Liberalism*. Oxford: University of Oxford Press.

Mills, Charles, and Carole Patman. 2007. *Contract and Domination*. Malden, MA: Polity Press.

Phillips, Anne. 1992. Must Feminists Give Up on Liberal Democracy? *Political Studies* XL: 68–82.

Schochet, Gordon J. 1975. *Patriarchalism in Political Thought: The Authoritarian Family and Political Speculation and Attitudes Especially in Seventeenth-Century England*. Oxford: Basil Blackwell.

Smith, Rogers M. 1997. *Civic Ideals: Conflicting Visions of Citizenship in U.S. History*. New Haven: Yale University Press.

Townshend, Jules. 2000. *C.B. Macpherson and the Problem of Liberal Democracy*. Edinburgh: University of Edinburgh Press.

Van den Berghe, Pierre. 1978. *Race and Racialism: A Comparative Perspective*. 2nd ed. New York: John Wiley & Sons.

West, Cornel. 1993. *Race Matters*. Boston: Beacon Press the chapter 'On Black-Jewish Relations,' 101–116.

Young, Iris. 1990. *Justice and the Politics of Difference*. Princeton: Princeton University Press.

CHAPTER 10

Urban Challenges

Macpherson's *The Life and Times of Liberal Democracy* is organized around four 'models' of democracy (protective, developmental, equilibrium, and participatory). Models for him are descriptions of the basic nature of an existing or sought for political society and evaluations of its desirability or practicality, including conceptions of human nature:

> So, in looking at models of democracy—past, present, and prospective—we should keep a sharp look-out for two things: their assumptions about the whole society in which the democratic political system is to operate, and their assumptions about the essential nature of the people who are to make the system work. (L&T, 5, and see PI, 46–70)

Macpherson makes only some passing references to urban matters (EJ, 44, L&T, 103), but his approach to social and political theory and some specific theses are relevant to challenges in contemporary cities. In this chapter, two urban models analogous to Macpherson's models of democracy will be constructed: possessive-individualist and developmental-democratic.

As ideal-typical models, each of these is exemplified to varying degrees in actual cities; though in recent years elements of the possessive model are more often encountered in large cities than developmental features. As normative models, each incorporates recommendations about what cities should and realistically can aspire to be.

The Possessive-Individualist City

On this model the city is thought of generically as what the urbanist Kevin Lynch labels an 'economic engine' or 'patterns of activity in space which facilitate the production, distribution, and consumption of material goods' (1981, 331). More specifically, Lynch describes cities thus regarded as places where 'the multiple decisions of pure economic men tend to bring the spatial pattern to a balance and the most efficient production and distribution of goods, given the set of resources available.' (*ibid.*) Looked at from the point of view of urban governance, the possessive-individualist city combines what Jon Pierre criticizes as 'pro-growth' and 'managerial governance,' where public services are contracted out or privatized and 'service production is oriented more by "customer" choice than by political decisions.' (2011, 26–27)

Cities on this model are like individuals in economic competition, and there is a large literature on essential features of the 'competitive city' (e.g., the contributions to Iain Begg 2002). One manifestation of this orientation pertains to cities with global economic import or with pretences to become such. As Saskia Sassen, a pioneer on this topic, describes these cities, they: 'concentrate control over vast resources, while finance and specialized service industries have restructured the urban social and economic order. Thus a new type of city has appeared … it is the global city.' (Sassen 1991, 4) Global cities compete to attract industrial and financial capital, and an index of their strength is economic growth. In David Harvey's view growth is also motivated by a need of capitalist firms continually to create investment markets, in part by means of urban projects. From Baron von Haussmann's reorganization of Paris to Robert Moses's reengineering of New York, an overarching mandate of cities, on his view, is to help 'resolve the capitalist-surplus absorption problem.' (Harvey 2009, 316, and see his 2014, ch. 15)

Being global economic players brings cities into the domain of globalization with the result, as Jason Hackworth maintains, that their autonomy is threatened. His analysis is similar to those reviewed in chapter seven regarding nations. 'Recent discussions of urban governance,' he writes, have focused on 'the difficulty of providing municipal services in the context of heightened capital mobility' and on mandates of international institutions such as the World Bank and the International Monetary Fund (2007, 19–20). In Hackworth's analysis competitive cities tend to morph into what he calls, in the title of his book on this topic, 'the neoliberal city,' with attendant departure from regulation and public service:

> Even the most socially progressive municipalities were forced to follow the federal government's anti-Keynesian lead by cutting back social welfare expenditures and regulations during downturns. Local governments are now not only expected to ally with business to improve [their] plight, they are also increasingly expected *to behave* as businesses as well. (*ibid.*, 26)

The features Hackworth sees in this city are those of neoliberalism generally, and as such they are subject to the criticisms reviewed in chapter six.

Also characteristic of competitive cities is interurban competition for people with the skills thought necessary to make them if not global forces at least preeminent economic centres in their countries or regions. This is the focus of Richard Florida's *The Rise of the Creative Class*. (2002) He agrees with Sassen's thesis in holding that 'cities and mega-regions are the true economic units that drive the world forward' (Florida 2008, 61), and he urges that cities should create the economic and cultural climates attractive to those with appropriate talents and energy. This is the 'creative class.' Though this class includes technological experts, actors, musicians, and artists as well as entrepreneurs and business leaders (2012, 8–9), most read Florida's thesis with the latter two groups in mind.

Both global cities and cities that fall short of this status act or (for urban politicians and planners who attend to the market appeal of cities) should act in ways that attract residents, local business, and amenities in market-competitive ways. An example of this is what one critic, David Imbroscio, calls 'the mobility paradigm,' where 'there is a heavy reliance on moving people through metropolitan space as a means of addressing urban social problems' as opposed to a 'place making approach' that aims to make existing places conform to people's needs. (2012, 2) The mobility paradigm is akin to a touchstone proposal in market-focused approaches to urban theory by Charles Tiebout about how public goods may be distributed in cities.

Tiebout's proposal is to rely on diversity among cities and suburbs of cities with respect to provision of goods (high expenditures on schools vs on golf courses, in one of his examples). With enough diversity 'consumer-voters' will reveal and act on their preferences by moving to municipalities that best serve them (1956, 418):

> Just as the consumer may be visualized as walking to a private market place to buy his goods, the prices of which are fixed, we place him in the position of walking to a community where the prices (taxes) of community services are set. ... Spatial mobility provides the local public-goods counterpart to the private market's shopping trip. (*ibid.*, 422)

Aside from its merits as an abstract model (see Stiglitz, 1977, for a criticism), Tiebout's speculations about just how the model could work in practice depart from purely market-based solutions, but his recommendations can also be deployed in a neoliberal way: municipalities, in competition with one another for (tax-paying) residents, will strive to make themselves attractive to selective constituencies and through time the market will make for an efficient distribution of city types with respect to citizen preferences. Something like this thinking can be seen in the ways that municipalities market themselves to highlight, for example, one or more of provision of single-family housing on spacious lots, high-end cultural facilities, major sports venues, or condominium housing with promise of ever-increasing market value.

On both the global city and the citizen-consumer approaches, cities and urban provisions are themselves commodities, and regarding them as such by politicians, urban planners, architects, the civil service, the media, and citizens invokes the overriding project of making cities successful economic competitors. An example is in the extraordinary effort put into attracting major sports events or facilities to a city claiming that this will 'put it on the world map.' Much imagination is devoted to 'branding' cities the better to market them (see the contributions to Dinnie 2011). Developers not infrequently tout costly architectural ventures on the grounds that they will be of 'iconic,' global significance.

Treating cities as commodities spawns and is reinforced by treating their constituent parts (dwellings, infrastructures, common spaces, amenities, educational institutions, social services) as also commodities subject to market forces and often including privatization or public-private ventures. These things exacerbate problems for those who do not wish their cities to be treated as commodities. Four such problems lend themselves to analysis in terms of Macpherson's theories.

Gentrification. In almost all large cities gentrification is posing a nest of problems (explored in Loretta Lees *et al.* 2010). As already flagged in the early 1960s by Jane Jacobs (1992 [1961]), with the erosion of family-friendly dwellings and local businesses, gentrification threatens the community-sustaining functions of neighbourhoods. It also segregates cities into economically ghettoized regions (see the study of Toronto by David Hulchanski 2007) Most distressing is the contribution of gentrification to homelessness, as developers invade the poorer parts of cities, displacing those who live in them without they or city governments providing sufficient (or any) alternatives (Ella 2013). According to Hackworth gentrification is a key component of the neoliberal city:

> [G]entrification is much more than a politically neutral expression of the real estate market; it involves the replacement of physical expressions of Keynesian egalitarianism like public housing with a privately led segmentation of inner city space. (2007, 98)

Public spaces. Urban public spaces in a legal sense are places from the enjoyment or use of which nobody is legally excluded or, put positively, to which everyone has a right of use. Streets and public parks are the most often-given examples. In practice such use is informally limited by the number of people who can fit into a space; so when city-owned land is sold it is removed from a stock of potential public-space development needed to keep up with population growth. High-end gentrification erodes public space when neighbourhood sidewalks and parkettes are replaced by gated enclaves.

Some venues that are legally private property can approach being public spaces when they are affordably conducive to public enjoyment, such as pubs and restaurants or sports venues. These things count as (quasi-)public spaces when admission is free (as in the malls that are often the only public-like spaces available in suburbia, see Barber 1999) or their costs are low. Public access to these things is compromised when high rents drive up prices, costs of tickets dramatically rise, and malls employ private security to keep out homeless people, demonstrators, and others deemed inappropriate to their use. Those who decry the attrition of public space argue that the quality of life is thereby diminished. Public spaces are places of relaxation and fun, places where urban dwellers from a diversity of ethnic, class, and other backgrounds interact, and sites for public expression of opinion as in political demonstrations. Pertinent treatments are by Kohn (2004), Cunningham (2009), and the contributions to Low and Smith. (2006)

Consumerism. In the words of one critic, Maya Oppenheim, consumerism:

has become integral to the evolution of cities, and as it has changed the urban landscape, the way we experience and inhabit the city has radically altered. With consumer outlets now dominating the centres of our cities, the built environment has been increasingly co-opted by consumer needs (2014).

In his discussion of this topic, Benjamin Barber identifies its main aspects. Consumerism nurtures 'a culture of impetuous consumption necessary to selling puerile goods.' (2007, 81) It turns attention from 'public spiritedness' towards the unreflective satisfaction of immediate individual wishes (126). Echoing the critique by Naomi Klein (2002), Barber adds that personal identity becomes 'a reflection of "lifestyles" that are closely associated with commercial brands.' (167) And consumerism homogenizes popular culture: it is 'totalizing rather than pluralistic, because pluralism offers space to something other than shopping.' (220)

In his commentary on capitalist cities of the early twentieth century (through an interrogation of Paris and taking its arcades as archetypes) Walter Benjamin sees consumerism as an instance of the myth of eternal return—that everything repeats itself infinitely—which while viewed positively by Friedrich Nietzsche represented for Louis-Auguste Blanqui the futility of human endeavours. Benjamin sees this as a feature of hell, being stuck in a nightmare world, unable to awaken. (1996, 25–26) In cities this is manifest in a fixation on acquiring ever new consumer goods. It is 'the quintessence of that false consciousness whose indefatigable agent is fashion' where the 'semblance of the new is reflected, like one mirror in another, the in the semblance of the ever recurrent.' (*ibid.*, 11, 22)

Democratic citizenship. According to Gerald Frug, when public services are privatized and urban life is geared to consumption 'values associated with democracy—notions of equality, of the importance of collective deliberation and compromise, of the existence of a public interest not reducible to personal economic concerns—are of secondary concern, or no concern at all, to consumers.' (1999, 172) In the possessive-individualist city a high premium is put by its citizens on being left alone to pursue their private interests, and city officials resist citizen input to the making and implementing of policies. Instead, they attend to the impact of market forces and pay special attention to the demands and bribes of major economic players. When citizens in this model are proactive is it often selfishly to resist things like public housing in what is often described as a not-in-my-backyard (NIMBY) way. (Though it should be registered that the charge of NIMBYism is more often than not levelled by private developers or in support of city mega projects without regard to the merits of neighbourhood concerns.)

One might come at the conceptualization of these challenges from a variety of (not mutually exclusive) directions: psycho-dynamic, political-economic, sociological, ideological, historical, and so on. Macpherson's theories provide one such conceptualization. In particular: the ideas of a *market society*, *property* as an exclusive right, the *infinite consumer*, and thinking of democracy on the analogue of a business, or *catallaxy*.

Market society. Recall that Macpherson appropriates a version of Karl Polanyi's notion of a market society as one in which 'a whole society' is 'embedded in the mechanisms of its own economy' (Polanyi 1977, 9) or, as Macpherson puts it, where 'exchange of commodities through the price-making mechanism of the market permeates the relations between individuals.' (PI, 55) Macpherson's main focus is on the way human labour is a commodity so that people's powers can be transferred to others. But these powers are not the only things that are commodified in a market society, since virtually everything else is as well. Insofar as urban marketization is all-encompassing, it makes the possessive-individualist city a neoliberal city.

To the extent that cities approximate this model, they are not just victims of neoliberalism, but also drivers of it. Cities, as is argued in a collection of essays on this topic by Neil Brenner and Nik Theodore, 'have become increasingly central to the reproduction, mutation, and continual reconstitution of neoliberalism itself during the last two decades.' (2002, 28) They list 12 categories of neoliberal elements in cities, including: 'Dismantling of earlier systems of central government support for municipal activities'; 'Assault on traditional relays of local democratic accountability'; 'Privatization and competitive contracting of municipal services'; 'Introduction of market rents and tenant-based vouchers in low-rent niches of urban housing markets'; and 'Retreat from community-oriented planning initiatives.' (*ibid.*, 22–25) All these features are prominent components of market societies as conceived by Polanyi and Macpherson.

Macpherson's critique of market societies applies as well when priority is given to a city's gaining competitive advantage by achieving high ranking based on economic factors like its share of a country's GDP and on the magnitude of its financial institutions. A ranking by the Globalization and World Cities (GaWC) project follows the convention of sorting cities into Alpha, Beta, or Gamma categories. By this ranking Macpherson's

Toronto was in the middle of a pack of Alpha cities in 2016 behind the top cities of London and New York, but ahead of Amsterdam, San Francisco, Berlin, and other generally highly regarded cities (made possible by the presence in Toronto of the head offices of most of Canada's banks). Toronto also ranked significantly higher than the Beta city of Copenhagen (GaWC 2017).

Rankings are different if alternative criteria are employed, for example, those of the 'Best Cities for Families' produced by an international real estate association. Prominent among its 15 indices are education, safety, cost of living, employment, level of pollution, health care, transportation, and activities for children. Of 100 cities ranked by it in 2017, Copenhagen came in first, New York 47th, and London 30th (Homeday 2017). Macpherson's prioritization of the 'quality of life' over 'the crass materialism of the market society' (DT, 6) is apt in choosing between these two ways of evaluating cities.

A related critique of the competitive global city model is in recent work by Florida. In a rare approach to a *mea culpa* by an academic scholar, he describes as 'the new urban crisis' a situation where 'the affordable housing and transit that we so badly need do not get built, where the causes of concentrated poverty remain unaddressed, and where our socioeconomic classes harden into castes.' (2017, 214) Florida describes this crisis 'as the product of our new age winner-take-all urbanism' (*xx*), where the 'concentration of talent and economic activity in fewer and fewer places not only divides the world's cities into winners and losers but ensures that the winner cities become unaffordable for all but the most advantaged' (33), and he proposes seven 'pillars' for meeting the crisis: reformed zoning, infrastructure development, affordable housing, turning low-wage service jobs into family-supporting work, directly addressing poverty, helping development in poor countries, and empowering local communities (17). Absent from this list is 'making cities attractive to the creative class.'

Finally, regarding the 'mobility paradigm' by which spatial mobility is supposed to provide efficient distribution of public goods within urban regions according to Tiebout's free market model, his assumptions for the model to have application are noteworthy. These are that (1) 'consumer-voters' are fully mobile; (2) have full knowledge about revenues and costs in different locales; (3) there are many communities from which to choose; (4) there are no restrictions on employment opportunities among the locales; (5) public services 'exhibit no external economies or diseconomies among communities'; (6) amenities in each community are either optimal, where this means adequate to service the size and wishes of its population; or (7) a community will strive to attract or to discourage residence movement to attain this size. (1956, 419) Unless the invisible hand of the market is supernaturally dexterous it is very hard to see how free market competition could provide for conditions (4) and (5), and it is a stretch to imagine how the other conditions could be assured just by the operation of a market either. (See Loren King's revision of Tiebout's scheme to incorporate fairness and democratic contestation, 2004.)

Exclusive property. In *Democratic Theory* Macpherson argues that in a possessive-individualist society property 'is equated with private property—the right of an individual (or a corporate entity) to exclude others from some use or benefit of something' (DT, 123), which right 'is not conditional on the owner's performance of any social function' (126). When public spaces and other assets are sold off they become the property of their buyers who thereby acquire the right to exclude others from their use. Such exclusion is correlated with gentrification and the proliferation of gated communities. It is all-too-evident in the case of the chronically unemployed when they lack homes, and their plight is even worse, as Jeremy Waldron laments, when they are also denied use of public space: 'some people have no private space—not even the temporary privacy that public shelters or public toilets would afford—to come out of or to return to.' (2000, 395)

The infinite consumer. It will be recalled from chapter six's discussion of neoliberalism that from the advent of a capitalist market society it came to be assumed that 'unlimited desire' in the form of an insatiable effort to accumulate consumer goods beyond what is required to meet basic needs and lead a fulfilling life (Benjamin's hell) is 'rational and morally acceptable.' (DT, 18) Macpherson echoes Aristotle in the latter's criticism of the *pleonexic* personality or the person who never has enough possessions to be satisfied (Aristotle 1984 [350 BCE], 1782). As noted earlier this disposition is a psychological aberration for Aristotle, but a normal feature of personal values in a market society for Macpherson, where, similar to Harvey's analysis, unlimited consumption serves the need of enterprises for ever-expanding markets and where the 'cult of growth' is a prominent feature of popular culture. (DT, 18–19, 1971, 35)

Catallaxy. Also, as noted earlier, the term 'catallaxy' was coined by Friedrich von Hayek to describe the application of economic principles to political behaviour. The concept is central to two of the models of democracy Macpherson criticizes—equilibrium and protective—which, he allows, more or less accurately correspond to the way that what is called democratic government actually functions in a market society. Equilibrium democracy is a political arrangement whereby political elites, through political parties, are supposed to achieve a balance among the interests of competing individuals and interest groups, and this task is all that democracy is. (L&T, 78, DT, 187–192)

On the protective-democratic model 'the political system should both produce governments which would establish and nurture a free market society and protect the citizens from rapacious governments.' (L&T, 34) In this model there is no enthusiasm for democracy in a fuller sense. It is premised on the assumption that 'man is an infinite consumer' mainly concerned to 'maximize the flow of satisfactions, or utilities, to himself from society' and democratic government is needed 'for the protection of individuals and the promotion of the Gross National Product, and for nothing more.' (*ibid.*, 43)

These elements of a possessive-individualist model of a city—market infused, focused on property, general commodification, catering to the infinite consumer, and governed as a business—reinforce one another and constitute a coherent whole. Just as locating sexism and racism within a market-society matrix (as discussed in the last chapter) helps to understand and combat these things, so does approaching these challenges from the vantage point of this ensemble contribute to understanding their nature and force. The core element of a market society that everything is an actual or potential commodity facilitates gentrification and the contraction of public spaces. The related treatment of constituent parts of cities as exclusionary property facilitates gentrification and selling public spaces, as well as making protection of private property a prime responsibility of government. Consumerism is an unavoidable concomitant of infinite desire for goods. There is no room in protective and equilibrium democracy for robust and civically minded citizen participation.

The elements of possessive individualism include both the requirements Macpherson specifies for any social model, namely, 'their assumptions about the whole society' and 'their assumptions about the essential nature of the people who are to make [the society] work.' (L&T, 5) Market society with its thoroughgoing commodification and its emphasis on exclusionary property provides a holistic conception of urban life and governance. The drive for infinite consumption is exemplified in the widespread consumerist behaviour described by Barber and is typically taken to be an ineradicable feature of human nature. Catallactic governance is portrayed as a normal and necessary response to a presumed self-interested and competitive urban citizenry.

The Developmental-Democratic City

Some urban theorists employ at least the developmental dimension of what Macpherson describes as a developmental-democratic vision in their conceptions of a good city. In a passage that almost exactly duplicates Macpherson's description 40 years earlier, Harvey endorses a humanistic world view 'that measures its achievements in terms of the liberation of human potentialities, capacities, and powers. It subscribes to the Aristotelian vision of the uninhibited flourishing of individuals and the construction of "the good life."' (Harvey 2014, 283) Similarly, Susan Fainstein looks to the capabilities approach of Amartya Sen and Martha Nussbaum as offering 'a way to devise rules that can govern the evaluation of urban policy and provide content to the demand of urban movements.' (2010, 54, see Sen 1993) Also in this vein is the vision of Ash Amin and Nigel Thrift. (2002, 143–144) Several themes in Macpherson's approach to developmental democracy are relevant to this urban model.

Democracy. Fainstein's project in her book on the just city is to apply the three aspects she sees as definitive of urban justice—democracy, equity, and diversity (2010, 54–55)—to aspects of city life and problems. In the course of this endeavour she prioritizes equity over democracy (175), and with respect to democracy she focuses on representation: 'Realism … points to calling for better representation rather than broader participation.' (177) On a conception of the developmental-democratic city inspired by Macpherson, by contrast, democratic participation and equity are inextricably conjoined. 'Developmental democracy' is partly defined for him by reference to equity: 'The good society is one which permits and encourages *everyone* to act as exerter, developer, and enjoyer of the exertion and development, of his or her own capacities.' (L&T, 48, emphasis added, and see Macpherson's criticism of J.S. Mill for failing to be a thoroughgoing egalitarian, *ibid.*, 58–62)

Also counter to Fainstein's opinion, for Macpherson democracy should always prominently include direct citizen participation both in formal governance and in civil-societal activities. Recently, urbanists have been revisiting the work of Henri Lefebvre, and in particular his notion of 'The Right to the City.' Alternative readings of this work have been given (surveyed by Kohn 2016, ch. 9), one of which is in the spirit of Macpherson's views on urban participation. This is that the city is an ongoing *oeuvre*, or what might be called a work in progress, in which citizens should have a right to participate and thereby for Lefebvre, as for Macpherson, be able to transform their city in a progressive and ultimately socialistic way. (Lefebvre 1996 [1967], 154)

From another tradition, Macpherson's view is also compatible with that of Aristotle. The citizen, in Aristotle's seminal definition:

> is one who shares in governing and being governed. He differs under different forms of government, but in the best state he is one who is able and willing to be governed and to govern with a view to the life of virtue. (1984 [350 BCE], 2037 [1283–1284])

The inclusion of governing as well as being governed connotes the participatory dimension of this conception (though it must be corrected for Aristotle's lamentable exclusions of women and his sanctioning of slavery). The notion of governing and being governed with a view to a life of virtue runs counter to the amorality of possessive-individualist citizenship. Among other virtues, this includes promoting public goods. In accord with this conception, the urban citizen on the developmental-democratic model is the opposite of the consumer citizen in the possessive-individualist city. The latter wishes just to pursue self-regarding interests and values democracy, in its catallactic version, only insofar as it permits voting against politicians who do not serve these interests. (A treatment of Aristotle on this topic and its contemporary urban applications is in Cunningham 2011, and see Amin and Thrift 2002, 146–154.)

Regarding constriction of citizen participation in favour of representative governance on the supposed basis of realism, Macpherson's view on 'trade-offs' is germane. He criticizes the habit in much liberal theory and policy to think in terms of trade-offs, for instance, between inflation and employment, and challenges claims of their inevitability. (EJ, ch. 4) In one of the few places where he refers to urban matters, Macpherson also gives the examples of a putatively unavoidable trade-off between 'neighbourhood amenities endangered by property developers and the enhanced assessments and tax revenues expected from the developer's projects' or 'in determining the best size for semi-autonomous municipal or regional authorities [asking] how much democratic responsiveness should be traded for how much administrative efficiency.' (EJ, 44) Championing citizen participation need not mean ignoring ongoing challenges to it, for example, those discussed by Meg Holden—externally imposed limitations, income and other disparities among citizens, possibilities of manipulation, resistance of many to any public engagement. However, Holden sees these not as proof against participation, but in the spirit of pragmatism as problems to be frankly recognized and addressed. (2017, 58–61)

As noted in earlier chapters, Macpherson's approach to problems confronting developmental democracy generally is similarly pragmatic. Regarding the urban trade-offs he mentions, one can identify ways of reforming urban governance so that at all its levels there is enhanced democratic input with avenues for interaction among citizens at different levels (an example of pertinent literature is Shah and Shah 2006). A relatively free hand can be given to urban planners and policy makers provided there are also institutionalized provisions for transparency and for appropriate citizen involvement. Also, just as trade-offs in some versions of welfare liberalism between democracy and individual freedom are exacerbated by attending to the needs of corporate capitalist individuals (EJ, 51–52), so, as Warren Magnusson maintains, does channelling popular democratic participation into political party and pressure group politics by anti-urban, statist assumptions diminish the potentials of effective citizen participation. (1997, see 67)

Trusteeship. Some of the resources necessary for everyone in a city to have realistic opportunities for developing their potentials may be provided by city governments—education, transportation, health-care facilities, libraries, community centres, and so on—and some are provided to urban citizens by one another, such as employment, good working conditions, and free time. Adequate and affordable housing, environmentally sustainable living and work conditions, recreational facilities, and many other things may be made available by both municipal governments and informally.

In all cases, provision of quality resources requires that citizens who have discretion over the resources' distribution comport themselves as their trustees and that they demand the same comportment from elected officials and city agencies. This means not just that citizens and officials are trustees for their family members or those from whom they receive financial support. Urban leaders and citizens are, rather, trustees of their cities' resources for all urban inhabitants including for the benefit of future generations. Evidently, trusteeship is incompatible with viewing such resources as commodities to be marketed for individual profit.

Inclusive property. Viewing oneself as a trustee of resources for anonymous fellow urban citizens, present and future, is compatible, if barely, with thinking of these possessions as private property. But then these provisions are subject to individual whim, or compliance is forced by often resented and resisted legislation. Trusteeship is much more secure in the developmental city when it flows from a popular culture where property is viewed as a 'right not to be excluded from the use of benefit of the accumulated productive resources of the whole society.' (DT, 133)

An example of the potential use of Macpherson's theory of property with respect to urban challenges is its *actual* employment to this end by Nicholas Blomley in his approach to a severe crisis of low-cost housing in a district of Vancouver, its Downtown Eastside, which is exacerbated by increasing depletion of affordable housing due to gentrification and loss of public housing. Blomley aims to provide urban-theoretical support for the efforts of a Downtown Eastside action committee to create a 'social justice zone' where 'low-income people and their basic human and social needs "have priority over profit."' (2016, 92)

Blomley characterizes housing in the district as a potential 'commons,' but he does not wish to situate its conception in the rational choice tradition associated with the 'tragedy of the commons' problematic, even when approached in the progressive manner of theorists like Elinor Ostrom, who argues on rational choice grounds for domains where resources for specified groups are protected (2000, 335–336). Though he does not disagree with this conclusion, Blomley finds that, as a product of self-interested calculation, it fails to reflect the 'moral, affective and political commons, that deploys a language of rights and justice.' For this purpose he invokes Macpherson's stance on common property, which 'is created by the guarantee to each individual that he will not be excluded from the use or benefit of a thing.' (Macpherson 1978, 5, quoted in Blomley, *ibid.*)

Affordable housing in the district would be the common property of those living in the area. Whether as units in refurbished single-room occupancy hotels, cooperatives, or some other form of housing, occupants would be trustees of their dwellings for other and future low-income residents, just as the city would be a trustee for ensuring continued inclusive property. Similarly to Imbroscio's advocacy of a place-making paradigm and drawing on the work of Donald Kreukeberg (1995), Blomley wishes to take the question of affordable housing out of a traditional planning framework, which focuses on the question 'where do things belong?' and place it in the context of 'the more pressing question: to whom do things belong?' (95) He sees support in Macpherson's views on property for this framing:

> [Macpherson] argues for the merit of using property ... to articulate broader claims relating to democracy and a right to a kind of society, suggesting that these claims 'will not be firmly anchored unless they are seen as property.

For, in the liberal ethos which prevails in our liberal-democratic societies, property has more prestige than almost anything else. And if the new claims are not brought under the head of property, the narrow idea of property will be used, with all the prestige of property, to combat them. (Blomley, 96 quoting Macpherson, DT, 138)

This orientation provides as a 'strategic advantage' the chance 'to talk back against' exclusionary property discourse in defence of inclusionary property rights. We shall return to another advantage Blomley sees in Macpherson's approach, namely, that it relates the topic of publicly accessible housing generally to that of market-society capitalism.

Individual diversity. If there is a paradigmatic fault line among urban theorists, planners, politicians, and activists it is between pro- and anti-utopians: le Corbusier versus Jane Jacobs. In turn, this is a species of an opposition in ways of conceptualizing a good city going back to ancient times:

> When the institutions of a society make it most utterly one, that is a criterion of their excellence than which no truer or better will ever be found. (Plato 1961 [350 BCE], 1325 [739d])

> Is it not obvious that a [city] state may at length attain such a degree of unity as to be no longer a state?—since the nature of a state is to be a plurality. ... So that we ought not to attain this greatest unity even if we could, for it would be the destruction of the state. (Aristotle 1984 [350 BCE], 2001 [1261a])

Some of the classic urban thinkers, including Charles Fourier (1968 [1934]) and Benjamin (1999 [1927–1940]), and many contemporary ones—Iris Young (1990), Harvey (1989), Frug (1999), Amin and Thrift (2002), Fainstein (2010), Kohn (2016), Holden (2017)—look to encourage city visions and institutions that preserve diversity ('social differentiation without exclusions,' in Young's parlance, 238–239) while uniting urban citizens around common values: 'solidarism' for Kohn (*passim*); individual/city authenticity in Holden's treatment (ch. 4); or 'community building' projects (Harvey, 233–235; Frug, 173–177). The extended arguments given by these authors illustrate the theoretical complexity of this task. Macpherson's version of individualism provides, for those who accept its premises, a straight forward way if not to square a Platonic/Aristotelian circle, at least to approach it. (For an effort focused on the utopian/anti-utopian opposition, see Cunningham 2010.)

Macpherson is an individualist in that the aim of a developmental-democratic society is to provide each of those in it with the opportunities and resources to develop his or her potentials to the fullest. But his announcement at the beginning of *Possessive Individualism* that he wishes to 'bring back a sense of the moral worth of the individual, and combine it again with a sense of the moral value of community' (PI, 2) reflects his wish to combine his individualism with a pro-communal orientation.

The sense of community compatible with his individualism that Macpherson has in mind is close to John Dewey's notion of a 'public,' that is, a constellation of people whose actions affect one another in an ongoing way and who confront common problems requiring coordination among them to be resolved. (1984 [1927]) Such a constellation typically includes people who are anonymous to one another and among whom there are different and sometimes conflicting interests and world views, but it is to be valued nonetheless to the extent that its members recognize themselves as a public and essay to cooperate in resolving their common problems. A pragmatic, urban-problematic orientation is the pivot of Jane Jacobs's approach where cities are taken as 'problems in organized complexity,' and urban 'variables are many, but they are not helter-skelter.' (1992 [1961], 433)

Another way that valuing community-embedded social relations is essential to individuals' development for Macpherson is that certain *sorts* of communities are indispensable for this end. Referring specifically to the potential for participatory democracy, Macpherson notes that this 'does not fit an unequal society of conflicting consumers and appropriators' whereas a society of people who see themselves 'as exerters and enjoyers of the exertion and development of their own capacities' brings with it 'a sense of community which the former does not.' (L&T, 99) Moreover, the development of some potentials is essentially social. This is obviously so regarding potentials for friendship and love but also for such things as intellectual or artistic pursuits (as argued in this book's chapter on intellectual property—chapter eight) and maybe all the others in Macpherson's sample lists. (DT 4, 54) Finally, and crucially for Macpherson's characterization of truly human potentials, there is the thesis that has centrally figured in the treatment of all the contemporary challenges that these potentials are such that their development and exercise by some are not at the expense of others, but thrive on cooperation. (DT, 54)

Against this background it is clear that from the perspective of Macpherson both diversity and unity can be *conceptually* accommodated in a city or any other kind of public. In the developmental-democratic city individuals will strive to develop potentials or packages of potentials unique to each of them, and to do so in a variety of ways (diversely). At the same time, a criterion that any such endeavour must meet is that the exertion of one person's talents not be unavoidably at the expense of others' exerting theirs (a precondition of unity). A unity/diversity combination can also be accommodated *in practice* provided there are realistic measures for overcoming obstacles to everyone developing their potentials.

One example is education, which must be strong and supple across all segments of a society. Ash and Thrift outline several realistic proposals to this end (2002, 144–147), and Aristotle's extensive treatment in the *Politics* of educational principles conducive to good citizenship is by no means utopian. (1984 [305 BCE], 2121–2129 [1337a–1342b]) Fainstein lists workable measures (16 in all) to further each of her components of urban justice, for instance: regarding equity, provision of low-cost housing; inclusionary zoning to further diversity; and appropriate forms of democratic consultation in planning. (2010, 174–175)

Capitalist market society. Several of the themes in Benjamin's reflections on modern cities are informed by the view of Georg Simmel that these are populated by a multitude of individuals who for the most part are unknown to one another and who lack the traditions of small towns to regulate their interactions. A virtue of large-city anonymity is that it opens space for much more personal freedom than do smaller locales where, as Simmel puts it, there 'is such a narrow cohesion that the individual member has only a very slight area for the development of his own qualities and for free activity for which he himself is responsible.' (2002 [1903], 15)

This advantage is offset for Simmel (though not necessarily so for Benjamin) by another feature of the modern metropolis, money:

> To the extent that money, with its colourlessness and its indifferent quality, can become a common denominator of all values, it becomes the frightful leveler—it hollows out the core of things, their peculiarities, their specific values and their uniqueness and incomparability in a way which is beyond repair. (*ibid.*, 24)

Elsewhere in his seminal essay, 'The Metropolis and Mental Life,' and examined at length in his *The Philosophy of Money*, Simmel makes it clear that money is not just a leveller of commodities but of individual personalities as well. Emotional life is replaced by instrumental intellectualism (*ibid.*, 12–13), and 'the more money dominates interests and sets people and things into motion, the more objects are produced for the sake of money and are valued in terms of money, the less can the value of distinction be realized *in men* and in objects.' (1978 [1907], 391–392, emphasis added)

The advantage metropolitan anonymity has for individuality as described by Simmel is compatible with the central value of developmental democracy in Macpherson's sense. But while Simmel sees the levelling power of money as an inevitable feature of urban life, in Macpherson's perspective, as in Benjamin's, this is true only of a city dominated by a capitalist market. The point is argued by David Harvey, who devotes a section of his book on *The Urban Experience* to Simmel on money. (1989, 161–170) While agreeing with Simmel about the homogenizing nature of money, Harvey sees this as peculiar to a capitalist society where individualism 'attaches to money uses in freely functioning markets' (231). Likewise, for Macpherson it is not anonymity that drives a culture of monetarization, but the commodification of people's capacities. From this standpoint, therefore, the benefits for individual development afforded by urban life can be reaped without incurring the levelling effects of money to the extent that a city is not a market society.

* * *

A definitive feature of the developmental-democratic city is that it is not infused with the policies and culture of economic markets, and while in the current, largely neoliberal, era freeing cites from market domination is challenging, it is not impossible. Just as Macpherson portrays developmental democracy as already prefigured in the history of political thought and social comportment (his 'retrieval' thesis), so features of past and existing cities exemplify developmental democracy.

The aforementioned Copenhagen, like several other Scandinavian cities, places a higher priority on the quality of life of its citizens than on economic competitiveness. In one of his examples of neighbourhood and community movements that challenge possessive individualism, Macpherson includes those 'against expressways.' (L&T, 103) This is certainly a reference to a successful effort, in 1971, to stop construction of an expressway through Toronto's centre (Jane Jacobs, by then living in Toronto, was an organizer). This movement provided impetus to election of a reform city council that pursued projects in keeping with developmental democracy (including social housing, neighbourhood renewal, curbing the powers of the development industry, and environmental protection). Participatory budget policy formation in Brazilian cities is another example. Or there are the sometimes successful projects of not-for-profit organizations such as the Tenderloin Housing Clinic in San Francisco, which has provided substantial low-cost housing from 1980.

There are many more examples of these sorts of undertakings, all of which illustrate the realistic possibility of making democratic-developmental advances in cities. None of them, however, has been easy or without capitalist push-back. They therefore also illustrate that success requires understanding the limitations imposed in a market society. This point can be illustrated by returning to Blomley on property.

Another advantage he sees in applying Macpherson's theory to the dearth of low-cost and public housing in his city is that 'as a political economist, Macpherson situates the right to exclude, and the right to not be excluded, within a capitalist market economy. It is this that makes the right to not be excluded particularly pressing,' and he quotes Macpherson on this point:

> Denial or limitation of access is a means of maintaining class-divided societies, with a class domination which thwarts the humanity of the subordinate and perverts that of the dominant class; this is a condition which neither any amount of 'consumers' sovereignty,' nor the fairest system of distributive justice can offset or remedy .... The extent and distribution of that access is set by the system of property. (Macpherson, DT, 120, quoted in Blomley, 97)

Whether this *is* an advantage depends on whether it is thought that a capitalist market society can be effectively challenged, and some urban thinkers who locate themselves broadly on the political left are at least cautious about confrontation with capitalism.

Fainstein disagrees with Harvey's contention that 'acting within the existing capitalist regime' will only mitigate 'the worst outcomes at the margins of an unjust system'; while her own view is that there is 'sufficient leeway [in this regime] that reform backed by political mobilization can produce significant change.' (Fainstein 2010, 170–171, quoting Harvey 2009, 46) Kohn expresses doubt that capitalist enterprises can be replaced and holds that while 'the goal is to transform the structure of capital, in practice this involves encouraging alternative economies to fill the gaps created by the dominant modes of production and exchange, and this leaves much of the power of capital intact.' (2016, 196)

An even more pro-capitalist approach is taken by Barber, who thinks it possible to 'moderate' consumer capitalism and to 'help capitalism survive and prosper by serving real rather than faux needs.' (2007, 314) Citing a thesis of C.K. Prahalad and Stuart Hart (2004), he recommends 'redirecting capitalism by utilizing its flexible potential for change' and turning 'the world's poor into paying customers' treating them 'as a capitalist "growth opportunity."' (Barber, *ibid.*) Referring to Harvey's view that 'a Just City has to be about fierce conflict all of the time,' Fainstein proposes reforms 'which do not depend upon revolutionary change for their realization' as an alternative to 'unending fierce conflict.' (2010, 171, citing Harvey 2009, 47) This opposition reflects just one perspective on the relation between reform and revolution, and one not likely shared by Macpherson, whose orientation on this matter, as suggested in chapter one, is closer to that of Gramsci than of Lenin.

Macpherson's critique of capitalist societies entails that subordination to their imperatives is not in the best long-range and seldom in the short-range interests of cities and that accommodation with capitalism in confronting an urban public's problems are forced upon it. This perspective is squarely at odds with Barber's enthusiasm for capitalist potentials. Whether it is also incompatible with the comments of Fainstein and Kohn depends upon whether one sees a specifically capitalist market, with its core elements of profit seeking, competition, and commodification, as a dependable ally in confronting urban challenges or if one regards accommodation to capitalism as an unfortunate and challenging obstacle.

As an example, on the first perspective, reliance on privatization or public-private partnerships in the provision of social housing, transportation, delivery of municipal services like waste removal, and so on is often depicted not just as opportune but as an improvement over public provision of these things: costs to a municipal government are reduced, and the presumed unavoidable inefficiencies of city bureaucracies in managing them avoided. On the second, reluctant, perspective, reliance on the private sector may be necessitated by shrinking resources, often due to inadequate support for municipalities by higher levels of government. Bureaucratic inefficiencies in this perspective can be recognized but seen as political and administrative problems amenable, contrary to neoliberal claims, to being overcome.

None of this is to deny that in some cities (including Macpherson's) there are no well-meaning, even civically virtuous, capitalist developers or that there are never opportunities for cooperation with them and other capitalist entrepreneurs. But a viewpoint on capitalism that Macpherson shares with Harvey and with Marx is that the impediments of capitalism are not functions of the personal values of capitalists but structural. This is why, in a common example of public-private partnerships in mixed-class housing complexes, these often start off with both private and public partners envisaging, even sincerely, that a majority of units will be set aside for subsidized housing, but through (not much) time the balance shifts to a majority of high-end, market value units.

Due to pressures of competition, capitalist enterprises cannot function as charities. Because private sector partners require profit, constant pressures to increase fees to 'citizen consumers' and to cut corners regarding standards will always have to be resisted. On this perspective, then, there should be no let-up in seeking sources of public funding and maintaining extensive, vigilant regulation and public oversight (by officials not beholden to moneyed interests).

Macpherson's original optimism that eventually capitalism and hence capitalist market society could be eliminated was tempered, if never repudiated, by the end of his life. However, while he did not shun reform efforts within the confines of capitalism, he held that they will always be constrained. Models of a possessive-individualist and a developmental-democratic city constructed out of Macpherson's theories, then, provide, in the one case, a negative example of things that urban theory, institutions, planning, and politics should wherever possible avoid and, in the second case, a positive vision of a city to be approximated and, one might hope with Macpherson, sometime to be fully achieved.

References

Amin, Ash, and Nigel Thrift. 2002. *Cities: Reimaging the Urban*. Cambridge: Polity Press.

Aristotle. 1984 [c350BEC]. *Politics*. In *The Complete Works of Aristotle*, vol. 2. Princeton: Princeton University Press.

Barber, Benjamin. 1999. Malled Mauled and Overhauled: Arresting Suburban Sprawl by Transforming Suburban Malls into Usable Civic Space. In *Public Space and Democracy*, ed. M. Héfnaff and T. Strong, 201–220. Minneapolis: University of Minnesota Press.

———. 2007. *Consumed: How Markets Corrupt Children, Infantilize Adults, ad Swallow Citizens Whole*. New York: W.W. Norton.

Begg, Iain, ed. 2002. *Urban Competitiveness: Policies for a Dynamic City*. Cambridge: Polity Press.

Benjamin, Walter (1999 [1927–1939]). *The Arcades Project*. Cambridge, MA: Harvard University Press.
Blomley, Nicholas. 2016. The Right to Not Be Excluded: Common Property and the Right to Stay Put. In *Releasing the Commons: Rethinking the Futures of the Commons*, ed. Ash Amin and Philip Howell, 89–106. London: Routledge.
Brenner, Neil, and Nik Theodore. 2002. Cities and the Geographies of "Actually Existing Neoliberalism" in Space. In *Spaces of Neoliberalism: Urban Restructuring in North America and Western Europe*, ed. Neil Brenner and Nik Theodore, 2–32. Oxford: Blackwell Publishing.
Cunningham, Frank. 2009. Public Spaces and Subversion. In *Rites of Way: The Politics and Poetics of Public Space*, ed. Mark Kingwell and Patrick Turmel, 85–99. Waterloo, ON: Wilfrid Laurier University Press.
———. 2010. Triangulating Utopia: Manfredo Tafuri, Walter Benjamin, Henri Lefebvre. *City: Analysis of Urban Trends, Culture, Theory, Policy, Action* 14 (3): 268–277.
———. 2011. The Virtues of Urban Citizenship. *City, Culture, and Society* 2 (1): 35–44.
Dewey, John. 1984 [1927]. *The Public and Its Problems*. In *John Dewey: The Later Works*, vol. 2, 235–372. Carbondale, IL: Southern Illinois Press.
Dinnie, Keith, ed. 2011. *City Branding: Theory and Cases*. New York: Palgrave Macmillan.
Ella, Howard. 2013. *Homeless: Poverty and Place in Urban America*. Philadelphia: Temple University Press.
Fainstein, Susan S. 2010. *The Just City*. Ithaca: Cornell University Press.
Florida, Richard. 2002. *The Rise of the Creative Class*. New York: Basic Books.
———. 2008. *Who's Your City*. New York: Basic Books.
———. 2012. *The Rise of the Creative Class Revisited*. New York: Basic Books.
———. 2017. *The New Urban Crisis: How Our Cities Are Increasing Inequality, Deepening Segregation, and Failing the Middle Class—And What We Can Do About It*. New York: Basic Books.
Fourier, Charles. 1968 [1834]. *Modification à introduire dans l'architecture des villes* in *Oeuvres Complètes de Charles Fourier*. Vol. 12. Paris: Éditions Anthropos.
Frug, Gerald E. 1999. *City Making: Building Communities Without Building Walls*. Princeton: Princeton University Press.
Globalization and World Cities. 2017. Classification of Cities: 2016. Available at: http://www.lboro.ac.uk/gawc/world2016t.html.
Hackworth, Jason. 2007. *The Neoliberal City: Governance, Ideology, and Development in American Urbanism*. Ithaca: Cornell University Press.
Harvey, David. 1989. *The Urban Experience*. Baltimore: The John Hopkins University Press.
———. 2009. *Social Justice and the City*. Athens, Georgia: University of Georgia Press.

———. 2014. *Seventeen Contradictions and the End of Capitalism*. Oxford: Oxford University Press.
Holden, Meg. 2017. *Pragmatic Justification for the Sustainable City: Acting in the Common Place*. New York: Routledge.
Homeday. 2017. Best Cities for Families. Available at: https://www.homeday.de/en/family-index-international/#results.
Hulchanski, David. 2007. The Three Cities Within Toronto: Income Polarization Among Toronto's Neighbourhoods 1970–2005. *University of Toronto Cities Centre Research Bulletin*, no. 41.
Imbroscio, David. 2012. Beyond Mobility: the Limits of Liberal Urban Policy. *Journal of Urban Affairs* 34 (1): 1–20.
Jacobs, Jane. 1992 [1961]. *The Death and Life of Great American Cities*. New York: Random House.
King, Loren A. 2004. Democratic Hopes in the Polycentric City. *The Journal of Politics* 66 (1): 203–233.
Klein, Naomi. 2002. *No Logo*. 2nd ed. New York: Macmillan Picador.
Kohn, Margaret. 2004. *Brave New Neighborhoods: The Privatization of Public Space*. New York: Routledge.
———. 2016. *The Death and Life of the Urban Commonwealth*. Oxford: Oxford University Press.
Kreukeberg, Donald A. 1995. The Difficult Character of Property: To Whom Do Things Belong? *Journal of the American Planning Association* 1 (3): 301–309.
Lees, Loretta, Tom Slater, and Elvin Wyly, eds. 2010. *The Gentrification Reader*. London: Routledge.
Lefebvre, Henri. 1996 [1968]. *Writings on Cities: Henri Lefebvre*, ed. Eleonore Kaufman and Elizabeth Lebas, 147–159. London: Wiley Blackwell.
Low, Setha, and Neil Smith, eds. 2006. *The Politics of Public Space*. London: Routledge.
Lynch, Kevin. 1981. *A Theory of Good City Form*. Cambridge, MA: The MIT Press.
Macpherson, Crawford Brough. 1962. [PI] *The Political Theory of Possessive Individualism: Hobbes to Locke*. Oxford: Oxford University Press. Reissued with an Introduction by Frank Cunningham. Toronto: Oxford University Press, 2010.
———. 1973. [DT] *Democratic Theory: Essays in Retrieval*. Oxford: Oxford University Press. Reissued with an Introduction by Frank Cunningham. Toronto: Oxford University Press, 2012.
———. 1977. [L&T] *The Life and Times of Liberal Democracy*. Oxford: Oxford University Press. Reissued with an Introduction by Frank Cunningham. Toronto: Oxford University Press, 2012.
———. 1978. The Meaning of Property & Liberal Democracy and Property. Introductory and concluding essays in *Property: Mainstream and Critical Positions*, ed. C.B. Macpherson, 1–13 and 199–207. Toronto: University of Toronto Press.

———. 1984. [EJ] *The Rise and Fall of Economic Justice*. Oxford: Oxford University Press. Reissued with an Introduction by Frank Cunningham. Toronto: Oxford University Press, 2013.

Magnusson, Warren. 1997. *The Search for Political Space: Globalization, Social Movements and the Urban Political Experience*. Toronto: University of Toronto Press.

Oppenheim, Maya. 2014. Who Shapes Cities and for Whom? *New Left Project*, February 26. http://www.newleftproject.org/index.php/site/article_comments/who_shapes_cities_and_for_whom.

Ostrom, Elinor. 2000. Collective Action and the Evolution of Social Norms. *The Journal of Economic Perspectives* 14 (3, Summer): 137–158.

Pierre, Jon. 2011. *The Politics of Urban Governance*. New York: Palgrave Macmillan.

Plato. 1961 [360 BCE]. *Laws* in *The Collected Dialogues of Plato*. New York: Pantheon Books, 1225–1511.

Polanyi, Karl. 1977 [1954–1964]. *The Livelihood of Man*. New York: Academic Press.

Prahalad, C.K., and Stuart Hart. 2004. *The Fortune at the Bottom of the Pyramid*. Upper Saddle River, NJ: Wharton School Publishing.

Sassen, Saskia. 1991. *The Global City*. New York: Princeton University Press.

Sen, Amartya. 1993. Capability and Well-Being. In *The Quality of Life*, ed. Martha Nussbaum and Amartya Sen, 30–53. Oxford: Clarendon Press.

Shah, Anwar, and Sana Shah. 2006. *The New Visions of Local Governance and the Evolving Role of Local Governments' Local Governance in Developing Countries*, 1–46. Washington, DC: World Bank Publication.

Simmel, Georg. 1978 [1907]. *The Philosophy of Money*. London: Routledge.

———. 2002 [1903]. The Metropolis and Mental Life. In *The Blackwell City Reader*, ed. Gary Bridge and Sophie Watson. Oxford: Blackwell.

Stiglitz, Joseph E. 1977. The Theory of Local Goods. In *The Economics of Public Services*, ed. Martin Feldstein and Robert Inman, 274–333. New York: Macmillan.

Tiebout, Charles M. 1956. A Pure Theory of Local Expenditures. *The Journal of Political Economy* 64 (5): 416–424.

Waldron, Jeremy. 2000. Homelessness and Community. *University of Toronto Law Journal* 50 (4, Autumn): 371–406.

Young, Iris. 1990. *Justice and the Politics of Difference*. Princeton: Princeton University Press.

Correction to: The Political Thought of C.B. Macpherson

CORRECTION TO

© The Author(s) 2018
F. Cunningham, *The Political Thought of C.B. Macpherson*,
Critical Political Theory and Radical Practice,
https://doi.org/10.1007/978-3-319-94920-8

An error in the production process unfortunately led to publication of the book prematurely, before incorporation of the final corrections. The version supplied here has been corrected and approved by the author.

The updated original online version if this book can be found at
https://doi.org/10.1007/978-3-319-94920-8

© The Author(s) 2019
F. Cunningham, *The Political Thought of C.B. Macpherson*,
Critical Political Theory and Radical Practice,
https://doi.org/10.1007/978-3-319-94920-8_11

Index

A
Aboriginal peoples, 28, 160
Affirmative action, 159–160
Ake, Claude, 122
Alberta, *see* Social Credit Party
Allen, Theodore, 160
Amin, Ash, 185, 187
Anarchism, 12
Angus, Ian, 68
Aristotle, 10, 61, 67, 75, 99, 146, 154, 179, 182, 185, 187
Autonomy
  of cities, 172
  of individuals, 27, 47, 161
  of nations, 118–119

B
Barber, Benjamin, 175, 176, 190
Beck, Ulrich, 118
Benjamin, Walter, 176, 179, 185, 187
Bentham, Jeremy, 30, 49, 99, 142
Berlin, Isaiah, 13, 19–20, 32, 57, 63, 67, 78

Black capitalism, 166–167
Blomley, Nicholas, 184, 189
Bourgeois feminism, 166–167
Bowles, Samuel, 100
  with Herbert Gintis, 100–101
Brenner, Neil, 177
Buchanan, James, 103
  with Gordon Tullock, 105
Bull, Hedley, 122

C
Canada, 24, 31
Capabilities ethics, 75
Capitalism, 41, 87, 189–191
Catallaxy, 102–103, 121, 177, 179–180
Chile, 103
Cities
  and capitalism, 189–191
  and creative class, 173
  developmental-democratic model, 181–188
  and diversity/unity, 185–187

Cities (*cont.*)
   and gentrification, 164, 174–175, 179, 184
   global, 172
   and market societies, 177, 180
   and mobility paradigm, 173, 178
   possessive-individualist model, 172–180
   and property, 183–184, 189
   rankings, 177–178
Citizenship, 176, 182
   global, 125
Civil liberties, 5, 34, 42, 49
Collins, Patricia Hill, 163
   with Sirma Bilge, 164
Colonialism, 160
Commodity fetishism, 102
Communitarianism, 27, 82, 83
Community, 9, 24, 47, 49, 82, 113, 156, 186
Conflict, 32, 83
Consumerism, 99, 126, 131, 159, 175–176
Consumption, infinite, 100, 122, 179
Contract theory, 64–65
Corporatist/plebiscitarian state, 7, 13
Cosmopolitanism, 119
Culture, 91, 122–123, 131–133

D

Dahl, Robert, 102, 121
Democracy
   ecological, 132
   models of, 11, 179–180
   participatory, 11–12, 31
   representative, 31
de-Shalit, Avner, 44, 130
Desires/wants/needs
   creation of, 47, 99–100
   and endogenous/exogenous preference formation, 100–101
   infinite, 47
   and true and false needs, 73–74

Developing countries, 9
Developmental democracy, 11
   definition, 9
   and racism/sexism, 158
   spirals in, 111
Dewey, John, 26, 61, 69, 84–85, 128, 156, 186
Downs, Anthony, 102

E

Eckersley, Robyn, 132
Eco-dictatorship, 132
Economic growth, 80, 103, 122, 129, 131, 172
   cult of, 44, 49, 159, 179
Education, 187
Efficiency, 12, 107–110, 112, 146, 182
   as Pareto optimality, 107–108
Eisenstein, Zillah, 154–155, 157
Engels, Friedrich, 153, 162
Environmental degradation
   and democracy, 131–132
   and neoliberalism, 129–130
Environmental philosophy, 133
Equality/egalitarianism, 40–41
Ethics, 62, 75
   and meta-ethics, 62–64
   and morality, 62–66
   perfectionism, 75
   phronesis, 67
Eurocommunism, 50
European Union, 119–120, 127
Exploitation, *see* Net transfer of powers

F

Fainstein, Susan, 181, 185, 189–190
False consciousness, 79–80, 159
   loopholes in, 80, 93, 128–129
Fatalism, 10, 103, 110–111, 123, 125
Florida, Richard, 173, 178

Foundationalism, 87–89, 149
Friedman, Milton, 95, 98, 103
Frug, Gerald, 176, 185

G
Giddens, Anthony, 118
Glasbeek, Harry, 28, 150
Globalization, 118–121
  and culture, 122–123
  and extortion, 125–127
  and intellectual property, 139–141
Goldberg, David, 155
Gould, Carol, 69, 88, 119
Gramsci, Antonio, 10, 190

H
Habermas, Jürgen, 54, 60, 119
Hackworth, Jason, 172–173
Hansen, Phillip, 59–60, 68, 70
Harrington, James, 17–18
Harris, Cheryl, 160
Hart, H.L.A., 63, 74
Harvey, David, 172, 181, 185
Hayek, Friedrich von, 45, 95, 102–103
Hegel, Georg Wilhelm Friedrich, 61, 149–150
Held, David, 119, 124
Held, Virginia, 29, 155–156, 158
Herrenvolk, 162–163
Historicism, 85–87
Hobbes, Thomas, 8, 14, 15, 64, 85, 98, 101, 112, 113, 144, 161
Holden, Meg, 182, 185
Humanism, 112
Human powers/potentials, 10
  and capabilities ethics, 75
  extractive/developmental, 161
  impediments to development of, 76, 79, 158–159
  loose list of, 75
  transfer of, 41, 43
  truly human, 29, 74–79
Hume, David, 63

I
Imbroscio, David, 173, 184
Individual/individualism, 26–30, 82–85
  atomistic, 26, 144
  compatibility with community, 27, 84, 186
Innis, Harold, 5
Intellectual property
  defenses of, 141–142
  and efficiency, 146
  and exclusionary property, 143
  and incentives, 146
Intersectionality, 164–165

J
Jacobs, Jane, 174, 186, 188
Jaggar, Alison, 157
Jung, Hwa Yol, 130, 134
Justice, economic, 12–13

K
Kagan, Shelly, 62
Kant, Immanuel, 68, 149
Kohn, Margaret, 185, 189
Kontos, Alkis, 6, 60, 66, 73
Kymlicka, Will, 28, 121, 124

L
Laclau, Ernesto, 34
  with Chantal Mouffe, 24, 87
Lange, Lynda, 161, 162
Laski, Harold, 5, 11–12

Leiss, William, 7, 43, 132–133
Levellers, 8, 16
Levine, Andrew, 23, 39
Liberal democracy, 25–26
  and capitalism/socialism, 23
  contested concepts of, 24–26
  and developmentalism, 25
  and racism/sexism, 154–157
Liberalism
  paradox of, 33
Liberty
  positive and negative, 27, 31–32, 67, 78–79
Light, Andrew, 134
Lindsay, Peter, 33, 43, 54, 75
Locke, John, 8, 15–17, 27, 30–31, 65, 140, 147
Losurdo, Domenico, 156, 162
Lukes, Steven, 29–30, 60, 70, 75
Luxemburg, Rosa, 13

M
MacIntyre, Alasdair, 27, 67, 82
Macpherson, Crawford Brough
  and Canadian Civil Liberties Association (*see* Civil liberties)
  as engaged theorist, v, 4, 70, 91
  feasibility of recommendations (*see* Realism)
  feminist criticisms of, 155, 158, 161–162
  as intellectual historian, 16–20
  life, 4–6
  as political-economic-cultural theorist, 4, 40, 57, 68, 91, 131
  pragmatism of, 69, 89, 183
  and structures, 158, 191
Macpherson, Kay, 6–7, 154
Marcuse, Herbert, 11, 47, 60, 79
Markets, 44, 103–104
  and consumer information, 45–46
  and efficiency, 108
  and socialism, 45
Market socialism, 44–45
Market society, 4, 12, 16–17, 43–44, 46, 53, 88, 92, 95–96, 100–103, 109–110, 122–123, 157–158, 161, 177, 180, 187–188
  as matrix of domination, 163–164
  and quasi-market society, 43
Marxism, 52–54
Marx, Karl, 27, 61, 156
  with Fredrich Engels, 70
Mason, J.W., 121–122, 124
May, Christopher, 141
  with Susan Sell, 139–140
McKay, Ian, 7, 13, 19
Meynell, Robert, 60, 61, 68, 70, 83
Miller, David, 13, 15, 19–20
Mill, John Stuart, 26, 29–31, 154, 156, 181
Mills, Charles, 28, 153, 155, 165–167
Models, 171, 180
  of cities, 191
  of democracy, 11
Morality, *see* Ethics

N
Nations
  and autonomy/sovereignty, 118–119
  and nation-centrism, 120, 123–125
Native peoples, *see* Aboriginal peoples
Needs, *see* Desires/wants/needs
Neoliberalism
  all encompassing, 101–103
  and bad people, 105–106
  and catallaxy, 102–103
  and cities, 177
  confronting, 109–111
  defenses of, 103–108

and democracy, 106–107
and efficiency, 107–108
and globalization, 120, 127
and humanism, 112
and incentives, 105
and neoclassical economics, 96–97
and pleonexia, 99–101
subjectivism, 97–98
Net transfer of powers, 53
Nussbaum, Martha, 75

O
Ontologies, 4, 66–67
Ophuls, William, 131
Oppenheim, Maya, 175–176

P
Paehlke, Robert, 131–132
Panitch, Leo, 39, 54
Parekh, Bikhu, 82
Pateman, Carole, 31
Perfectionism, *see* Ethics
Phillips, Anne, 156
Philosophy, 60
  and agnosticism, 69–70, 88
Plato, 185
Pleonexia, *see* Neoliberalism
Pluralism
  political-scientific, 10
  of values, 31–32
Pocock, John, 13, 18
Pogge, Thomas, 119, 123
Polanyi, Karl, 46, 95–96, 110, 177
Political economy, 5, 91, 104, 112, 157
Political parties, 7–8, 12, 42, 51, 102–103, 106–107, 121, 180
Political theorists, 12, 32, 47, 53–54, 79, 84
Populism
  right-wing, 7, 13, 125–126

Possessive individualism
  by default, 86, 105, 111, 126
  definition, 3
  relation to developmental democracy, 11
Poster, Claire, 146
Property, 31, 142–145
  and cities, 183–184, 189
  exclusive/inclusive, 143
  as means/rights, 81–82, 142–143, 148
  and sexism/racism, 165–166

Q
Quality of life/work, 12, 49, 126–127, 159, 178, 188

R
Rational/collective choice theory, 112, 184
Rawls, John, 10, 33, 65
Ray, B.N., 7, 35
Realism, 50–52, 76–77, 127–129, 159, 188–189
  and revolutionary radicalism, 92–93
  and utopianism, 51
Realists
  political-scientific, 51
  revolutionary, 51–52
Retrieval, 10, 157, 188
Revolution
  of consciousness, 40
  proletarian, 49, 53
Rights
  group/individual, 28, 84
Rousseau, 23, 83, 100

S
Sandbrook, Richard, 123–124
Sassen, Saskia, 172

Scarcity, 13, 32, 46–47, 76, 87, 113
Schochet, Gordon, 161
Schumpeter, Joseph, 51, 102
Schweickart, David, 43–45
Self-ownership, 15–16, 61, 81–82, 101, 157, 166
Sell, Susan, 141
Sen, Amartya, 75, 118
　with Martha Nussbaum, 181
Simmel, Georg, 187–188
Skinner, Quentin, 13, 16
Social conservatives, 112–113
Social contract theory, 64–65
Social Credit Party, 7, 13
Social democracy, vi, 39, 41, 109, 125
Socialism, 9
　aspects of, 39
　economic institutions of, 42–47
　and feminism, 157–158
　political institutions of, 42
　transition to, 48–50
　vision of, 39–41, 50–51
Socialist countries, 8–9
Social movements, 47–49, 80, 81, 106, 124, 128, 133, 153, 163
Soviet Union, 9, 33, 45
State, theories of, 53–54
Strange, Susan, 120
Svacek, Victor, 41, 52

T
Taylor, Charles, 26–27, 83
Technology, 13, 46–47, 63, 87, 93, 130, 133
Theodore, Nik, 177

Thrift, Nigel, 185, 187
Tiebout, Charles, 173–174, 178–179
Toronto, 175, 178, 188
Townshend, Jules, 7, 13, 43, 133
Tradeoffs, 12, 182
Trade-Related Aspects of Intellectual Property Rights (TRIPS), 140
Trade unions, 29, 49
Truly human potentials, *see* Human powers/potentials
Trusteeship, 143–145, 183
Tully, James, 13, 15–16

V
Vancouver, 184
Vanguardism, 33–36, 52
Visions, 4, 12, 39, 51–52, 66, 92

W
Walras, Léon, 97–98
Welfare capitalism, v, 10, 42–43, 46, 96, 125, 183
Wood, Ellen, 39
Workers' self-management, 44
Working class, 48–49
World Intellectual Property Organization (WIPO), *see* Trade-Related Aspects of Intellectual Property Rights (TRIPS)

Y
Young, Iris, 159, 164, 185

The manufacturer's authorised representative in the EU is Springer Nature Customer Service Centre GmbH, Europaplatz 3, 69115 Heidelberg, Germany. If you have any concerns regarding our products, please contact ProductSafety@springernature.com

Printed and bound by CPI Group (UK) Ltd, Croydon, CR0 4YY

23/03/2026

02076736-0004